HUM R

A Dictionary and Catalog
of African American Folklife
of the South

A Dictionary and Catalog
of African American Folklife
of the South

Sherman E. Pyatt and Alan Johns

Greenwood Press
Westport, Connecticut • London

Library of Congress Cataloging-in-Publication Data

Pyatt, Sherman E.
   A dictionary and catalog of African American folklife of the south
/ Sherman E. Pyatt and Alan Johns.
     p.   cm.
   Includes bibliographical references and index.
   ISBN 0–313–27999–3 (alk. paper)
    1. Afro-Americans—Southern States—Folklore—Dictionaries.
2. Afro-Americans—Southern States—Social life and customs—
Dictionaries. 3. Folklore—Southern States—Bibliography.
4. Folklore—Southern States—Discography. 5. Southern States—
Social life and customs—Bibliography. 6. Southern States—Social
life and customs—Discography. I. Johns, Alan, 1949– .
II. Title.
GR110.A47P93   1999
398'.08996075—dc21   97–26906

British Library Cataloguing in Publication Data is available.

Library of Congress Catalog Card Number: 97–26906
ISBN: 0–313–27999–3

First published in 1999

Greenwood Press, 88 Post Road West, Westport, CT 06881
An imprint of Greenwood Publishing Group, Inc.
www.greenwood.com

Printed in the United States of America

The paper used in this book complies with the
Permanent Paper Standard issued by the National
Information Standards Organization (Z39.48–1984).

10 9 8 7 6 5 4 3 2 1

Dedicated to

Sean, Shomari, Marilyn, Loretta,
Gloria, and Mary E. Johns

Contents

Preface   ix

Acknowledgments   xiii

Abbreviations   xv

Dictionary   1

1. General Works   57

2. Folk Medicine   75

3. Folk Music   79

4. Folk Material   115

5. Witchcraft, Superstitions, Voodoo, and Hoodoo   129

6. Myths, Tales, and Customs   137

7. Folk Literature and Religion   151

Appendix 1.   Festivals   169

Appendix 2.   Libraries and Archives   173

Appendix 3.   State Folk Cultural Programs   177

Appendix 4.   Interviewees   181

Index   183

A photo essay follows page 56

Preface

A race must respect itself before it can win the respect of other races. There has been a tendency on the part of some African Americans to despise whatever is peculiarly their own, and this tendency has been most unfortunately fostered by ridicule, caricature, ragtime and coon songs of the coarsest type. In the past many African American children were taught to forget all that reminded them of the long, hard years of slavery. African American children of today are, for the most part, still unaware of their people's cultural contributions in song, dance, art, and literature. A priceless part of these children's existence slowly disappears with the demise of each of the communicators.

One of the main thrusts of this work is to show how African Americans possess an enormous wealth of folklife, which they should take pride in preserving in their annals, not only because it may be interesting or picturesque or it may throw light upon their origin, but because it will allow them to understand themselves better and to be better understood by other races. This work is not intended for humor, amusement, or ridicule, but rather for instruction and thoughtful insight into a race's culture.

Folklife or folklore has always been an intrinsic part of African American society. In particular, southern African American folklife has directly and indirectly influenced the entire mood of U.S. society. It is the heart of southern culture. Southern African American folklife includes music, narratives, and material cultural traditions that are passed on orally from generation to generation. It should be noted that African American folklore or folklife was generally ignored for many years, and it was not until the early 1940s that interest started to develop in this unique, rich source of information. Melville Herskovits has been credited with documenting the authenticity of African American folk roots and demonstrating it in his classic study *The Myth of the Negro Past*. However, one would be remiss not to mention the name of Zora Neale Hurston (1893–1960) for her groundbreaking work in the area of folklore, anthropology, and African American literature.

Since then, extensive research has been done on African American music, folk arts and crafts, tales, customs, and literature. For example, a work entitled *Afro-American Folk Culture* lists nearly 1,400 articles and books focusing on southern African American folklife. What is really fascinating is the fact that a unique culture evolved from people who were removed from their culture and placed in a new environment yet still managed to maintain a large portion of their individuality.

We are all aware that the institution of slavery on these people made the transition to the New World even more difficult. Though the Africans who were brought to the New World were forced to adapt and incorporate many of the ways of their slaveholders, they were able to cling to some of the more intrinsic values that had allowed them to endure for centuries.

There were those who argued that the African Americans did not have a distinct culture for two reasons. First, the capture and enslavement of these people did not allow them to continue with their customs, beliefs, and religion. Second, the acculturation of the Africans in American culture led to the adaptation of many customs, beliefs, and lore of the dominant group.

Yet, through all of the indignities, dehumanization, and deplorable conditions, they survived and developed a folklore rich in spirit and vitality. Generally speaking, their culture or lore can best be described as resilient. What has transcended over the years since Africans were brought to North America as slaves is an absolute phenomenon in the development of their unique folkways. It should be noted that this is not a comprehensive book, and there are several others that one should consider as a source of information for African American culture or folklife. Consult chapter 1 for additional sources.

Overall this work is arranged in three parts. The first part focuses on selective subjects gathered from our interviewees and secondary sources. The secondary material comprises monographs and serials. These sources were acquired through computer-assisted literature searches and visits to libraries and archives. The topics or subjects in the "Dictionary" section are followed by an entry number or numbers for further clarification of the subjects. A subject without an entry number indicates that it was taken from an interviewee. The entry numbers are located in the bibliography section of this work. For the most part, each of the subjects or topics have at least two or more entry numbers referring to either books or journals. Please consult the "Sources" catalog for a complete listing of secondary material.

The interviewees listed in this work were chosen based on their knowledge and expertise in the area of African American folkways. All of them were interviewed in person, and some were interviewed more than once. Selection of these interviewees was based on two methods. First, our contact people in various states recommended individuals based on their knowledge of the subject(s) as perceived by the people in their community. Second, we chose other inter-viewees based on our personal knowledge of each individual's expertise. Several of the interviewees are either friends or relatives of one of the authors. As of this writing, all of the interviewees are alive and well, with the exception of Mr. Vernon Sands, Loretta Pyatt, and Gloria Mitchell. In most cases, the inter-viewees were at least fifty years old; some are up to ninety-three years of age. The exception were those who perfected a particular craft, in which case age was not a criterion.

The same questions were asked of all the interviewees. The majority of them were interviewed in the privacy of their homes, and others at their place of business. The subjects cover material that explores the remedies, customs, tales, artisans, musicians, and practices of African Americans in the South. The cov-erage is from the late 1800s through the present.

It should be noted that because of the sensitive nature of some of the subjects and the request of many of the interviewees that their names not be associated with any of the information, we decided not to credit any informant directly with any of the subjects or terms listed. However, interviewees did agree to allow us to use their names in the appendix and, in some instances, their photos.

The second section of the book encompasses the catalog of sources, divided into seven chapters. Each chapter is categorized by monographs, articles, and (when relevant) recordings. Under "Monographs" are chapters within books and unpublished dissertations. "Articles" covers scholarly journals as well as dissertations from University Microfilm International. Chapters listing record-ings include spoken records and musical recordings covering the late 1800s through the present.

Chapter 1 contains numerous monographs and articles about the general over-view of southern African American folklife.

Chapter 2 contains information on medicine that explores some of the unique remedies that have been passed down from generation to generation, many of which are still used.

Chapter 3, the largest chapter, includes material that covers different aspects of folk music, and spiritual jazz. We excluded any references to minstrel music.

Chapter 4 focuses on material that deals with architecture, art, crafts, and various artifacts.

Chapter 5 explores the various practices and beliefs surrounding witchcraft, superstitions, voodoo, and hoodoo.

Chapter 6 pertains to myths and tales that have been told time and time again. The research will also include citations referring to various customs that were practiced by African Americans from slavery until the present.

Chapter 7 deals with the different aspects of literature that directly and in-directly encompass African American folklore. The same can be said for relig-ion, with its sermons and religious practices.

Each of the entries cited in the chapters were either observed firsthand or were verified by at least two different sources. Bibliographic references are included with each citation whenever possible. All in all, the citations present in this listing of sources are not inclusive of southern African American folklife; rather, we feel that it is a good representation of references that can be used by students and scholars alike. Moreover, we feel that the entire work can be utilized by a general audience. However, the layperson may find greater enjoyment with the first part of the book, while students and researchers will more than likely be most interested in the final parts.

This work includes a photo essay made up of various black and white photographs. The photos display the past and the present. Architecture, crafts, customs, and some interviewees appear in these photos. Many of these are from the collection of Sherman Pyatt, while the others are from various libraries and archives.

The appendixes list major festivals and holidays pertaining to African American culture, libraries and archives, state cultural programs, and interviewees.

Acknowledgments

We have received encouragement and support from many family members and friends. We would like to thank the following people for their time and assistance with this project: Joseph Jenkins, Gail Tolbert, Dru Welch, Muriel Kennedy, Gloria Mitchell, and Angela Brooks. We would also like to give special thanks to Janie Dingle for her excellent job in typing this work.

Among institutions, we would like to thank the staff of the libraries and archives of the Citadel, University of North Carolina, University of Alabama, Birmingham Public Library, University of Mississippi, Hampton University, Charleston County Library, Atlanta University, Tulane University, Amistad Research Center, Penn Center, and the Avery Research Center. Finally, we would like to thank the Citadel Development Foundation for their financial support.

Abbreviations

A Mu	*Art of Music*
AA	*American Anthropologist*
AAG	*Annals of the American Association of Geographers*
Afr Rep	*Africa Report*
AJS	*American Journal of Sociology*
Ala R	*Alabama Review*
All	*Allegro*
ALR	*American Literary Realism 1870–1910*
AM	*American Missionary*
Am Hist Rev	*American Historical Review*
Am J Phys Anthro	*American Journal of Physical Anthropology*
Am Lit	*American Literature: A Journal of Literary History, Criticism, and Bibliography*
Am Mag	*American Magazine*
Am Merc	*American Mercury*
Am Mu	*American Music*
Am Mus J	*American Museum Journal*
Am Q	*American Quarterly*
Am S	*American Studies*
Am Sp	*American Speech: A Quarterly of Linguistic Usage*
Ams	*Americas*
AN	*Art News*
ANQ	*American Notes and Queries*

Antiq	Antiquities
Ar	Arena
Art Am	Art in America
AS	American Speech
ASR	American Sociological Review
Atl	Atlantic Monthly
BALF	Black American Literature Forum
BB	Billboard
Bk	Bookman
Bl W	Black World
Black Ex	Black Experience: A Southern University Journal
Black Mag	Blackwood's Magazine
BlS	Black Scholar
BRH	Bulletin of Research in the Humanities
Brush & P	Brush and Pencil
BU	Blues Unlimited
Bul Bibliog	Bulletin of Bibliography
Bull Univ SC	Bulletin of the University of South Carolina
BW	Blues World
Ca Lit	Cahiers de Litterature
Callaloo	Callaloo: An Afro-American and African Journal of Arts and Letters
Car	Caravan
Carib Stud	Caribbean Studies
Cent	Century Magazine
CG	Common Ground
Christ Cen	Christian Century
Church Hist	Church History
CLA	College Language Association Journal
Comt	Commentary
Cur Lit	Current Literature
Cur Opinion	Current Opinion
Curr Hist	Current History
CWH	Civil War History
DAI	Dissertation Abstracts International
DBT	Downbeat
De Bow	De Bow's Commercial Review
Dialect N	Dialect Notes

DJM	Dwight's Journal of Music
Early Am L	Early American Life
Econ Bot	Economic Botany
ER	Evergreen Review
Ethmus	Ethnomusicology
Farm J	Farm Journal
FF	Fox Fire
FForum	Folklore Forum
Folk F Va	Folklore and Folklife in Virginia
GBM	Golden Book Magazine
GFM	Georgia Folk Medicine
GHQ	Georgia Historical Quarterly
GR	Georgia Review
Griot	Official Journal of the Southern Conference on Afro-American Studies
Harper	Harper's Magazine
Harper's Mag	Harper's New Monthly Magazine
Hea Se Me Hea Rep	Health Services and Mental Health Reports
HER	Harvard Educational Review
Hist Arc	Historical Archaeology
Hist Reflec	Historical Reflections
Hoot	Hootenanny
HWAY	Humble Way (Exxon)
Ind Folk	Indian Folklore
Inter BC	Interracial Books for Children Bulletin
IRM	International Review of Missions
J Am Stud	Journal of American Studies
J Black Stud	Journal of Black Studies
J Miss H	Journal of Mississippi History
JAFL	Journal of American Folklore
JAFLR	Journal of American Folklore Research
JASP	Journal of Abnormal and Social Psychology
Jazz R	Jazz Review
JB	Jazz and Blues
JEMFQ	John Edwards Memorial Foundation Quarterly
JIFMC	Journal of the International Folk Music Council
JJ	Journal of Jazz Studies
JM	Journal of Music Theory

JNE	*Journal of Negro Education*
JNH	*Journal of Negro History*
JPC	*Journal of Popular Culture*
JR	*Jazz Record*
JSH	*Journal of Southern History*
KFQ	*Kentucky Folklore Quarterly*
KFR	*Kentucky Folklore Record*
LA Hist	*Louisiana History*
LA Stud	*Louisiana Studies*
Lab Hist	*Labor History*
LAFM	*Louisiana Folklore Miscellany*
Land	*Landscape*
Lang Soc	*Language in Society*
LHQ	*Louisiana Historical Quarterly*
Lippinc	*Lippincott's Magazine*
Lit Dig	*Literary Digest*
Liv Blues	*Living Blues*
Mac	*Macmillan's*
Man Q	*Mankind Quarterly*
Mass M	*Massachusetts Magazine*
MAWA R	*MAWA Review*
MELUS	*Journal of the Society for the Study of the Multi-Ethnic Literature of the United States*
Ment Hyg	*Mental Hygiene*
MET M	*Metropolitan Magazine*
MF	*Midwest Folklore*
MFR	*Mississippi Folklore Register*
Mid-SF	*Mid-South Folklore*
Miss A	*Mississippi Architect*
Miss FR	*Mississippi Folklore Record*
Miss Q	*Mississippi Quarterly: The Journal of Southern Culture*
MLAN	*Music Library Association Notes*
MLN	*Modern Language Notes*
Mod C	*Modern Culture*
Mod Mus	*Modern Music*
MQ	*Musical Quarterly*
MR	*Music and Rhythm*

MT	*Musical Times*
Mu Ob	*Musical Observer*
Mus Mem	*Musical Memories*
Musc	*Musician*
N Eng Mag	*New England Magazine*
N Music R	*New Music Review*
NALF	*Negro American Literature Forum*
Nat	*Nation*
Nat An Rev	*National Antiques Review*
Nat Hist	*Natural History*
Natl Rev	*National Review*
NC FL	*North Carolina Folklore Journal*
NCB	*North Carolina Booklet*
NCF	*North Carolina Folklore*
NCHR	*North Carolina Historical Review*
Negro D	*Negro Digest*
Negro Hist Bull	*Negro History Bulletin*
New Rep	*New Republic*
Nine Ct	*Nineteenth Century*
NJ Folk	*New Jersey Folklore*
NLHAJ	*North Louisiana Historical Association Journal*
NS	*New South*
NY Folkl	*New York Folklore*
NYFQ	*New York Folklore Quarterly*
NYTM	*New York Times Magazine*
OUTL	*Outlook*
PAAS	*Proceedings of the American Antiquarian Society*
PADS	*Publications of the American Dialect Society*
Pap Bibl Soc Am	*Papers of the Bibliographical Society of America*
Ped Sem	*Pedagogical Seminary*
Penn Hist	*Pennsylvania History*
Phyl	*Phylon*
Plant Miss	*Plantation Missionary*
Poet	*Poetry*
Pop Mech	*Popular Mechanics*
Pop Mus & Soc	*Popular Music and Society*
Pop Sci	*Popular Science*

PQM	*Pacific Quarterly: An International Review of Arts and Ideas*
PRG	*Place Rogues Quarterly*
Proc Am Phil Soc	*Proceedings of the American Philosophical Society*
PTFS	*Publications of the Texas Folklore Society*
Q J Speech	*Quarterly Journal of Speech*
Q Pub Hist Phil Soc OH	*Quarterly Publication of the Historical and Philosophical Society of Ohio*
RC	*Review of the Churches*
Ri M	*Riverside Magazine*
RR	*Record Review*
SAQ	*South Atlantic Quarterly*
Sat R	*Saturday Review*
SC His Mag	*South Carolina Historical Magazine*
SCI	*Science*
Sci Mo	*Scientific Monthly*
Scrib M	*Scribner's Magazine*
Sew R	*Sewanee Review*
SFQ	*Southern Folklore Quarterly*
SI	*Sing Out!: The Folk Song Magazine*
SLJ	*Southern Literary Journal*
SLLR	*Sierra Leone Language Review*
SLM	*Southern Literary Messenger*
SO	*Soundings*
So Cul	*Southern Cultivator*
So HR	*Southern Humanities Review*
So Work	*Southern Workman*
Soc Prob	*Social Problems*
Social Forc	*Social Forces*
South Exposure	*Southern Exposure*
South Liv	*Southern Living*
South Med J	*Southern Medical Journal*
South V	*Southern Voices*
SQ	*Southern Quarterly: A Journal of the Arts in the South*
SR	*Southern Review*
Stud Lit Im	*Studies in Literary Imagination*
Stud Philol	*Studies in Philology*
SW	*South and West*
SWR	*Southwest Review*

Tarts	*Theater Arts Monthly*
TFSB	*Tennessee Folklore Society Bulletin*
TGM	*Theatre Guild Magazine*
Tran Pro Mod Lang Assoc	*Transactions and Proceedings of the Modern Language Association of America*
Trav	*Travel*
Tri A	*Trinity Archives*
Utah Hist Q	*Utah History Quarterly*
VF	*Vanity Fair*
WF	*Western Folklore*
William M Q	*William and Mary Quarterly*
Yale R	*Yale Review*
ZNHF	*The Zora Neale Hurston Forum*

Dictionary

A Long Road Has No End. One of our interviewees explained that just doing and saying things to get by will eventually cause problems. In other words, don't take the easy way out.

Adopted Child. This child brought good luck to the family of the house into which he/she was adopted. (0019, 0268)

All Saints' Day. In the Catholic enclaves of the South, and especially in New Orleans, the day after Halloween was a day to commemorate the dead. Tombs and sepulchres throughout the city boasted wreaths, conch shells, single roses, and other tributes to the departed. Even now, to make a wish come true, one must go to the cemetery on this day with a new white handkerchief, pick up a piece of dirt, and tie it into a corner of the handkerchief. Making a wish on this graveyard clod will make it come true. (0049, 0057)

Anansi Stories. Passed along first in the Caribbean by Creole nurses called nanas, these tales came directly from Africa. They featured animal fables and the spider, or nansi. "Nana," meaning "grandmother," comes directly from the Ashanti tongue in Africa. (0019, 1762)

Animals. Importance was often attached to the presence or appearance of domestic and other animals. For example, the first person gazed upon by a cat after it licked itself would be married. A blackbird was a sign of bad luck. Owls could also foreshadow ominous events. A black dog was seen as an evil thing, possibly a spirit or the companion of a spirit. *See* Birds; Cats. (0057)

Armstrong, [Daniel] Louis "Satchmo," 1900–1971. Jazz trumpet/cornet player and composer. As a boy Armstrong was sent to a reform school, where he learned to play the cornet. The New Orleans native performed in the **Storyville** red-light district as a youth. He joined **Kid Ory**'s Band in 1919, replacing his mentor **King Oliver**. After playing on riverboats for **Fate Marable**, he joined King Oliver's **Creole Jazz Band** in Chicago. Changing from cornet to trumpet in the mid-1920s, he became the leader of his own Hot Five Band with, among others, **Johnny Dodds** and **Kid Ory**. His **scat**-tinged vocal stylings, notably on "Heebie Jeebies," influenced later vocalists, among them **[Elizabeth] Bessie Smith**. Armstrong's early and influential songs included his version of "St. Louis Blues," "Potato Head Blues," and "Cornet Chop Suey." He later formed Louis Armstrong's All-Stars and achieved fame in television and movies. A mark of his stature is the park named after him in New Orleans. (Obituary in *New York Times*, July 7, 1971, p. 1) (0478)

Arthritis. Taking small dosages of a mixture of one cup of lemon juice, honey, and red vinegar was one of the best over-the-counter remedies. Also, wearing copper as a bracelet or anklet was considered to be a good remedy for this ailment. *See* Rheumatism.

Asfeddity. Made of red flannel, a bag full of asafetida worn around the neck helped save one from contagious diseases. *See* Flannel. (0383, 0392)

Ashe Cake. See Hoecake.

Aunt Dicey. Texas ex-slave. Many stories revolve around the person of Aunt Dicey, who was born a slave in the Galveston area. After **Juneteenth**, she and her husband went to live with and work for some German farmers nearby. Because of her habit of asking the mailman to bring her a dime box of Levi Garrett snuff every Saturday, the town was eventually called Dime Box, Texas. (1653)

Ax. If an ax or hoe was brought into a house and taken out again by a different doorway, it was bad luck. This tool was also placed under the bed of an expectant mother to cut or ease the labor pain. *See* Birth. (0376)

Backache. To cure the pain, it was to one's advantage to find a child whose father had died and have that child walk on one's back. Stepping in someone else's footprint was a sure means of getting a backache. If a person crossed a road where a snake had just passed, the person could end up with an aching back. However, the backache could be prevented if the person walked backward along that same road. (0057)

Bad Disposition. It was once thought that if one put one's left foot on the floor first when getting up in the morning, one would be in a bad mood the entire day.

Bad Luck. Throughout history, the African American has always expressed the views of good luck and bad luck in everyday life. Listed are a few examples given to us by several interviewees. If a child was carried downhill on its first journey from home, that baby would have bad luck for life. Also, when leaving the house, a baby's nurse or mother used to say, "Come Spirit," before closing the door. Otherwise, the baby would become fretful because its spirit stayed home. Placing a hat on the bed was not in one's best interest. Purple grackles, purple martins, starlings, and magpies meant bad luck. To call a coffin pretty was bad luck. It was bad luck to sweep or carry ashes out after sunset. It was also bad luck to sweep under anyone's feet. Sweeping under the bed of a sick person or a new mother and baby would curse the sweeper to die. (0212, 1637)

Baptism. In various Baptist congregations, people to be baptized gathered with other church members at the river. They wore long white robes. A "feeler" waded into the stream before the rest, carrying a pole to plumb the water's depths and avoid pitfalls. When a likely spot was found, the preacher immersed the applicants three times, and they emerged from the water shouting praises. On the shore, the other members of the church sang a slow, mournful hymn. (0057, 0139)

Basketry. Basketmaking can be traced directly from Africa to the United States. A common decorative thread, that of dark brown interwoven into the pattern, has been found in baskets from Southwest Africa. Types of baskets made in the Charleston area of South Carolina vary from the fanner to the sewing basket. A fanner, used to winnow the rice after it had been picked, was wide with a shallow, splayed edge. Examples of fanners from as early as 1730 can be found. Rice cultivation was a major industry in South Carolina until the hurricane of 1913 destroyed many of the paddies. Such coiled baskets were woven of different material than contemporary designs. The basketmakers who work along Highway 17 in Charleston County use sweet grass. Their ancestors employed palmetto butt or white oak to blind the coils instead of palmetto strips, although the patterns remained the same. Types of baskets made today include hot pads, church collection baskets, cord baskets, sewing baskets, cake baskets, clothes baskets, traveling baskets, picnic baskets, and spittoon baskets. Present-day basketmakers gather a handful of sweet grass into a quarter-inch bundle and tie one end into a knot to form the center of the base. A quarter-inch strip of palmetto is then wrapped around the bundle, and the coils are turned clockwise in larger circles. Alternating stitches clinch the grass into a tight bundle and tie each coil to the preceding one. A sharpened teaspoon handle is used to feed the palmetto strip through the coils, the ends of which have been sharpened with scissors. Some of the early styles were the fruit basket, place mat, bread basket and the ladies' purse. *See* Palmetto Tree Leaf. (1193, 1474)

Bay Leaf. The aromatic leaf of the laurel tree was dried and used as a spice in cooking. One of our interviewees guaranteed that if a person places one of these next to a dollar bill in his or her wallet or purse, that individual will always have money.

Beale Street. A thoroughfare in Memphis, it is the street from which **W. C. Handy** took the title of one of his most famous songs. It can also refer to a form of Southern urban **blues**. (0495, 0524)

Beech Tree. For a bad cold or pneumonia, water was boiled with some of the inside bark from this tree until the water darkened. This was given to children in teaspoon dosages. *See* Colds. (0383, 0389)

Belly Band. A device that was used mainly by midwives. Immediately after the birth of the infant, the band was tied around its abdomen to strengthen his/her back and hips so he/she might proceed to walk at an early age. (0392, 0393)

Bend Your Sap While They Are Young. Our interviewee indicated that parents should discipline children when they are young and they will be respectful and obedient when they are older.

Birds. Birds of auspicious omen included the skypoke (blue heron), whose feathers were used to make dusters and to bedizen cabins. The yellowhammer brought sickness or death if killed. Birds of good repute included cardinals, bluebirds, tanagers, vireos, and pink flamingos. An owl hooting in the day was a sign of death. To counteract death, pockets were turned inside out and a horseshoe was put on the fire if an owl was heard hooting. *See* Animals. (1650, 1767, 1773)

Birth. There were many omens and practices concerning the birth of a child. Our interviewees gave us the following. A child born with its face down was destined to be drowned, according to Charleston, SC, stories. A child born with a veil over its face was able to see spirits and had good luck. An ugly child grew to be handsome or pretty, and a pretty child would only get uglier. The seventh child was considered to be the wisest. Ashes from the coal of a fire were placed in a bucket and left in the room of the person who had just given birth. The ashes, as well as the woman, remained in the room for at least thirty hours. In some instances, it was customary for a woman to remain in the house for at least nine days after giving birth. A baby born at midnight had the second sight. Trousers placed over the bedpost would make a birth easier. If a baby died in infancy, in order to make the next baby live, it was buried face down. It was said that a baby delivered head first meant that the child would have good luck. Others contend that children born feet first were more likely to acquire a taste for traveling and had the ability to predict their own demise. *See* Birthmark. (0378, 0391, 1580, 1680)

Birthmark. This was produced when a pregnant woman who craved a certain food touched a particular part of her body before she got that food. In that case, the infant would bear a mark on him or her that resembled the craved food. Moreover, the mark would be in the area of the body that the mother had touched. *See* Birth. (0019, 0025, 0057)

Black Betty. Nickname for the bullwhip used on the inmates in prisons and prison farms throughout the South. It was also the subject of a song by the same name and a double entendre for "woman." (0021, 0233, 1650)

Blind Blake [Arthur Phelps]. 1890?–1933? Singer/guitarist. Reportedly born in the Jacksonville, FL, area, he moved to Georgia as a youth. He worked as a street musician throughout the South, riding the rails from town to town. He recorded in the early 1920s for Paramount, singing such songs as "Diddie Wa Diddie" and "Doing a Stretch." He influenced **"Big Bill" Broonzy**. (0470, 0473, 0495)

Blisters. A blister on the tongue meant that you had told a lie. And if one was found on your lip, it was an indication that you had been kissed. *See* Lies. (1498, 1528, 1582)

Blues. A form of secular African American music. The blues, which stresses improvisation, was derived from rural and urban experiences. Formalized into a 12-bar form by **W. C. Handy** and others, the blues reflect the experiences of coping with hard times, unfaithful partners, and alcohol/drug addiction. "Dallas Blues" in 1912 is considered the earliest blues song, and Handy's "St. Louis Blues" in 1914 was another popular early effort. **Mamie Smith** recorded the first blues record, "Crazy Blues," in 1920. **Blind Lemon Jefferson** created the Texas style in such numbers as "Match-Box Blues." The Mississippi Delta manner was begun by **Charley Patton** and carried on by women such as **Lucille Bogan.** "Big Bill" Broonzy developed Chicago-style blues. *See* W. C. Handy. (0436, 0440, 0473)

Boatbuilding. Dugouts were some of the earliest crafts constructed by African Americans. This type of vessel was made from a hollowed-out log. A special type of boat found in South Carolina, called a bateau, was made of cypress logs. Planking soon replaced logs, however, and these boats carried two masts. They averaged around fifty feet in length. (Davis, *The American Negro Reference Book*) (0064, 1306)

Bo-hound. This creature, encountered on lonely roads at night, has been described as a devil-dog. (1637, 1648)

Boils and Sores. A mixture of cabbage or pokeweed and vinegar were applied as poultices to cure these infections. *See* Poultices. (0376, 0383)

Bolden, [Charles Joseph] "Buddy," 1877–1931. Cornet player and band-leader. A New Orleans native, he first played in string orchestras before switching to **jazz**. He performed in **Storyville** and at local functions. Because of alcoholism, he was placed in the state mental institution in 1907, spending over two decades in and out of the asylum. He influenced **Bunk Johnson** and was praised by **Jelly Roll Morton** for the power of his playing. *See* Jazz. (0495)

Bowens, Cyrus, 1890?–1966. Woodcarver. He worked in the Sunbury, GA, area. His abstract grave markers of wood represented the human form and featured curved structures resembling snakes. The markers for the Bowens' family grave contained shingles bearing the names of those interred. (1232, 1256)

Brass Band. Musical groups consisting of brass instruments with a bass drum often were found on larger, wealthier plantations. Some of the slave-based groups could even boast of an imported conductor. (0469, 0495, 0744)

Breaking a Conjure. A method that was used to break a spell. A mixture of salt peter and bluestone was sprayed in the ground around a house to break any spell that might have been put down for the intended victim. *See* Dress or Dressing.

Brer Rabbit. The rabbit represented black folks in the animal fables told in the cabins at night. Although he was small and had no natural defenses, the hare used his wits to overcome his enemies. Brer Fox represented the slave owners, and he often found himself outfoxed by his cotton-tailed adversary. The most famous compilation of these fables was undertaken by **Joel Chandler Harris**, who called the teller of these tales Uncle Remus. In the Low Country, the rabbit was called Buh Rabbit. (1635, 1658)

Bringing Peace and Harmony. In some parts of Florida, it was believed that to ensure happiness in the home, it was a wise move to burn white candles and pray to God. Reciting the Twentieth Psalm was another method that individuals might have considered. This was done by reading the psalm seven times over a glass of water. A saucer was then placed over the glass, and the glass was turned over onto the saucer. The glass and saucer were placed on a shelf, and after three days total agreement would be found in home or business.

Broken Bones. For this ailment, a towel was heated in water and vinegar. The towel, along with mud, was placed on the broken area for several hours. Then, mud was wrapped and packed on the area for several days, during which time the bone would mend. *See* Sprained Ankle.

Broom. To thwart a witch, a broom was placed in the doorway of the bedroom. The witch could not come into the room until she had plucked each straw in the broom, which would take all night. *See* Hag. (1446, 1472)

Broonzy, "Big Bill" [William Lee Conley], 1893–1958. Guitarist, violinist, mandolinist, singer. The Delta-born performer was one of 17 children, whose parents had been born into slavery. As a boy in Pine Bluff, AR, he sang in churches and learned to play the fiddle from his uncle. He served in the army immediately after World War I and moved to Chicago in 1920. Only then did he learn to play the guitar, and he played backup for others in early blues sessions on such labels as Paramount. Fame came after World War II, and he performed with **Sonny Boy Williamson** in clubs and taverns around Chicago and all over the country. He toured Europe and appeared on television and in documentary films. He was influenced by **Blind Lemon Jefferson** and, in turn, influenced **Brownie McGhee** and **Memphis Slim**. His songs included "Back to Arkansas" and "Romance Without Finance." He was an inventor of the Chicago style of blues. (Obituary in *New York Times*, August 16, 1958, p. 17) (0455)

Buckeye. A shrub or a tree of the horse chestnut family, it resembles a chestnut and was sometimes used as a cure for rheumatism. It was also worn around the ankle and carried around in pants pockets as a means of relieving other aches and pains. (0376, 0377)

Buckra. (Afr.) White person. Blacks in the Low Country of South Carolina and the Sea Islands used this term as a respectful way of referring to their masters and mistresses and, after Emancipation, all white people. It could also describe a light-skinned black person. (0001, 0057)

Bull-Roarer. Also called an oro-stick, this toy is made of a flat strip of lath tied to a string and twirled around the head. It produces a roaring noise. In Africa, it was the "voice of Oro," an angry Yoruban god. (0020, 0495, 0685)

Bull Rush. A type of grass found in the marsh area along the coast of Georgia and South Carolina and primarily used to make sweet grass baskets. *See* Basketry.

Burial. Church members were buried with their feet to the east so that they would rise up on Judgment Day facing the sun as it came up. Sinners were buried facing the opposite direction, to avoid facing God. In Alabama it was believed that you must be buried with your head to the west, so that you will not have to turn around to rise up when Gabriel blows his horn at the Resurrection. If a horse neighed or laid down during the funeral service or the coffin slipped while being lowered into the grave, it meant that someone present would soon follow. To leave a grave before it was filled or to leave first from the service invited death. If someone pointed at a grave, his/her finger would rot off or the person's mother's teeth would drop out. After a funeral all cups, pans, and buckets were emptied westward, to discourage a spirit to remain and partake. A pregnant woman who looked down into a grave would never feel her baby.

Cups, saucers, and bottles of medicine used by the deceased were placed on the grave. There were some who felt that placing children over the casket of the deceased adult family member would prevent that person from coming back and harming the children. *See* Positioning the Body.

Burial Parades. It was a traditional New Orleans practice to accompany the hearse to the graveyard with a full brass band. Mournful on the way to burial, the music became jubilant on the way home from the burial. This approach was used by **Jelly Roll Morton** in "Dead Man Blues." (1713)

Burial Preparations. No family member could help prepare the body for burial. Coins held the body's eyelids shut (and were placed in the body's hand before burial), and a dish of salt was set upon the chest of the deceased. The salt prevented swelling, or purging. The hair of the deceased was combed out, and a female corpse's hair was never plaited because the devil would send his black-birds to unplait it, even after the lid was on the coffin. *See* Soda Water. (1658, 1738, 1785)

Butterflies. A white butterfly brought good news while a black one portended evil. (1637, 1767)

Buzzards. These animals are bald because the rabbit dunked their heads in hot grits. (1637, 1650, 1762)

Calabash. This was a special type of turtle cooked in the shell. The yellow-bellied terrapin was the favored type of ingredient for calabash. Many house-holds kept their turtles in a cooter pond covered with wire. (1233, 1237)

Camel-Back House. Dwelling. It has one elongated story in the front and two in the rear. (1278, 1329, 1363)

Candles, Meaning of. One of our interviewees explained how different colors of candles are used for various reasons. The use of some of these candles, with the reading of certain psalms, are said to bring interesting results. A white candle represents purity, rest, and communion and should be used while reading Psalm 112. Black denotes freedom from evil and works well with Psalms 7, 12, or 55. Reading Psalms 59 or 112 and burning a yellow candle depicts attraction and religion. If there is a desire for money or luck, a green candle along with reading the 4th or 61st Psalms will fulfill needs. And for those desiring love, affection, and good health, consider a red candle, along with reading Psalms 54 or 138 and 139. These are just a few examples of what the color of these candles represents. *See* Reading of Psalms.

Canes. Staffs carried by conjure-doctors had magical powers, much like Aaron's rod in the Bible. A James Island, SC, practitioner had a talking cane, which warned him one day while he was not home that his house was being robbed. (1589, 1627, 1702)

Can't to Can't. One of the interviewees from South Carolina explained that this generally referred to the amount of time a person worked in a given day. The person would work from can't see in the morning to can't see at night.

Carnations. Some contend that taking a bath in the petals of this flower is a good way to bring a loved one closer in spirit.

Catching Babies. A frequent way of saying that someone was going to or had helped deliver a baby. (0393)

Cats. Corpses attracted cats, so care was taken before burial that a cat did not spring onto the body and eat the eyes out of it. Some say that babies are vulnerable to cats, who like to suck the breath from the helpless infants. How was the cat created? One story says that Jesus was walking upon the earth and visited the home of an old woman. Her house was overrun with rats and mice and other pests. She told the Lord of her dilemma. He pulled off his right-hand glove and threw it on the floor. The glove turned into a cat, the four fingers of the glove becoming its legs and the thumb its tail. The cat then rid the house of the vermin. Therefore, it is not a good idea to kill a cat. A cat is good luck for a house. It was said from one interviewee from Alabama that if a cat ran through a room, it had the power to make the entire room shake. *See* Animals. (1727, 1738, 1767, 1807)

Causing Blindness. One method of causing blindness was to combine frog dust and salt, which was then placed in the hat of the person who was to be made blind. Another method was to use the remains of a dried-out snakeskin and place it between the pages of a book. When the book was opened, the dust would fly up into the person's eyes and blind him or her.

Causing Difficult Deliveries. One method of bringing about hard labor pains and labor was to tear apart the woman's underwear and bury it under her steps or house, which would result in the woman having a breech birth. A person would also secure a slip or piece of underwear of the intended victim and tie nine knots in it, cursing the woman with each knot. Next the item would be measured close to the length of an infant. This was knotted three more times and buried under the woman's doorstep. If she walked over the item nine times, she would have a miscarriage. (1503, 1521)

Causing Insanity. It was once said that securing a piece of hair of the person in mind, burning it slightly, and burying it would cause the individual to go insane. If a bird retrieved any of a person's hair, it was believed that the bird would make a nest with it and cause the individual to have terrible headaches.

Chicken Manure. It was dried, wrapped in white cloth, and used mainly as a tea to cure scarlet fever. (0389, 0390)

Chicken Pox and Measles. Sulfur and lard were mixed and used as a salve to relieve children and adults from the discomforts of these diseases, mainly the itching.

Children's Feet. One should never sweep over a child's feet because this would prevent him or her from ever marrying. (1498, 1503, 1528)

Child's Growth. If one stepped over a child, it was believed that it would stunt his or her growth. (1498, 1503)

Coffee. Corn was removed from the stalk and placed in a pot of hot water. This eventually turned the water dark brown, which was drunk as coffee. (0036)

Coffee Grounds. Some practitioners use these to predict the future. The process involves using the dried-out grounds left at the bottom of the cup of the person whose fortune is being told. The grounds are spread on a table, and from these the practitioner would forecast his or her future. Tea leaves are used as well.

Coffle Song. This plaintive song was sung by newly captured slaves as they were marched together in yokes, or coffles, from barracoons to the holds of the slave ships. *See* Slave, Prison, and Railroad Songs. (0429, 0495)

Coins. *See* Wearing of Coins.

Cold Weather. If the larger end of the Milky Way system pointed to the north, it was a sure sign that it would get colder. The crying of the killdee, or killdeer, in the late afternoon or early morning meant a dramatic drop in temperature. (1637, 1660, 1738)

Colds. A teaspoon of sugar mixed with a few drops of kerosene was a good way of curing a cold. Once the mixture had hardened, the individual would then suck on the product like a cough drop. A level teaspoon of sugar with nine drops of turpentine was also a very good cure. *See* Beech Tree; Hog's Hoof Tea; Mini Weed Tea; Peach Tree; Tar Tea.

Colic. One of the better known methods of curing colic was to prevent the baby's diaper from falling onto the floor. Another method was to give the child a half teaspoon of bourbon added to a bottle of water.

Color. Black people are the color they are because when they were asleep beneath the Tree of Life, God woke them up. They all ran to Him and started shoving and pushing. He said, "Get back!" They misunderstood him. (1637, 1660)

Confusion or Disturbance. For those who were interested in causing trouble in someone's home, they would do the following. First, they would combine cayenne pepper, sulfur, and crossing incense, which was placed in a new handkerchief or a clean piece of cloth. Next the mixture was sprinkled in the house of the intended person. Finally, once the house was swept, the powder would begin to take effect. Another method was to get some dirt from the graveyard and scatter it in different rooms of the house or around the house of the intended victim.

Conjure-Doctors. These individuals offered five distinct services to one who had been under the influence of a spell. They could (1) tell the person whether he or she had been conjured; (2) discover the identity of the conjurer; (3) search for and find the "trick" and destroy it; (4) cure the patient; (5) turn back the trick, at the patient's behest, on the person who made it. Upon first consulting with the victim, the conjure-doctor usually placed a small piece of silver into the hand or mouth of the sufferer. If the silver turned black, it indicated that the person had been conjured. Use of a cupper-horn, made from a cow's horn, drew corruption from the body, and often featured engravings of lizards, snakes, and toads. Another method involved a deck of cards, which the conjure-doctors always carried. After cutting the cards, the doctor could tell the persons who summoned him/her if they indeed were under evil influence. *See* Dress or Dressing; Toby. (1483, 1485, 1503)

Cooling Board. A device that was used to prepare the deceased before they were finally placed in the casket. *See* Burial Preparations; Funeral Customs.

Corn Songs. Call-and-response songs sung by slaves as they shucked the corn. These were among the earliest types to be documented. *See* Slave, Prison, and Railroad Songs. (0429, 0495, 0716)

Corns and Callouses. A mixture of baking soda and castor oil or lard was used to bring relief to aching feet. The mixture was made into a paste and wrapped in a cloth around the affected area. (0376, 0389, 0392)

Cortier, Eldzier, 1916–. Painter. Although trained in Chicago, he traveled to the Sea Islands in 1940 in search of new themes. Of the works inspired by that sojourn, *Southern Gate* stands out. It depicts a nude black woman, draped only in a striped cloth placed around her loins, standing before a plantation gate. This portrait symbolized both the beauty and the pain of the Sea Islanders. (1217, 1232)

Cotton. Sitting cross-legged on a bale of cotton assured a young man many children. Making love while picking cotton brought good luck. Wherever a wind-blown cotton ball landed, money would be found. For luck, the first boll picked each year in the Delta area was buried under the back doorstep. A boll of cotton in the sugar bowl also assured good luck, but cotton in the pocket kept money away. *See* Good Luck. (1593)

Counting Teeth. An interviewee suggested that one was always careful when smiling in the presence of an older person, because there was a possibility that that person might count the teeth in your mouth. If that happened, there was a chance that the person could be a hag and could visit you that night. *See* Hag.

Covering Mirrors. One important custom following the death of a person was to make sure that if there were mirrors in the house, they should be covered. Otherwise the mirrors would lose their color. If death saw a person's reflection, he would return for that person.

Cowan (Cow-an). This is a type of stew whose main ingredient just happens to be snapping turtle. The stew is prepared and served on Easter Sunday with potato salad and rice. This dish is prevalent in the Louisiana area. (1294, 1297)

Cracklin' Bread. It consists of cornmeal, salt, and crisp bits of fresh pork, called cracklin'. It is baked in a hot oven and resembles cornbread. (1308, 1333, 1348)

Creatures in the Body. Snakes were said to grow in an individual if someone placed the blood of a snake in the food or drink of a person he/she was interested in harming. Also earthworms were placed in fish just before frying and served to the individual whom one wanted to harm. In a matter of a week, the individual was supposed to have developed worms in his or her intestines. (1503, 1515, 1582)

Creole. Native, from Sp., *criollo*. Formerly it referred to a white descendant of French or Spanish settlers of Louisiana. It now is used to distinguish African American ways from those people of French or Cajun descent. (0019, 0028, 0032)

Creole Jazz Band. After **Storyville** was closed, **King Oliver** left New Orleans for Chicago. There, he formed the Creole Jazz Band, whose members included **Louis Armstrong** on cornet, Honoré Dutray on trombone, **Johnny Dodds** on clarinet, Lil Hardin Armstrong on piano, Bill Johnson on banjo, and Baby Dodds on drums. The band offered the first recording of New Orleans style in 1923. It was characterized by the use of mutes and was notable for Louis Armstrong's first recorded solo, "Chimes Blues."

Critter Stew. This delicacy is a mixture of dove, rabbit, squirrel, and sausage. It is then cooked as if preparing a gumbo. (1218, 1241, 1279, 1294)

Crudup, Arthur ["Big Boy"]. 1905–1974. Guitar player, A Mississippi Delta native, he taught himself to play the guitar. His early training was in gospel and church singing, and he left for Chicago in 1940. He performed on the King Biscuit Time show in the mid-1940s. During World War II he entertained the troops on Armed Forces radio. He was influenced by **Big Bill Broonzy**, and he performed with **Sonny Boy Williamson**. His songs included "Greyhound Bus Blues" and "That's All Right [Mama]." He was named the Father of Rock and Roll by many observers, having directly influenced Elvis Presley. (0470, 0495, 0531)

Cuts. Several interviewees noted that one means of stopping bleeding was to apply sugar to the affected area. Others were said to have used soot from the fireplace and a wad of chewing tobacco. A mixture of spider web and turpentine was considered to be a good healing agent for cuts. Placing what was known as fat meat, soot, and a copper penny on a piece of white cloth was good for healing abrasions.

Dance Band. The model for early jazz bands, the New Orleans dance band, ca. 1910, consisted of violin, cornet, clarinet, trombone, drums, double bass, and guitar. **Louis Armstrong**, Sidney Bechet, and **Jelly Roll Morton** performed in early dance bands, both at festive and somber events. (0469, 0495, 0531)

Dances. African Americans provided the sense of spontaneity in dancing, often lacking in European-based steps. In the 18th and 19th centuries, many dances were adapted by people of color, such as the *cakewalk*, a high-stepping, syncopated march that originated during slavery and derived its name from the prize of a cake, which the winning couple received from the masters. It was popularized during the **ragtime** era. Another dance of Afro-Caribbean origin was the *calinda*, which was danced in the slave quarters to the accompaniment of drums. When drums were forbidden by law as a means of illegal communication, this dance was all but suppressed. During the post-Emancipation, pre–Civil Rights era, other dances originated in the black community. **Ma Rainey** popularized the *Black Bottom*, a *shimmy*-style exercise, which may have originated in Atlanta or, perhaps earlier, in Nashville. The shimmy itself has been attributed to Tony Jackson, ca. 1900. The *Charleston*, another shimmy variety, was probably of Ashanti origin and was introduced in the 1923 black revue *Runnin' Wild*. In the 1930s and 1940s, the *jitterbug* evolved in the juke joints and at the Savoy Ballroom in Harlem. Since the rock and roll era, many popular dances have been the product of black artists. (0487, 0495, 0515)

Dancing. Not crossing the feet made any dance a religious dance. Crossing the feet while dancing made it secular, or sinful, dancing. Plantation dances often featured this song: "Hurrah, ladies, tow on de floor, here we go to Baltimore. Swing e lady roun' de town, sling 'em roun' de floor." *See* Shout. (0487, 0495, 0515)

Days of the Week. A woman was not supposed to enter your house on a Monday or a Friday until a man had entered that domain first. If she did, chaos would reign for weeks in that house. (1650, 1738, 1746)

Death Customs. After a death, the windows of the deceased were opened for a thorough airing. After the burial bedclothes and other clothes were burned or aired. The sickroom, or death room, was frequently painted. This was done to prevent bad spirits from entering the house of the deceased. (1593, 1650, 1726, 1785)

Decoration Day. Memorial Day. In the post–Civil War, pre–Civil Rights era, many in the black community celebrated this holiday by putting fresh flowers on the graves of Union soldiers. Gathering at the cemetery, they would listen to speeches and have a parade. (0049)

Delta Blues. The Delta is the geographic area between the Yazoo and Mississippi rivers, south of Memphis and north of Vicksburg. The region has nurtured innovators from **Charley Patton** to **Muddy Waters**. (0450, 0495, 0528)

Dett, R[obert] Nathaniel, 1882–1943. Canadian-born, classically trained (Eastman School) composer, pianist, and conductor, he was the director of music at the Hampton Institute 1913–1931. He developed the Hampton Institute Choir, famous for its **gospel** renditions. Dett founded the National Association of Negro Musicians. (Obituary in *New York Times*, October 4, 1943, p. 17) (0495, 0499)

Devil Shoe String. One interviewee stated that placing a piece of this root in your pocket would bring you good luck.

Diddy-Wah-Diddy. Mythological place. In that land, nobody had to work. Chickens appeared already cooked with a knife and fork, waiting to be eaten. Other food, from chitterlings to sweet potato pie, abounded for the asking. Nobody went without. (0021, 0025, 1637)

Dint. Another name for a spirit. Inhabitants of the Tidewater region of Virginia called ghostly visitors by this name. (1503, 1517, 1579)

Dirt. Graveyard dirt in the shoes prevented bloodhounds from picking up a person's scent. (1503, 1515, 1579)

Dirt Eating. In North Carolina and Georgia in particular, the habit of eating dirt or clay prevailed among some children. The type of clay found in these areas contained silex, oxide, iron, alumina, magnesia, and water. This kind of clay, especially abundant in Richmond County, GA, cannot be found north of the Mason-Dixon Line. The dirt-eating habit could be cured by feeding the children roast bat. *See* Yellow Clay. (0383, 0412)

Dixieland. Style of jazz. It developed as a two-bar form in the 1920s, performed by **Louis Armstrong** and **King Oliver**. It was disseminated by such bandleaders as Eddie Condon in New York. Swing and bop later arose from this form. New Orleans still boasts performers, among them the Preservation Hall Band. (0469, 0495, 0782)

Doctor Cat. A prominent voodoo doctor from New Orleans around 1912–1914. His real name was Joseph M. McKay, and he made a lot of money through his mail order business selling advice, gris-gris, and candles. His mail-order voodoo business was brought to a halt when federal authorities charged him with mail fraud. *See* Gris-Gris. (1483, 1521, 1529)

Dogtrot House. This type of construction was also called saddlebag, breezeway, or three Ps (two pens and a passage). It consisted of two separate one-room buildings set side by side and connected by a wide covered hall open at both ends. (1259, 1278, 1377)

Domino, Antoine "Fats," 1928–. Singer/pianist. Born in New Orleans, he was the son of a violinist. Teaching himself to play the piano, he worked for tips in local clubs. Throughout the 1940s, he toured in Kansas City, Los Angeles, and Philadelphia. The rock and roll craze elevated him to prominence in the mid-1950s, singing such songs as "Ain't That a Shame?" and "Walkin' to New Orleans." He was influenced by **Louis Jordan** and in turn influenced such performers as Chuck Berry. (0441, 0495)

Don't Sneeze. If you happened to sneeze while eating, it was viewed as a sign of death. *See* Sneezing.

Dorsey, Thomas A. 1899–1993. Georgia-born **gospel** singer, pianist, guitarist, and composer. He was called "our Irving Berlin" by **Mahalia Jackson**. As a youth, he worked with **Ma Rainey** and recorded secular music under the name of Georgia Tom. Dorsey started publishing his own gospel music in single sheets, called "dorseys." He founded, with Sallie Martin, the National Convention of Gospel Choirs and Choruses. Dorsey toured with the Gospel Choral Union from 1932 to 1944. Among many other songs, he wrote "Take My Hand, Precious Lord," "Peace in the Valley," and "In the Sweet Bye and Bye." (0505, 0539)

Dr. Ryngo. Called Doctor to the Dead, he lived on James Island, SC. He always wore a black soutane and had a reputation in the Charleston, SC, area for his command of occult knowledge. (1472, 1503, 1538)

Dragging on Your Dress. A term commonly used when a person has a baby. The saying meant that you were now responsible for someone besides yourself.

Dream. Many people still contend that dreaming about a wedding indicates a funeral, and vice versa. To dream of a rat is a bad dream. To dream of a snake is not a bad dream; and if you kill it, you conquer your enemy. Not killing it means that your enemy will conquer you. Moreover it is believed that if a dead person came to you in a dream and asked you for something and you gave it to him, you were giving away somebody in your family. However, if that person gave you something, it was good luck. If you dreamed of a person that you knew in a platonic manner and that person was naked in the dream, it was likely that someone in your family would soon die. *See* Dying Man or Woman. (1503, 1517, 1523)

Dream Books. Popular books that sold in drugstores. These books help provide the interpretation of dreams and are used frequently to determine the winning number of a lottery. (1503, 1517, 1523)

Dress or Dressing. Several interviewees stated that this referred to the fact that someone was putting root on or fixing an individual. *See* Conjure-Doctors; Uncrossing a Conjure.

Dying Man or Woman. One interviewee indicated that if one dreamed of a dying man, it was a strong indication that a lady was going to die and vice versa. *See* Dream.

Earache. It was customary to place a lock of hair in the ear that was ailing to render some relief from pain. Another method of treatment was to take the head off a cockroach, split it, and squeeze the juice into the ear.

Easter Rock. In certain parishes in Louisiana and districts in the Mississippi Delta, this church service took place usually among Baptists, who favored various types of sunrise services. The congregation began to assemble at around 10 P.M. on the Saturday night before Easter Sunday. Professions of faith, called "cul'ns," took place and then the collection plate went around. After this the central aisle of the church was cleared and a long table covered with a spotless white cloth was placed thereon. Both sides of the pulpit were curtained off and all the lamps, except one, were extinguished. At midnight the deacon ordered the congregation to "come quiet." "When the Saints Go Marchin' In" was sung while a procession entered through the rear of the church, headed by a man and woman carrying a banner. Twelve women, all dressed in white and carrying a lamp, followed these two. They proceeded to march endlessly around the table, after first placing the twelve lamps on it. They next "dressed" the table by placing twelve cakes and twelve bottles of "angel liquor" on it, followed by paper baskets containing three Easter eggs. Each of the twelve women, or "sancts," then chose a partner to sit with her at the table. They sang "They Crucified My Lord," "Little David," and "Won't You Set Down?" All the while, the congregation rocked and swayed while singing. The preacher began his sermon at sunrise, with proper responses from the congregation. He then commanded them to re-form the procession and circled the table before exiting through the back door. (0049)

Edmonson, William, 1870–1951. Stonemason. Working in the Nashville area, he began carving gravestones in the 1930s. Told by God to start carving stone, he began by carving simple tablets. As his work evolved, he added animal figures, notably the lamb, to the tops of his gravestones. He also made human figures, usually working in small pieces of limestone. His most famous figure represents Eleanor Roosevelt. (1218, 1231, 1232)

Egg in Hand. Hoodoo method of finding a murderer. It is told that when a young man killed his sweetheart in a jealous pique, he ran from justice. Since no posse could locate him, the conjure-doctor was consulted. He suggested that an *egg* be placed *in* the *hand* of the girl in her coffin. After three days, her killer surrendered. (1499, 1503, 1521)

Elbow. If you accidentally hit your elbow against something, it was very likely that you would see someone whom you had not seen in quite awhile. The interviewee was quite adamant about this.

Ellington, "Duke" [Edward Kennedy], 1899–1974. Composer, bandleader, pianist. Born in Washington, DC, he began his career there. In the 1920s, he moved to New York, working at the Cotton Club in Harlem. There his audience was wholly white. Radio boosted his fame, allowing him to collaborate with such composers as George Gershwin. His band members stayed with him loyally, from the **swing** era to his death. His compositions include his signature tune, "Take the A Train," and "Black, Brown, and Beige." He remains the premier composer of the jazz genre. (0489, 0495)

Emancipation Day. January 1 has been treasured by African Americans as a day marking freedom because on January 1, 1804, the slaves fighting for their freedom in Haiti were liberated by their leaders. On January 1, 1808, the importation of slaves into the United States was forbidden by Congress. The most significant January 1 was in 1863, when President Abraham Lincoln issued the Emancipation Proclamation. (0049)

Enemies. It was recommended by a voodoo doctor that a person wanting to get rid of enemies should put some sugar in a bowl and burn a brown candle. This was to be carried out before going to bed. The person would then take the remnants of what was left and throw it in the enemy's yard. (0389)

Every Grin Teeth Don't Mean Laugh. Beware of people who are always smiling with you; they are not always your true friends.

Every Tub Needs to Stand on Its Own Bottom. According to an interviewee, this means that each person needs to take full responsibility for his/her actions.

Evil Spirits. Throwing water through a screen door would rid a person's house of spirits. Blue doors and shutters kept evil forces away. (1650, 1734)

Fatherless Child. A child who has never seen his father brings good luck to the house because he has the power to cure sickness by the touch of his hands. (1787)

Field Holler. Sung by individual workers rather than a group while engaged in cotton picking, working on the levee, or mule skinning. Described as a "long, low musical shout, rising and falling and breaking into falsetto," it was common in prisons. *See* Street Cries. (0465, 0476, 0489)

Fig Milk. A remedy that is still used, this was produced by squeezing the end of unripened figs. The milk from this fruit was placed on the nipple of a woman who had just given birth. The breasts were then bound in white cloth. The cloth was left on until the breast milk had dried up.

Fingernails. It was believed that blacks with pink-colored fingernails were untrustworthy and deceitful. A child's fingernails were not cut before he/she was one year old. Otherwise, the baby would grow up to become a thief. We were told by one interviewee that white pigmentation under the nails represented how many girlfriends or boyfriends one had.

Fish. Several people in South Carolina explained that dreaming of fish meant that someone in the neighborhood was pregnant. A fish with scales meant that the baby was a girl and without scales meant the baby was a boy. *See* Dream.

Fisk Jubilee Singers. Organized in 1871 as the Fisk Singers, they worked by going on tour to raise money for Fisk University in Nashville, TN. George L. White, a music teacher, formed the group of nine singers and a pianist. They sang **gospel** they had learned as slaves. Their tour of the northern United States raised enough money to pay off their college's debts. The money raised also built Jubilee Hall, the first permanent building on the Fisk campus. **John W.**

Work then took over the direction of the choir and consolidated the group's stature. They first recorded in 1913 under the title of the Fisk University Jubilee Quartet. They continue to produce albums and tour. (0569, 0585, 0608)

Five Fingers Grass. In many parts of Louisiana, it was believed that hanging this plant in the house would ward off spirits. The plant is described as having a leaf divided into five segments. (1483, 1676)

Flannel. Red flannel worn next to the skin helped ward off rheumatism, and a bit in the lamp kept the kerosene from exploding. Red flannel in the shape of the sacred heart of Jesus was placed at the foot of a sickbed to help cure the patient, or at least delay death. (0382, 0414)

"Frankie and Johnny." Popularized in 1928 by **Mississippi John Hurt**, this song depicts the inevitable demise of the unfaithful lover. Published in 1912 under this title, the song has over 300 variants. Traced to a Scottish folk song, some individual lines have been identified from as early as 1863. One real-life version has Frankie Baker of St. Louis shooting her man in 1899. It is also called "Frankie and Albert." (0001, 0020)

Friday Night. Executed convicts walked on this night because they had never seen the light. The custom was to hang felons with a black hood over their face. Thus they were blind. On Fridays they visited people who died on sickbeds. These people led the blind ones where they wished to visit. (1650, 1738, 1754)

Fuller, [Albert Fulton] "Blind Boy," 1909–1941. An eastern, or Piedmont-style, blues singer and guitarist. A North Carolina native, he worked with Rev. Gary Davis and **Sonny Terry** on such albums as "Rag Mama Rag" and "Pistol Slapper Blues." He was often accompanied by harmonica and washboard. (0542, 0572)

Funeral Customs. The watch night took place immediately after a death. Friends and relatives sat up with the corpse and ate, drank, and sang. The body was placed on a cooling board, which was two planks supported by a saw-horse on each end. A sheet covered the cooling board, hanging to the floor. Another sheet covered the body, and a separate sheet covered the face. Mourners lifted this sheet and addressed the body. A plateful of salt and ashes was placed under the cooling board, to absorb the disease. These ashes were carried to the grave and thrown into the grave at the phrase, "ashes to ashes." Mourners threw dirt on the coffin, singing. During the funeral sermon the men kept their hats on. When someone with a small child died, the young child was passed over the coffin, to prevent the parent from returning from the dead to fetch the child. (0295, 0349)

Geechee. This term is associated with people (African Americans) from the Sea Island and surrounding area who include rice as a part of their daily diet. *See* Gullah. (0227, 0270, 1966, 1979)

Gee's Bend. An all-black community in Wilcox County, AL, the community is located along a deep bend of the Alabama River. Situated in the "Black Belt" region, this community's history stretches back to pre–Civil War plantation days. Slaves were originally brought into the area to work the cotton fields. Many former slaves then chose to work in the area as tenant farmers rather than venturing outside the Bend. (0004, 0023, 0038)

Ghosts. One way of seeing ghosts was to look back over one's left shoulder. It was believed that looking through a mule's ear or putting a small hole in your own would produce the same results. If one should eat a little fat meat or grease at night, one could see witches, ghosts, and all sorts of half-visible occupants of the atmosphere. Moreover, wiping off a rusty nail and putting it in one's mouth would result in ghosts and spirits coming forth. When a person died, the spirit rode the coffin to the grave and then came back to its earthly house and stood behind the door for three days. All cups, buckets, and pans were emptied in the house of one recently deceased to discourage the spirit from lingering. (1680, 1722)

Gig. Around New Orleans, this was well known as someone playing the illegal numbers game, better known as the lottery.

Gillespie, "Dizzy" [John Birks], 1917–1993. Trumpeter, bandleader, composer. A native of Cheraw, SC, he started playing music as a boy, under the tutelage of his father, a musician. When the family moved to Philadelphia, he joined a band and began his career. During the 1930s he played with several groups, including that of Cab Calloway. In the 1940s, in Harlem, he collaborated with Charlie "Bird" Parker and Theolonius Monk. After developing bop, he worked with such performers as Duke Ellington. He formed his own band in 1945. His songs include "Groovin' High" and "Blue 'n Boogie." (0495, 0524, 0630)

Going Home. Several interviewees said that this phrase was used constantly by a person who was ill for a period of time and either wanted to die or was about to. "Home" represented the departure to heaven.

Good Luck. The bones of a black cat were considered to be lucky. The bones were obtained by boiling a black cat (not even a single white hair was allowed) alive and throwing the remains in a stream. The bones that stayed behind were the lucky ones. Young women were supposed to have good luck when fishing.

If a person's left hand itches, to make a wish come true, the saying goes, "rub your ass and it will come to pass." *See* Cats. (1670)

Goofer Bag. This contained goofer-root, cloth, strands of hair, needles, and graveyard dirt. Stepping over one that was buried somewhere would "goofer" the victim. Hair taken from a camel by the conjure-doctor added potency to the bundle. Shaking hands with one who had rubbed theirs in goofer dust would put one under their spell. Goofer dust was taken from the lid of the coffin to be fully effective. *See* Dress or Dressing. (1483, 1499)

Goofer Dust. Taken from a graveyard, this dust was used in **voodoo** ceremonies. (1483, 1499)

Gospel. African American religious music. It is characterized by pre-Emancipation "sorrow songs" ("Steal Away") and post-Emancipation "jubilee spirituals" ("In That Great Gettin' Up Mornin' "). Often based on the same texts as white sacred music, African American gospel developed its own flavor and forms, using syncopation, blue notes, and call-and-response delivery. The African Methodist Episcopal [AME] Church and the National Baptist Convention were the strongest organized influences on church-based singing. The modern performance style originated in the Pentecostal Church of God in Christ in Memphis around the turn of the century. By the efforts of **Thomas A. Dorsey, Mahalia Jackson**, and Rosetta Tharpe, gospel became a popular and recognizable format. Its influence remains apparent in the later work of such commercial performers as Sam Cooke and Aretha Franklin. Contemporary performers include Rev. James Cleveland, the Staple Singers, and Andrae Crouch. (0457, 0495)

Granny and Grannymother. A term commonly used when referring to the midwife of a community.

Grave Decorations. In the Low Country and Sea Islands, seashells often decorated graves. Broken cups and saucers, vases, and plates were also found on graves. In some locales, a lattice hut protected the grave. *See* Burial Preparations. (1658, 1738, 1785)

Green Sally Up. A clapping game that went something like this: "Green Sally up, Green Sally down, Green Sally bake her possum brown. Asked my mama for fifty cents, to see that elephant jump the fence." (0141, 0601)

Gris-Gris. Charm. Of African origin, this concept refers to the potency of the magic possessed by an individual or inflicted upon him. *See* Goofer Bag. (1483, 1499)

Grits Tea. An interviewee from South Carolina explained that when she was a child, her mother would fry day-old grits until they were browned. Water was then poured over the grits, and this produced tea.

Guitar. Some of the early identifications of this instrument were described as follows: ''negroes would cut lengthwise through the middle of a calabash (fruit) and stretch a goat skin over it. They adjusted around the edges with little nails, they made two holes in the surface; then a piece of flat wood made the handle of the guitar. Finally, three cords of some type of hemp were stretched across the instrument and it was finished.'' Fiddles were constructed in a similar manner. As reported by a former slave who reached Canada in 1855, ''In Virginia, we generally made our fiddles by catching ground hogs and tanning the hides. It was then stretched over a piece of timber fashioned like a cheese box.'' *See* Instruments. (Conaway, *The Afro-American Traditions of the Folk Banjo*) (0485)

Gullah. Considered the most conservative form of black English spoken in the South today. This term is used to depict the language of the African American Sea Island people. Gullah preserves features of African language brought in by plantation slaves as far back as 300 years ago. It is applied to a special group-type of Negroes, limited historically and geographically to the Sea Islands and the narrow tidewater strip bordering the coastal counties of Georgia and South Carolina and a small section of northeast Florida. *See* Geechee. (0227, 0270, 1966, 1977)

Gullah Jack. Also called Jack Pritchard, he was born in Angola. Denmark Vesey, who planned an uprising of slaves in Charleston, SC, in 1822, used Pritchard's reputation as a **conjure-doctor** to recruit conspirators and assure their silence. On the morning of the attack his troops were supposed to eat nothing but parched corn and ground nuts. And to protect themselves from being hurt or killed, they were to hold crab claws in their mouths. After the collapse of the conspiracry, which was squelched before it started, Gullah Jack was hanged with Vesey and others. (0220, 0390, 0409, 0422)

Gumbo Ya-Ya. From Angolan *kinkombo*, hen party. A gathering with many voluble women. (0175, 0301)

Hag. Old men or women who had the ability to get out of their skins, assume different forms, and ride people in their beds. The hag was caught in a bottle and placed in the ashes under a fire, which caused an agonizing death. Ways to keep hags from entering the home included turning the key sideways in the lock, placing the handle of a broom across the doorway, and turning stockings inside out before going to bed. Mustard seeds sprinkled around the bed kept hags away. A hag could be identified by his or her refusal to step over a broom. If a hag could be caught out of its skin, salting it would allow it to be seized.

Hambone. A rhymed chant, it was first practiced by slaves. Sometimes it involved the uncrossing of hands on knees, while fanning to and fro. It was derived from children's rhymes, with the same set of verses applied to different songs. A record of "Hambone," released in 1952, became a best-seller. (0489, 0495)

Hampton Folklore Society. This group was founded at the Hampton Normal Institute in Hampton, VA. The charter stated that its purpose was "the education of the colored people to do their own observing and collection; to watch the little things peculiar to their own race, and to record them and place them where they can be made of permanent value." Reports were published in the *Southern Woman*. George Washington Cable, Booker T. Washington, and Alice Mabel Bacon were founding members. (0432, 0489, 0495)

Hampton Quartet. This singing group from Hampton Normal Institute, Hampton, VA, sang African American spirituals. Under the direction of **R. Nathaniel Dett**, they garnered worldwide recognition for **gospel**. (0432, 0489, 0525, 0526)

Handy, W. C. [William Christopher], 1873–1958. Alabama-born, the composer, conductor, publisher was the father of jazz notation. As a youth, he was active in minstrel shows and formed his own brass band, playing the cornet. A college graduate, he abandoned teaching for music. He toured the South with the Mahara Minstrels and in the course of his travels, he heard the folk music that later became **blues, jazz**, and **ragtime**. He wrote a campaign song for Boss Crump of Memphis, which was published as "Memphis Blues" in 1912. With Harry Pace he formed a music publishing company, responsible for such numbers as "Yellow Dog Blues" in 1914, "Beale Street Blues" in 1917, and "Harlem Blues" in 1922. Handy was responsible for the emergence of the African American vernacular in American popular music. (Obituary in *New York Times*, March 29, 1958, p. 17) (0563, 0564, 0565)

Hardy, John. A steel driver, he worked on the building of the Big Bend Tunnel of the C & O Railroad in West Virginia in the 1870s. The John Henry ballads are based partially on him. He could drive more steel than any other two men of his day. A massive person, he stood 6' 2" and weighed 225 pounds. In a quarrel over a woman while gambling, he killed a man and was later hanged. (1637, 1650, 1670)

Harris, Joel Chandler (1848–1908). *Uncle Remus: His Songs and Stories* was published in 1881. Therein, he related animal fables featuring **Brer Rabbit** and his adversary, Brer Fox. Harris labored as a newspaperman for the *Atlanta Constitution* and offered many of the stories in that paper. He created a composite of an ex-slave, Uncle Remus, to tell these tales. They were based on stories the young Harris heard while growing up on a Georgia plantation. His use of dialect helped propagate stereotypes. (0105, 0106, 0112, 1764)

Heart Condition. An interviewee from Alabama claimed that drinking one teaspoon of ground nutmeg mixed in a small glass of water once a week was considered to be a very good cure for heart ailments.

Heart of a Cat. It was believed that by eating the heart of a black cat, one could prevent any harm from bullets or knives. (1483, 1499)

Hen and Hawk. A popular game played in Charleston, SC. It had the following rhyme: "Chickame, Chickame, Chimescrow, I went to the well to wash my toe; when I came back, my chick was gone. What o'clock, old witch?" (0141, 1638, 1641)

High John the Conqueror. Hero of black folk stories. Gifted with superhuman powers, he was so bold that he eloped with the daughter of the devil. Confronted by Satan, he didn't back down but instead seized Lucifer by his arm, ripped it off, and beat him with it. Before leaving hell, High John passed out ice water to the damned and turned down the damper. (0319, 1725, 1934)

Hoecake. There were some people from South Carolina and Alabama who stated that this bread was made from a mixture of cornmeal, salt, and water rolled into a paste and then patted into a cake. Placed under hot coals in the fireplace, it was baked all day and served with butter.

Hog's Hoof Tea. Several interviewees from Alabama said that the debris from the hog's feet were scraped and placed in a white piece of material. It was then submerged into a pot of boiling water until the water had darkened. This was given to those with flu symptoms, whooping cough, or a cold.

Holler. Field hands sang this precursor of the **blues** solo. A pre–Civil War traveler described them as a "long, loud, musical shout, rising and falling and breaking into falsetto." Hollers recorded by **Alan Lomax** at Parchman, Mississippi, include "Whoa Red" and "Levee Camp Holler." *See also* Street Cries. (0465, 0476, 0489)

Hoodoo. A variation of **voodoo**. The word first appeared in 1885 in *Dynamiter*, by Robert Louis Stevenson. (1483, 1488, 1512)

Hooting Owl. This was considered to be a sure sign that death was close to the person the owl was near. (0220)

Hoppin' John. A dish that is still eaten on New Year's Eve and New Year's Day. It consists of cowpeas or field peas, rice, and pork meat. Eating this dish is said to bring good luck and money. (1308, 1333)

Horseshoe. Nailed in the fireplace, it kept hawks from catching a person's chickens. Placing this item over the doorway prevented ghosts from entering a house. (0065)

House, Son, 1902–. Singer/guitar player. A Mississippi Delta native, he was the son of a musician. As a youth he preached. A self-taught guitar player, he performed at informal settings throughout the 1920s and 1930s and recorded for the Library of Congress. He was influenced by **Charley Patton** and he in turn influenced the great **Robert Johnson**. During the folk music revival of the 1960s, he was rediscovered. His songs included "Levee Camp Moan" and "My Black Mama." (0470, 0528)

How to Kill Someone. It was said that if one wanted to bring about the demise of an individual, one could do so by obtaining some of the feces of this person and placing it in a jar with some graveyard dirt. While burying the jar, the person would curse it as well. This would bring about constipation, and the intended victim would die within a week to ten days. Another method was the use of a sock or stocking of the intended victim. Graveyard dirt was placed in the sock or stocking of the victim and buried under the intended individual's steps or house. Within a month the victim would supposedly die an unexplainable death. (1490, 1503, 1521)

Howlin' Wolf [Chester Arthur Burnett], 1910–1976. Singer and guitar/harmonica player. Born in the Mississippi Delta, he sang in church as a boy. Self-taught, he performed on tour with **Robert Johnson** and **Sonny Boy Williamson**. During the depression, he often had to turn to farming to survive. Serving in the Army during World War II, he entertained the troops. First in Memphis, then in Chicago, he established himself as a top club performer. He influenced many rock musicians, including ZZ Top and the Yardbirds. He sang many hits, such as "Natchez Burnin' " and "Howlin' Blues." (Obituary in *New York Times*, June 12, 1976, p. 30) (0470, 0528)

Hunting Peanuts. An Easter custom from Charleston, SC. The peanuts were concealed in the pockets of the older folks, and the children had to search for them. The child finding the most peanuts got a prize. (1787, 1880)

Hurston, Zora Neale, 1893–1960. Author/folklorist/anthropologist. Born in Eatonville, Florida, she attended the local public schools before she eventually
entered Howard University, where she studied from 1921 to 1924. In 1928
Hurston received a fellowship and private grant to do research in African American folklore at Columbia University and in her native state. She produced a
program of African American spirituals and work songs. In addition, she did
extensive research in the British West Indies and Haiti. Her travels and research
produced several books. (2062)

Hurt, [John Smith], "Mississippi," 1893–1966. Delta-style singer, guitarist,
and harmonica player. He recorded "Avalon Blues" in 1928 and returned to
farm and railroad work in Mississippi. He made no further commercial efforts
until his rediscovery in 1963. He recorded for the Library of Congress. His
stylings were characterized by a light beat and rapid fingerwork. He was influenced by Jimmie Rodgers. His work remains important because of its fidelity
to roots. (Obituary in *New York Times*, November 4, 1966, p. 39) (0470, 0528).

Hush Puppies. Called monobilies in certain parts of the South, these delicacies
consisted of corn meal, flour, baking powder, onions, and water, rolled into
croquettes and fried in leftover fish fat. One cook in Florida swore she invented
them, inspired by a dream of Jesus. She called them p'noblums, perhaps a
version of monobilie. (1233, 1241, 1308, 1311)

If I Had Your Hand. As explained by an interviewee, it was a compliment
that was paid to an individual by another regarding his/her social and economic
status in the community.

Instruments. The *banjo* originated in Africa, evolving from an instrument called
the banza, or banjar. It consisted of a parchment membrane stretched over a
circular frame, with an open bottom, a bridge, and a long neck. Original banjos
had four strings and detachable necks. Thomas Jefferson took note of them in
his observations on the daily lives of the slaves. Throughout the 19th century,
it was the characteristic American instrument. However, its role in African
American music was taken over by the double bass in bands. The *jug* was played
to produce a tubalike sound by blowing across the opening. It became a mainstay
of the improvised groups called jug bands. The washtub was used in jug bands
to form the bottom of a basslike stringed instrument. It was accompanied in
those bands by the *washboard*, which was rapidly rubbed up and down for
rhythmic effect. *Bones* are really flat hardwood sticks but originally were made
of ox rib. A pair was held in each hand, one between the thumb and index
finger and the other between the index and middle finger. Flicking the wrist
made them click. *See* Guitar; Jug Band. (0469, 0495, 0630, 0685, 0876)

Ironwork. The Mandida people of West Africa had a tradition of working with metals. When brought as slaves to the United States, they found work as ornamental ironworkers and smiths. In Charleston, SC, by 1848, African American smithies outnumbered whites. In fact, Charleston, Savannah, Mobile, and New Orleans became noted for ornamental ironwork, often made by African Americans. *See* Simmons, Philip. (1173, 1289, 1235, 1349)

Itching Hands. If the left palm itches, a person will receive a letter; if the right palm itches, money is on the way. However, to make these things happen, people should spit on their right hand or scratch on wood. *See* Good Luck.

Jack-MUH-Lantern. Entity feared by Low Country inhabitants. He wandered through the swamps at night, carrying a lantern and leading the unwary traveler to death in a bog or quicksand. Almost human in form and covered in hair like a dog, this being boasted ear-to-ear lips and eyes like locomotive lamps. It could outpace a horse, so the only charm against it was not to outrun it, but to take off one's shirt or coat and put it back on inside out. (1767, 1787)

Jackson, Mahalia, 1911–1972. Singer. Called the Queen of Gospel Singers, she was born in New Orleans. She grew up from adolescence in Chicago, working with the Johnson Gospel Singers before starting solo work in 1935. Her first hit, in 1947, was "Move On Up a Little Higher." She was associated with the National Baptist Convention and Dr. Martin Luther King, Jr. She popularized gospel through her radio and TV shows and set the style for succeeding gospel singers in the more restrained NBC method. (Obituary in *New York Times*, January 28, 1972, p. 1) (0495, 0568, 0609)

Jazz. It is a music form with roots in the African-American experience, emphasizing rhythm, pulse, syncopation, and improvisation. Rising up in New Orleans around the turn of the century, African American musicians expressed themselves outside the rigid forms of traditional European music. **Ragtime** was a predecessor of the form, and other evolved styles include boogie-woogie, **blues, dixieland, swing**, bop, third stream, free jazz, and fusion. Originally spelled "jass," it was a street term for copulation. Now it is the chosen form of most contemporary African American and other composers. (469, 495)

Jefferson, Clarence "Blind Lemon," 1897–1929. A Texas-born blues pioneer, Jefferson became one of the street singers in Dallas to survive, having been born sightless. A guitar player par excellence, he sang shout-style blues, sometimes with **Leadbelly**. He developed the Texas style, as distinct from Delta and Piedmont blues. In Chicago in the mid-1920s, he recorded a series of records, including such self-composed songs as "Long Lonesome Blues" and "Blind

Lemon's Penitentiary Blues.'' He influenced many, including **Louis Armstrong**, Bunk Johnson, and **Bessie Smith**. Jefferson died in Chicago, by some accounts frozen to death in the street. (0475, 0495)

Jenkins Orphanage. This orphanage for destitute African American children was founded by the Rev. Daniel J. Jenkins in Charleston, SC, in 1891. It sponsored a brass band, which went from offering street concerts to touring Europe and major U.S. cities. The orphanage is still open as of 1998. (0477)

Jimson Weed. Tied around the head and the ears, this herb is said to bring the body temperature down from a fever.

Jive. A word synonymous with deception, fooling, etc. It was used by **Louis Armstrong** in a 1928 song, "Don't Jive Me." Later it became associated with jazz and the jitterbug style of dancing. (0430, 0431, 0495)

John Domingo. The black constable of Charleston, SC, Domingo bore the fame of being a greater **conjure-doctor** than Gullah Jack. He lived on Mazych Street in the Holy City, where he enforced his own brand of justice and intimidated his fellow blacks through his magic. John was tall and heavyset, wearing an old Union Army coat year-round. His hair stuck up in tufts secured by shoestrings, and he wore a silver ring shaped like a snake. He was walking down Market Street one evening with a felon in each huge hand when he suddenly said, "I'm jus' like Jesus Christ, a thief on my lef' and my right." For this blasphemy, he was struck down by an unseen hand. (1738, 1787)

John Henry. Legendary character, subject of songs and stories. **Alan Lomax** and Carl Sandburg traced the song named after him, wherein he competes with a steam-driven pile driver, using only his nine-pound hammer. He beats the machine but dies of exhaustion. The Big Bend Tunnel on the C & O Railroad is one of the settings for the song. Ribald tales have risen about his prowess with women. See also Slave, Prison, and Railroad Songs. (1725, 1790)

John Kuners. Christmas personality. He was usually the slave who led the Christmas parade among the inhabitants of the Outer Banks of North Carolina and elsewhere. Slaves from the Guinea coast originated the tradition. These individuals were to be found in Wilmington, Edenton, and Hillsboro, NC, at Christmas. Their presence has been noted as far back as 1720, and they faded away around 1900. Marching down the main street, they wore colorful, tattered costumes. They danced and played the bones, cow's horns, and juice harps. Some dressed as women and wore masks called kuner faces. The leader carried a bullwhip to playfully keep back curious urchins. They chanted "Hah! Low! Here we go!" and "Kuners come from Denby." Onlookers watched as they capered and performed comic antics. (1876)

Johnny the Conqueror. A type of gris-gris that was described as a twisted root with a long prong. The female John was distinguished with a short prong and male with the longer prong. Johnny was considered to be very good for gambling and love affairs. If a man was having problems with his lover, he was told to mix Johnny with cayenne pepper and sugar and put it under her bed. The result was unending love for the man as long as he wanted her. The same thing was done by the husband if he thought his wife was having an affair, except the Johnny was placed under her pillow. *See* Love Charms. (1446, 1466, 1467)

Johnson, Robert, 1911–1938. Singer. Born in Clarksville, MS, he performed throughout the South before dying under mysterious circumstances (perhaps poisoned by a jealous woman friend) in San Antonio. He wrote and sang his own songs, playing the guitar. Famous for his walking bass line, he influenced many who came after, including most rock guitarists. His singing was noted for its intense emotion, tinged by falsetto phrasing. Famous songs include "Kind-hearted Woman Blues," "Hellbound on My Trail," "Preaching Blues," and "Me and the Devil." Johnson's career gave rise to the legend of the bluesman who sold his soul to the Devil for musical talent. (0470, 0474)

Johnson, William Geary "Bunk," 1889–1949. Jazz trumpeter/cornetist. Born in New Orleans, he worked as a youth for such groups as the Original Superior Orchestra, who all wore resplendent military-style uniforms. His career was spent in doing everything from circus bands to minstrel shows until he performed with the Evan Thomas band. A murder involving band members forced him to lay low and subsist by giving lessons. Enterprising researchers rediscovered him in the 1940s, and he left a record of what early jazz sounded like. After World War II, he performed with his old friend Sidney Bechet. (Obituary in *New York Times*, July 9, 1949, p. 13 (0470, 0478, 0489)

Johnson, William H., 1901–1970. Painter. Born in Florence, SC, he moved to Harlem, where he studied art. Upon graduating from the National School of Design, he left the United States to live in France. He returned to the United States in 1938. Thereafter he drew upon his South Carolina roots to produce such works as "Early Morning Work," depicting a rural black family in the South. He worked for the government during World War II and went back to Europe after the war. His mental processes declined because of syphilis, and he died in a New York state hospital. (1263, 1265, 1277, 1278)

Joplin, Scott, 1868–1917. **Ragtime** pianist-composer. Joplin was a native of Texarkana, TX. His music was composed for and distributed on piano rolls (before the invention of the Victrola). The form consisted of a 2/4 rhythm, with the left hand performing the bass beat and the melody taken from folk music dances. Although others established ragtime, Joplin perfected it. His better-known compositions included "Magnetic Rag" and "Maple Leaf Rag." A consummate musician, he also composed the opera *Treemonisha*. He influenced **Jelly Roll Morton** and Fats Waller. Joplin died in a mental institution. (0469, 0524)

Jordan, Louis, 1908–1975. Bandleader, singer, composer, saxophonist. Born in Brinkley, AR, he played music from childhood and joined a band in Hot Springs as a youth. He went from Philadelphia to New York, where he worked the Savoy ballroom in Harlem, recording first with Chick Webb. In 1938, he formed his own band, the Tympany Five, which added rhythm to the blues. He wrote such songs as "Is You Is or Is You Ain't My Baby?" and "Don't Burn the Candle at Both Ends." He was known also as "King of the Jukeboxes." (Obituary in *New York Times*, February 6, 1975, p. 36)

Juba. Precursor of "Hambone." A rhyme from Virginia says, "Juba boys, Juba, Juba up, Juba down, Juba round Simmon town. Juba dis, and Juba dat, Juba round de simmon vat." "Simmon" refers to persimmon beer. *See* Persimmon. (1638, 1641)

Jug Band. Folk string band. The name derives from the use of a jug as an instrument. These bands usually contained a guitar, a fiddle, a bass, a harmonica, a kazoo, and sometimes a piano. The characteristic sound came from blowing air across the mouth of the jug to produce a tubalike noise. Early recordings by the Memphis Jug Band ("K. C. Moan") and **Ma Rainey** ("Black Cat, Hoot Owl Blues") accompanied by the Tub Jug Washboard Band made the sound distinct. *See* Instruments. (0489, 0585)

Juke Joint. A rural southern meeting place. Unable to afford costly entertainment, many poor African Americans frequented these establishments. They were often housed in ramshackle buildings or even tents. During Prohibition liquor could be bought and musical entertainment and dancing were provided. Many joints were little more than brothels. The jukebox gets its name from these places. This term reputedly originated in the turpentine camps in Florida. (0019, 0021, 0057)

Jumping the Broomstick. When slaves were not allowed to be married by rites of the churches, they developed the custom of jumping the broomstick to solemnize their vows. The couple stood together while witnesses held a broomstick a few inches above the floor. The couple then hopped over the broomstick together. Oftentimes the bride and groom and the older men present would notch the door of the bedroom with their initials or marks. (0021, 0057)

Juneteenth. Among the African Americans of Texas, June 19 was celebrated as the day on which slavery was abolished. A festive occasion, it always featured music, dancing, and picnics. On June 19, 1865, General Gordon Granger occupied Galveston, TX, proclaiming the freedom of all slaves in the region. This day was then celebrated in the African American community in Oklahoma, Arkansas, and Louisiana, as well as Texas, as Juneteenth. Since the Civil War ended in April, many reasons were given for the delay in getting the news to Texas. One has it that an ex-Union soldier from one of the "colored" regiments rode a mule from Washington, D.C., west to spread the word. (0049)

Keeping a Woman Faithful. Men who were suspicious about their wives or lovers having affairs had a few methods of preventing this from happening. One way to end the female's affair was to secure a strap from the woman's slip or brassiere and tie one knot in it for each of nine nights. This item was kept in the man's pocket at all times. It symbolized that she was tied to him and she would not end the affair because of those ties. Another method was to have intercourse with the woman and afterward wipe himself with a new handkerchief. The handkerchief was then placed in a bottle or jar and sealed. The female's sexual desires would remain dormant as long as the bottle remained sealed. (1482, 1495, 1499, 1515)

Kentucky Folklore Society. Founded in 1912 at Lexington, this group at first consisted of college professors. They worked closely with schoolteachers throughout the state, concentrating on music—notably mountain ballads and African American folk songs and spirituals. The group publishes the *Kentucky Folklore Record.* (0030, 0064, 0072)

Knife and Fork. The crossing of a knife and fork while standing behind a door will permit someone to see the Devil beating his wife. If a person had dropped either of these items on the floor while eating, it was an indication that someone was coming to the person's house seeking food. *See* Sunshine and Rain.

Leadbelly [Huddie Ledbetter], 1885–1949. Blues singer. Born in Louisiana, he wandered throughout Texas and his home state, picking up songs from every sort of group. His material covered everything from cowboy songs to spirituals. While serving time for murder in Angola Penitentiary, he was discovered by **John and Alan Lomax** on a song-gathering expedition for the Library of Congress. Possessed of a powerful voice, he accompanied himself on the 12-string guitar. His recordings included "Good Morning Blues," "Goodnight Irene," and "Rock Island Line." (Obituary in *New York Times*, December 7, 1949, p. 36) (0434, 0470, 0473)

Lies. A sore on the lip was a pretty good indication that one had lied. Biting one's tongue while talking was a sign that one was lying at that very instant.

Lightning. Many blacks would not continue to work in the fields with horses or mules during a storm because they felt that the eyes of these animals drew lightning. Moreover, it was a good idea to cover all the mirrors in the house during lightning because the evil spirits would otherwise get people. It was believed that burning the wood from a tree that had been struck by lightning would cause a house to burn or to possibly get struck by lightning. (1608, 1618)

Lion's Mouth. "When you have your hands in the lion's mouth, play with it until you get it out." That saying means you shouldn't argue with someone who has control of the situation at that time.

Lock Jaw. Several informants remarked that if a child encountered a hag, this would have been his/her ultimate fate. *See* Hag.

Lofton, "Cripple" Clarence, 1887–1957. Blues pianist. Born disabled in Kingsport, TN, he moved to Chicago in 1917. In that city, he worked at rent parties and other informal entertainments. He served as a sideman on many records in the 1920s and 1930s. During this time, he owned and operated the Big Apple Tavern. With **Pine Top Smith** he developed the boogie-woogie style of piano playing. During the post–World War II period, he left music. His songs included "Brown Skin Gals" and "Streamline Train." (0457, 0470, 0495)

Lomax, Alan. 1915–. Folk song scholar. Born in Austin, TX, he went on to study at Harvard, Texas, and Columbia. He then started to work with his father, John A. Lomax, at the Archives of American Folksong at the Library of Congress. He helped to compile *American Ballads and Folksongs* in 1934 and has written and researched extensively in the field. (0165, 0168, 0225)

Lomax, John, 1867–1948. The prime folklore collector of the century. The Mississippi-born scholar studied music at the University of Texas. He founded the Texas Folklore Society. Able to endure hardships on the trail, he traveled on horseback and in a "tin lizzy" to record folk songs on an Ediphone cylinder recording machine. His first book, *Cowboy Songs and Other Frontier Ballads*, came out in 1910. He worked with his son at the Library of Congress, giving over 3,000 songs to that institution. Among his discoveries was **Leadbelly**. (Obituary in *New York Times*, January 27, 1948, p. 26) (0165, 0168, 0225, 0227)

Lost Tooth. A dream of a lost tooth meant that a friend would die.

Louisiana Folklore Society. The New Orleans Branch of the American Folklore Society was founded by Alcée Fortier and others in 1892. After the death of Fortier in 1914, the Louisiana Folklore Association faded away. In 1956, the organization was revived by the English Department Folklore Committee of LSU. It publishes the *Louisiana Folklife Miscellany*. (0165, 0168, 0225, 0227)

Love Charms. A woman was able to win the affection of a man by putting his tracks under her bed. A woman could bring discomfort to an undesirable mate by putting his tracks or prints on an ant bed. Some believed that one could put some blood on a piece of candy, give it to your beloved to eat, and he/she would return your affection. A woman could wear a piece of meat under her arm for about two days and then squeeze the juice of the meat into a bottle of alcohol that she sprinkled on the man's shirt or jacket. This was followed by a hand-kerchief being tied in knots at the end of each corner. When making love, the woman would place the handkerchief in a position to catch some of the semen. The handkerchief was then buried, and the man could no longer have an erection for another woman. *See* Menstrual Blood. (1521, 1575)

Malaria. As a preventive measure against malaria, many people wore a string with 16 knots around their waist.

Mamma Onesy. A few people from the Sea Islands noted that a mother used this term when she referred to her only child.

Mandinga. (Afr.) Fetish. Many Blacks wore them to protect themselves from evil. (0380, 0384, 0388, 0389)

Mandrake. If used the correct way, this root could be administered to someone as a source of harm or pain. (0380, 0384, 0388, 0389)

Mardi Gras Indians. African Americans of New Orleans, long barred from taking part in the Krewes of the main parade, formed their own groups of "tribes" dressed in feathers. Among the twenty or so such bands, the Wild Magnolias were noted for their color and style. They consisted of Spy Boys, Flag Boys, a Wild Man, Trail Chiefs, the Queen and her court, and the Big Chief, Bo Dollis. They rehearsed for weeks each year and competed with other "tribes" for the crowd's adulation. (0019, 0032, 0033)

McGhee, "Brownie" [Walter Brown], 1915–. Banjo/guitar/jazz-horn/kazoo/piano player and singer. A native of East Tennessee, he learned to play the guitar from his father. He worked at different itinerant jobs as a young man, including a stint with the Rabbit Foot Minstrels. In the 1930s, he sang in the Golden Voices' Gospel Quartet with his father. He met **Sonny Terry** in North Carolina in 1939, and they performed the blues together afterward. He set up his own blues music school in New York in the 1940s and appeared on Armed Forces Radio during World War II. He toured extensively with Sonny Terry thereafter and worked with all the great bluesmen. His songs include "Me and Sonny" and "I Gotta Look Under Your Hood." (0518, 0521)

McTell, "Blind Willie" [Willie Samuel], 1901–1959. Blues accordion/guitar player. Growing up in Statesville, GA, the Milledgeville native learned to play the guitar from his mother. He ran away from home and performed with medicine shows and the John Roberts Plantation Show. Living in Atlanta, he performed sporadically throughout the South during the depression. His jobs included being a singing car hop at an Atlanta drive-in restaurant. At the end of his life he was a preacher at Atlanta's Mt. Zion Baptist Church. His notable songs included "Blues Around Midnight" and "Statesboro Blues." (0518, 0521)

Marsh Tacky. African for "horses." They were on St. Helena Island and were wild, thriving on marsh grass. (0220, 0287)

Memphis Minnie [Lizzie Douglas], 1897–1973. Guitar/banjo player. Although born in Algiers, LA, she grew up in Mississippi. She ran away from home and played with the Ringling Brothers circus. Finally settling in Memphis, she became a fixture on **Beale Street** in the 1920s. She recorded with the Memphis Jug Band. During the next twenty years she lived and worked in Chicago with **Big Bill Broonzy**. She retired in the 1950s. Her songs included "Bumble Bee" and "Queen Bee." She has been called the "most popular female country blues singer of all time." (0476, 0521, 0526)

Memphis Slim [Peter Chatman]. 1915–1988. Memphis-born blues singer. A songwriter, he played the boogie-woogie piano. He started singing at age 16, emphasizing the shout style and working with Roosevelt Sykes. Moving to Chicago, he started playing piano with **Sonny Boy Williamson** and **Big Bill Broonzy**. He formed his own group in 1944, the House Rockers, playing such songs as "Maybe I'll Lend You a Dime" and "I Believe I'll Settle Down." (0489, 0495)

Menhaden Chanteymen. They were organized in 1988, nearly fifty years after many of the members first sang the work songs associated with North Carolina's important menhaden fisher. Like the chanteys of British tradition, the worksongs were nautical, but with an African American flavor. The singers came together to share and relive the sound of work songs on the water. (0459, 0585)

Menstrual Blood. Several women stated reluctantly that if a woman was trying to prevent her husband or lover from having an affair, she would mix some of her menstrual blood into his food. Usually, it was mixed into red rice, okra soup, or any other dish that was red in color. *See* Love Charms.

Midsummer's Day. Also called St. John's Day, June 23 was the traditional time of the major voodoo celebration in New Orleans. This tradition arose with Sanité Dédé, a quadroon from Santo Domingo who came to Louisiana in the 1820s. She was the first of many voodoo priestesses who presided over the rituals in New Orleans. *See* Voodoo. (1495, 1499, 1503, 1519)

Mini Weed Tea. In Alabama we were told that this was administered to cure the common cold. It was made by placing dried cow manure in a piece of white cloth, which was then placed in boiling water. Sometimes turpentine or whiskey was added to this brew just before it was given to the infirmed.

Mirrors. An interviewee from South Carolina remarked that as soon as a member of the family died, the mirrors were turned facing the wall, else they would tarnish and hold a permanent picture of the corpse. Another theory is that the dead person would see the reflection of a living person and return to get them.

Mississippi Folklore Society. The society was founded in 1927 at the University of Mississippi. It ceased functioning in 1930. However, in 1966, it was reactivated and reorganized again at the University of Mississippi. It publishes the *Mississippi Folklore Register.*

Missouri Folklore Society. Organized in 1906, the society met first in St. Louis. Mary A. Owen became the lifelong president in 1908. Washington University in St. Louis was the center of the early activities. Leaflets featuring African American ballads were published. The group ceased meeting in 1920. (0020, 0021)

Mistletoe. Like the cottonwood tree, the mistletoe was reputed to be the wood of the cross at Jesus' crucifixion. To show the love of Jesus at Christmas, it is hung inside the house so people can kiss each other in brotherly love. (0383, 0386, 0389)

Morton, "Jelly Roll" [Ferdinand Joseph Le Menthe], 1890?–1941. Jazz pianist/composer. A New Orleans native, he worked as a youth in **Storyville** playing the piano in bordellos. Influenced by **Scott Joplin**, he took his inspiration from a lagniappe of sources, including **ragtime** and the **blues**. He transformed ragtime into **jazz,** originating the break and the riff, which came to characterize jazz performances. He often stated that the piano should always be an imitation of a jazz band. Like Joplin, he composed for piano rolls. Working with the Red Hot Peppers band in the 1920s, he wrote such songs as "King Porter Stomp" and "Sidewalk Blues." He wound up in Washington, DC, during the depression after a notable career in New York. **Alan Lomax** found him in a shabby club in 1938 and asked him to make some recordings for the Library of Congress. These remain a definitive version of **scat** and blues singing and piano playing. (Obituary in *New York Times*, July 12, 1941, p. 13) (0462, 0472)

Moss. Several interviewees noted that by placing this in shoes one could prevent high blood pressure. However, if the moss pulled from the tree fell onto the ground before it was placed in one's shoes, one had to throw it away and use a different piece of moss.

Mud Dauber. A tea was made from the nest of this insect along with a mixture of gunpowder to ease the pain during labor and to accelerate the delivery of the baby.

Mulatto. From Sp. *mulato*, young mule. This described in the past the gradation of African American blood in which one of the child's parents was black and the other was white. This term is also used when referring to quadroons and octoroons, second- and third-generation offspring of a Negro and a white person. (0066, 0073, 0118, 0160)

Mullen Leaves. More than one interviewee revealed that pine needles or the leaves of the mullen plant were administered as a tea for healing individuals with measles.

Mumps. It was a widely known belief that fat meat or butt meat along with a penny was placed on each jaw and held in place with a piece of white cloth tied to the top of the head of a person with mumps. This was worn until the swelling subsided.

My Spirit Meets You. An interviewee explained that this saying indicated that a person liked the demeanor or characteristics of another individual from the very first encounter.

Nail Bone. A flat-shaped metal instrument resembling a table knife that is used to construct sweet grass baskets. During the days of slavery, slaves were not allowed to have metal, so they used animal bones. *See* Basketry.

Names. Naming a child after a deceased person would surely have brought bad luck to that child.

Negro Caesar. This slave from South Carolina was given his freedom and an allowance for life for discovering the benefits of the root of the plantain plant. His prescription consisted of the juice of the plantain and wild horehound, along with applying tobacco soaked in rum to the wound. This was used as a cure for the rattlesnake bite. (0218, 0220, 0270, 0287)

North Carolina Folklore Society. Started in 1913, this group was founded in Raleigh. It consisted of the governor, the state education superintendent, and professors. James F. Royster of the University of North Carolina was the first president. (0265)

Nose. If the inside of a nose itches, someone will visit. A burning sensation from the nostrils indicates that someone is talking about a person.

Nose-Um. A South Carolina interviewee noted that this was a card game in which the loser was hit on his nose with a deck of cards.

Obi Hut. The home of a voodoo priest, it contains his pharmacy. Also called obeah hut. *See* Voodoo. (1490, 1499, 1506)

Octoroon. This is a pseudo-Latin word describing a person of color who had a quadroon and a white parent. This person is described as having a mixture of ⅞ white and ⅛ black blood. *See* Mulatto. (0025, 0032, 0057, 0165)

Ogeechee River. Georgia stream. Those who came from the Ogeechee River area were called Geechees. It referred to the manner of speech—a mixture of English and African and particular vowel pronunciations. *See* Geechee. (0094, 0165)

Oliver, Joe "King," 1885–1938. Cornet player. In his native New Orleans, he worked with **Kid Ory**'s Brownskin Babies before the demise of **Storyville**. Afterward, he left for Chicago and formed his own band, the Original Creole Jazz Band. This group boasted any number of luminaries, from **Louis Armstrong** to **Johnny Dodds**. He used a mute to produce the characteristic "wah-wah" sound on such numbers as "Dippermouth Blues." After the breakup of this band, he formed the Dixie Syncopaters and produced such hits as "Dead Man Blues." Musical innovations passed him by, however, after the 1920s, and he ended up as a janitor. (0495)

One Rain Won't Make a Crop. People have to keep striving and working hard in order to succeed. If people fail while trying to accomplish a goal or task, they should pick themselves up and try again.

One-Strand. This is a stringed instrument based on the African earth bow and musical bow. It consists of a string or wire stretched over a board and often has a tin cup resonator. It is played by plucking the string and running a slider along the wire to vary the effect. Such techniques were later adapted to produce the bottle-neck method of guitar playing in the Delta. *See* Banjo; Guitar. (0485, 0524, 0585)

Ory, Edward "Kid," 1886–1973. Trombonist. Born in La Place, LA, he invented the "tailgate" style of trombone playing, which stressed the use of glissandi. He also played many other instruments, including the banjo. After the exodus of jazz musicians from New Orleans in the late teens, he went to California, helping to establish jazz on the West Coast. From there he journeyed to Chicago, joining **Louis Armstrong** in the Hot Five band. They produced such songs as "Muskrat Ramble" and "Gutbucket Blues." He returned to Los Angeles in 1930, playing there for 25 years. (Obituary in *New York Times*, January 24, 1973, p. 44) (0495)

Page, "Hot Lips" [Oran Thaddeus], 1908–1954. Trumpet/mellophone player and singer. Born in Dallas, he worked with Ida Cox, **Ma Rainey,** and **Bessie Smith**. He toured Texas and the Midwest with the Walter Page Blue Devils. During the course of his career he worked with Count Basie and Artie Shaw. His songs included "Ashes on My Pillow" and "Big D Blues." (Obituary in *New York Times*, November 7, 1954, p. 88) (0495)

Palmetto Tree Leaf. Also known as mada (may-dah), it is a greenish fanlike leaf that is used when constructing sweet grass baskets. *See* Basketry.

Pan of Water. There were several people from South Carolina who agreed that this was usually placed under the bed to lower the temperature of a person who had a fever.

Parsons, Elsie Crews. 1875–1941. A pioneer folklore collector, she helped sustain the American Folklore Society. Her work carried her to the Sea Islands and the Caribbean. Her unique conceptual framework viewed folk studies of African American groups in an anthropological light as serious scholarly subjects. She avoided the curiosity element and downplayed dialect in her recountings. (0165, 0189, 0337, 0338)

Patton, Charley [Chatmon], 1887–1934. Singer/guitarist. The Mississippi Delta native spent his career working in informal settings, from logging camps to **juke joints**. His many influential songs included "High Sheriff Blues," "Magnolia Blues," and "You're Gonna Need Somebody When You Die." He influenced **Son House** and **Howlin' Wolf**, among many. (0470, 0475, 0495)

Pay for What You Get. One interviewee from South Carolina gave this bit of advice. He said, "Whenever people take a root or plant from the ground, they should never leave that spot empty. They should always place rice, grass, leaves or something in that spot."

Peach Tree. The inside bark of this tree was placed in boiling water and administered as a tea to babies for colds and the flu. *See* Colds.

Peach Tree Leaves. The leaves were moistened and placed over the person's body. This was done to bring a fever down or lower the body temperature. *See* Weak Kidneys.

Persimmon. A sprout of this plant buried under the front steps kept a wife faithful to the marital bed. Beer was often brewed from the berries of this plant. *See* Love Charms. (0381, 0384, 0392)

Persimmon Beer. Persimmons were fermented in a barrel of warm water to produce this brew. *See* Persimmon. (0381, 0384, 0392)

Pine Straw. Several informants told us that one could produce a tea by adding pine straw to boiling water. Drinking this tea would help cure the common cold. *See* Colds.

Pink Candle. They say that if a man burns this candle for at least nine days, for an hour each time, on the ninth night he will have the woman that he has desired. *See* Love Charms. (1523, 1529)

Plat-Eyes. Failure to give the departed a proper burial meant dire consequences. The idea developed on the basis of African beliefs that a soul needs the direction given by correct rites, and that untended spirits haunted particular places. These places included graveyards, lonely roads, crossroads, and surviving friends and relatives. Plat-eyes took on multifarious shapes, from headless corpses to black dogs to nameless entities. Animals could perceive them faster than people could.

Pocketbook. One female interviewee told us that women never placed this on the floor because this would prevent them from ever having money.

Pockets. Turned inside out at night, pockets warded off ghosts and witches.

Pointing at Graves. It was believed that if a person pointed at a grave, there was a possibility that the person's fingers would rot off or, even more disastrous, his/her mother's teeth would fall out.

Positioning the Body. Several Sea Island residents explained that it was a known practice to turn the head of the deceased to the right immediately after death. *See* Burial.

Possum-A-La. A type of song or dance that was recorded in Alabama in 1937. The words are those of a little African American girl. It goes something like this: ''Put your hands on your hips and let your mind roll forward, back, back, back until you see the stars. Skip so lightly, shine so brightly, that is the Possum-a-la.'' (0141)

Posthumous Child. These children supposedly had the ability to cure digestive disorders of other children by blowing down their throats. (0001, 0019, 0025)

Pot Liquor. Residue. This water remains after greens and salt meat or ham have been boiled. (0392)

Pottery. A jealously guarded craft by its white practitioners, pottery was disdained by many male slaves as a woman's task. However, the shortage of white workmen and the increasing demand for pottery in the nineteenth century brought many slaves into the craft. Edgefield, South Carolina, was a center of the production of alkaline-glazed stoneware, and it is probable that this form originated there. Potters in Edgefield Country produced vessels with applied faces. Other potters had inscribed poetry on their pottery, the most notable efforts being those of Dave, a slave who made large storage jars with horizontal slab handles. Monkey jars in the Caribbean are shaped like teakettles. Those from Edgefield can have the shape of a human head with movable eyes and teeth. The origin of this form can be traced to Barbados and thence to South Carolina, first settled by Barbadians. (1255, 1256, 1277)

Poultices. For bruises and other pains, red clay softened with vinegar helped. Elm bark reduced inflammation. Mutton suet and beef tallow rubbed on the chest eased a cold. Another type of poultice was a mixture of an okra blossom and octagon soap. *See* Rub Her Up.

Praise House. Church. Plantations in many small communities, especially in the Sea Islands of Georgia and South Carolina, boasted such a dwelling. Some have interpreted the name to mean "pray's house," because of the Gullah syntax. (1969, 1979, 1989)

Problems. *See* Solving Problems.

Protecting a Baby. The name of a new baby was called when leaving his/her house, so that his/her spirit would not wander in a strange place. (0020, 0057, 0060)

Protection. In sympathetic magic, it was the bag worn around the waist to protect one from being "fixed" by an evil root doctor. Men carried it in the wallet. It contained such items as **asfeddity** and other herbs or talisman-like objects. *See* Toby. (1479, 1496)

Quilts. Because of the climate in Africa, the quilt was unknown there. When Africans were brought to America, they often were given the job of making quilts for their masters. Thus, they adapted their own design sense to previously unknown tasks. Quilts can be divided into three types: (1) plain quilts, made of single pieces of material front and back, usually of a single color or printed pattern; (2) appliquéd quilts, which have tops of whole cloth to which are applied forms cut from a contrasting color of cloth and stitched down; and (3) pieced quilts, whose tops are made of pieces of material stitched together to form patterns and borders, frequently of a geometric design. The string quilt is an example of the latter, wherein a strip element runs the entire length of the quilt top. The strip quilt thus incorporates elements of design taken directly from African textile traditions, with nonpatterned strips and eschewing straight lines. Evil was thought to travel in straight lines. (1233, 1271, 1280, 1282, 1286)

Rabbit Tobacco. Also known as life everlasting. It was first used by the Native Americans for medicinal purposes. This plant was used as a tea as a cure for the flu.

Rabbits. As told by an interviewee from South Carolina, everyone knows that when a person makes a sudden jerk or feels a slight chill, a rabbit just ran across his/her grave.

Ragtime. Music of African American origin popular in the early twentieth century. Louis M. Gottschalk, a Creole, received retrospective credit for the first ragtimelike compositions. "Harlem Rag" by Thomas Turpin was the first rag by an African American. The typical rag contained an opening flourish, which was followed by contrasting sections. Syncopation became a feature, especially under Scott Joplin who stipulated that his rags not be played too fast. Rags were always associated with dancing, especially with the cakewalk. It remained essentially piano music. (0467, 0476, 0489)

Railroad Bill. Morris Slater of Alabama was a bad man who killed his white boss on a road building job. Hiding from justice, he lived with a hoodoo doctor and learned black magic from him. He started a career of robbery and got his nickname because he liked to travel by freight train. He eluded the posse by changing his shape to that of a dog, a sheep, or some other animal. However, eventually he was surprised by a posse and shot before he could say the spell to change his visage. (1637, 1657, 1671)

Rainey, "Ma" [Gertrude Melissa Pridgett], 1886–1939. Singer/dancer. Born in Columbus, GA, she was the daughter of minstrel troupers. She married William "Pa" Rainey at age 18 and spent many years touring, billed as Ambassador of the Blues. She worked with Bessie Smith and Thomas A. Dorsey. She started recording in 1923, offering such songs as "Ma Rainey's Black Bottom," "Shave 'Em Dry Blues," and "Sweet Rough Man." She retired to Rome, GA, in the early 1930s, where she managed theaters. (0487, 0495)

Rainy Weather. Many believed that if the moon was shaped like a saucer, it was full of water and could drain at any time. This was a sure sign of rain.

When the new moon was tilted on its side, the water was pouring out and that also produced rain. When smoke came out a chimney and went straight to the ground instead of going up, it would rain soon. (1680)

Rattle. As reported by several interviewees, this was the sound made when a person was about to die. The sound was described as if someone was attempting to gargle.

Reading of Psalms. An interviewee remarked that the reading of certain psalms helped an individual to benefit from particular misfortunes. The 27th Psalm was read to rid oneself of the blues, while the 37th was good for increasing financial wealth. Psalm 126 was a source of inspiration if one were worried about a job, and the 91st would ease the feeling of lonesomeness. *See* Candles, Meaning of.

Reception by the Dead. It was customary for a corpse to be dressed as if for a festival, in its best clothing. The usher announces, ''The corpse will now receive his friends.'' Those present enter and depart with greetings and farewells, given as if the dead person were capable of communication. *See* Burial. (1713, 1738, 1785)

Red Legs or Red Bones. One of several names designated to a group of people having white, Native American, and African American heritage. The majority of these are located in the South. Physically, they vary in appearance from fair to dark brown skin, and hair texture will appear kinky, straight, wavy, and/or frizzy. They are sometimes referred to as Brass Ankles, Buckheads, Clay-Eaters, and Yellow Hammers. *See* Mulatto. (0165)

Red Oak Tree. The bark of this tree was used to make a tea and administered whenever someone had a fever or the chills.

Red Pepper. A female interviewee from Alabama explained that it was once believed that using this type of pepper as a tea was supposed to prevent a woman from having a baby. Drinking ginger tea or castor oil (to help the fetus slide out) was a means of aborting the fetus.

Reincarnation. Belief that blacks with a displeasing disposition would return as mules after death.

Rheumatism. Relief from this condition was controlled by carrying a white potato in the pocket, rubbing the afflicted area with rattlesnake oil, or wearing a ring made of a bent nail. *See* Arthritis.

Rhythm and Blues. Style of music combining elements of jazz and blues. The term came into vogue in 1949 when *Billboard* magazine changed the names of its charts. Louis Jordan developed the style and others refined it. Also known as the jump blues, this style featured the amplified electric guitar, tenor sax, and gospel-tinged stylings. Los Angeles was the city that first produced the sound, with such artists as T-Bone Walker and Charles Brown. By 1953, with the Orioles' "Crying in the Chapel," it had reached national fame. Fats Domino, Little Richard, and Chuck Berry helped turn it into rock and roll, as their songs were recorded by white singers, such as Elvis Presley and Bill Haley. (0487, 0489, 0495)

Right Eye Jumping. It is a sure sign of good luck whenever the right eye jumps.

Ring Shout. A southern form of worshipful singing and dancing rhythmically in a counterclockwise circle. Its origins can be traced along the South Carolina and Georgia sea islands. *See* Sandy Ree. (0716)

Ringworm. An interviewee from Alabama revealed that the juice squeezed from green walnuts and placed directly on the affected area was considered to be a good remedy for ringworm.

Robin. The robin got its red breast because it carried water to pour on the eternal fire of Hell. *See* Birds.

Rooster. The yard rooster crowing with his head toward the house meant that company was coming. When he crowed with his head turned away from the house, somebody would soon die. If a rooster crowed after sundown, it indicated imminent death in the household. (0019, 0020)

Rub Her Up. In order to correct the positioning of the uterus of a woman who had just given birth, many midwives used a particular poultice. It consisted of a mixture of lard, petroleum jelly, and turpentine. The mixture was placed in a sterilized piece of cloth and inserted into the vagina. A small piece of string was left hanging from the end of the cloth, so it could be removed after the woman had slept with it inserted overnight. (0393, 0414)

Safety of Children. There were those who believed that people could provide extra protection for their children by cutting a piece of each child's hair and keeping it with them. Everyone knew that children would not die without all of their hair. (1483, 1499)

Salt. Spilling salt was bad luck, which resulted in anger or a quarrel. Salt was thrown over the left shoulder or tasted before speaking to avoid these catastrophes. Throwing salt behind someone who had done you wrong would be an assurance that the person would never return.

Salt Bath. Salt acts as a cleanser and should be used to rid oneself of confusion or troubling thoughts. Add enough salt to cover the top of the water in the tub. Afterward, light a white candle and get in the water. Affirmations to God should follow for the next few hours in order to get the best results. One interviewee still recommends this practice as a means of bringing peace to the mind and soul.

Sandy Ree. Much like the **ring shout**, except it was "step, step, step, chug." The step itself was an elaboration of the secular shout step. The word itself may have originally been "sangari," an African term, but the people from the Sea Islands say that the name came from the way one's feet "scrooch up the sand" when the Sandy Ree step is done. (0141)

Scat Singing. Style of singing using syllables, but not words. It apparently was invented by Louis Armstrong in 1926, when he dropped the sheet music for his recording of "Heebie Jeebies" and ad-libbed. The voice imitates a jazz instrument, and this method became standard in the repertoire of such singers as Ella Fitzgerald and Mel Tormé. (0478)

Sea Breeze Hotel. A South Carolina interviewee said that this was the name given to the city jail in Charleston. It was called Sea Breeze because of its location on the Cooper River.

Seeing Spirits. An interviewee from South Carolina told us it was possible to do this by looking through the hole of a button at the casket where the deceased was resting. If the deceased was a bad person, one would be able to see his/her spirit sitting atop the casket.

Seeking Jesus. Especially in the Sea Islands, the people congregated in a darkened meetinghouse and called out "Where is Jesus?" Somebody would then answer, "Here is Jesus," and the others would rush to him. "He is not here" would come the reply. This practice could take place all night and end in frenzied testimony. Also, several Sea Island residents explained that many African Americans sought their confirmation with God by going out into the wilderness or a secluded area and praying for several hours. (2196, 2261)

Seventh Child. This child was said to be the wisest and to possess an extraordinary amount of healing power. (1671, 1738)

Sewing Clothing. One interviewee suggested that it was to a person's advantage to put a piece of wood in his/her mouth when sewing something that he/she was wearing at the time. If not, one would have headaches, and every stitch that was sewn would cause harsh words to be spoken about the person.

Sexual Intercourse. It was said that a man would lose his strength if he had sex with a pregnant woman. (1676, 1781)

Shout. A style of dancing that is denoted by a fast-paced shuffling two-step. The back foot closes up to but never passes the leading foot: step (R), close (L), step (R), close (L). The term is derived from the Arabic "saut," meaning "to dance around the Kaaba." The word was also associated with West African Muslims as a "holy dance" around the pulpit. A singing style in the **blues**, it marks a change in emphasis from the earlier style of moaning by such artists as **Robert Johnson** and **Bessie Smith** to a more assertive mode. **Big Joe Turner** made this style popular. *See* Dancing; Sandy Ree. (0057, 0897)

Signs of Death. If a dog lay on his back with his feet in the air, somebody in the house would die. A mourning dove indicated death unless a knot was tied in each corner of an apron. (0060, 1671)

Simmons, Philip, 1912–. Ironworker. A native of Charleston, SC, he started as a blacksmith. He has created decorated iron gates throughout the city, notably his "snake" gate at Gadsden House. His door panels, pilaster posts, and grilles remain models of their kind. *See* Ironwork. (1349, 1350, 1351)

Sitting Up. This was commonly known as the wake. When a person died, people from the area would come to the deceased person's home the night before the funeral to pay their last respects. *See* Wakes.

Slave, Prison, and Railroad Songs. This type of work song was regarded as a means of pacing workers and helping to pass the time. It was believed that slave owners considered slave songs to be beneficial to greater work output and usually demanded fast, lively music. *See* Corn Songs; Field Holler. (0585, 0600, 0611, 0613)

Smelling. An interviewee from Florida noted that this term was sometimes used to describe a person who had the ability to detect spirits. The smell of different spices, such as cinnamon, nutmeg and ginger, was present when spirits were around.

Smiling. If smiling while asleep, a baby was said to be talking to angels. (0019, 0189, 0265, 0268)

Smith, Clarence "Pine Top," 1904–1929. Boogie-woogie piano player. Born in Troy, AL, he moved to Birmingham as a youth. Self-taught on the piano, he moved to Pittsburgh in the 1920s. He toured with, among others. **Ma Rainey**, before settling in Chicago in 1928. While attending a dance at the Masonic Lodge Hall, he was accidentally shot and killed. He sang with a peculiar high-pitched voice and made such songs as "Jump Steady Blues" and "Pine Top's Boogie Woogie." (0470, 0475, 0521)

Smith, Elizabeth "Bessie," 1894–1937. Singer. The often proclaimed Empress of the Blues was born in Chattanooga, TN, the daughter of a part-time preacher. She developed her singing technique in the church choir and perfected it while working for **Ma Rainey** and the Rabbit Foot Minstrels. She first recorded in 1923, singing such songs as "Down Hearted Blues." She toured the Negro vaudeville circuit. By the 1930s, though, her gifts began to be blighted by alcoholism. She died as a result of a still-controversial car wreck. Among her favorite songs were "Weeping Willow Blues," "Cold in Hand Blues (The Empress)," and "Nobody Knows You When You're Down and Out." (0495, 0518)

Smoke in a Bottle. One informant stated that the practice of blowing smoke from a tobacco pipe in a baby's bottle helped to relieve an infant's colic.

Snake Root. The most striking thing about this plant is the snakelike, twisted, curled root that is brown on the outside. It is used as a tea to help increase a child's appetite.

Snakes. All snakes except the black snake were able to whistle. Cornfield adders had the ability to puff up and flatten. If a black snake got into a fight with a moccasin, the black snake always won. A milk snake would charm children. It would also suck a cow dry. A coach snake could whistle like a man. It wrapped itself around its victims and whipped them with its tail. Greasing the hands with the fat of a graveyard snake made it possible to steal without being discovered. If a person killed a snake on the first day of the year, the person had killed his/her enemy. It was said that by tying a snakeskin around the waist, power was given to overcome evil. (1528, 1534, 1573)

Sneezing. If a person sneezed seven times in a row, it meant a ghost had risen from the dead. *See* **Don't Sneeze**. (1655, 1670)

Soda Water. A piece of cloth was submerged in this water and placed over the face of the deceased to prevent the dead skin from turning darker before being buried. Silver coins instead of copper were placed over each eyelid because the copper usually turned the skin green. *See* Burial Preparations. (1658, 1713, 1738)

Solving Problems. Mix a pinch of sugar and nutmeg together while reciting affirmations to God. Throw the mixture into the air in any room of the house; clap the hands once and say "peace." This should bring better clarity to problems. The interviewee stated that this practice was passed down to her from her grandmother.

Sore Throat. It was once said that one should tie a piece of string around the highest lock of hair of the person with the ailing throat to make it better. (1650)

South Carolina Folklore Society. Reed Smith was elected president of the group upon its founding in 1913 at the University of South Carolina. Efforts concentrated on Gullah and other indigenous subjects, and the group worked closely with the WPA in the South Carolina Writers' Program. The documents gathered in this process were donated to the South Carolina collection at the University of South Carolina. They merged with the Southeastern Folklore Society in 1934. *See* Southeastern Folklore Society. (0165, 0220)

South Carolina Negro Folklore Guild. When the white folklore society faded away in the 1930s, no statewide organization existed to promulgate folk traditions. J. Mason Brewer suggested in 1944 that such a body be created. It originated at Claflin College in Orangeburg at a meeting of the Negro Jeanes Teachers of the state. Its objective was ''the assembling of folk items that will be suitable for use in the projection of a statewide movement in intercultural education.'' Charter members included J. B. Randolph, W. A. Schiffley, J. P. Burgess, and Cora V. Green. (0165, 0220)

Southeastern Folklore Society. Founded at the University of South Carolina in 1934, this organization elected Maurice Matterson as its first president. Early supporters included Mellinger Henry and Julia Peterkin. The group published the *Southern Folklore Quarterly. See* South Carolina Folklore Society. (0165, 0192)

Spasm Band. Band using homemade instruments. Such bands were particularly popular around the turn of the century and usually used jugs, washboards, bones, and other household implements as music makers. Emile ''Stale Bread'' Lacoume of New Orleans led a notorious group called the Razzy Dazzy Spasm Band. A magazine article in 1919 gave Lacoume credit for inventing jazz. *See* jug band. (0489, 0585)

Spinning the Bible. Two of our interviewees from South Carolina confirmed that to detect whether a person had lied or stolen something, a grandfather's clock key, a long piece of string, and a Bible were needed. The string was placed between the pages of the Bible and closed. The key was then placed on the back outside cover of the Bible, and the string was tied around the Bible and the top half of the key. The Bible was then placed in the right hand while two fingers on the left hand held the top part of the key. The following was repeated: ''By St. Peter, By St. Paul, By God who made us all.'' The suspected person's name was then repeated. If the person were guilty of any infraction, the Bible would begin to turn.

Spirits. Sprinkle sulfur all around the outside of the house and in the rooms as a means of preventing spirits from entering.

Spousal Arguments. If chaos persisted between husband and wife, it was advised that as soon as a spouse entered the room, the other should place a piece of straw from a broom in his or her mouth. This would guard against any harsh words being said to the other. Also, if the argument continued, salt was sprinkled on the floor, and that would bring peace.

Sprained Ankle. A mixture of red clay and vinegar could be placed on the area that was hurt, and it would ease the pain and swelling of a sprained ankle.

Stammering. This was said to be brought on because that person was tickled when he or she was a child. (0019, 0025, 0026, 0057)

Stocking and Kerosene. Another well-known treatment for a cold was to soak a sock or stocking in kerosene and tie it around the throat. *See* Colds. (0019, 0025, 0026)

Storyville. District in New Orleans. Between Canal and Basin Streets, this 38-block section of the city was from 1896 to 1917 designated as a place where prostitution, though not legal, was tolerated. The inhabitants named it after the alderman who worked for the passage of the law. Every form of vice flourished, from stark ''cribs'' to elegant townhouses. To entertain the customers between times, the madames would hire talented musicians, among them Jelly Roll Morton and Louis Armstrong. The U.S. Navy closed down the area in the spring of 1917 in order to protect sailors from venereal diseases. (0489, 0495, 0524)

Stove-Up. It indicated that a person was feeling tired or a little run down. Our South Carolina interviewees confirmed this saying.

Street Cries. Black peddlers in Southern cities hawked their wares with various cries. One such from Mobile, AL, said, ''I sell to the rich, I sell to the poor. I sell to the pretty girl that stands by the door.'' *See* Holler. (1668, 1957)

Sty on the Eye. It was sloughed off by standing at a crossroad and chanting, ''Sty, sty, come off my eye; light on the next one passing by.'' (1650, 1738)

Sulfur. Ingesting a teaspoon of sulfur was said to be an excellent laxative. One of our interviewees from Birmingham said that this was the only laxative she was ever given as a child. Another interviewee from Alabama told us that a mixture of sulfur, turpentine, and a little sugar was rolled together and taken together as a ''spring tonic.''

Sulfur and Turpentine. An interviewee from Alabama informed us that a mixture of these two items along with a little sugar was rolled together and taken for medicinal purposes every spring.

Sunshine and Rain. When it rained as the sun shined, the Devil was beating his wife. Sticking a pin or needle in the ground and placing your ear close to it would allow one to hear the screams of Satan's wife. (0221, 0246, 0287)

Sweeping. It was a known fact that one never swept under the bed of a sick person because the patient would surely die. One would definitely bring bad luck upon oneself if one swept after dark. Sweeping under a girl's feet would end any chances of her ever marrying. (0221, 0246, 0287)

Swing. A style of jazz. It supplanted **Dixieland** around 1930. Based on solo improvisation, larger horn sections, and Tin Pan Alley lyrics, it was also called "four-beat jazz." Four beats of the bar often marked the style, and the loss of the tuba and banjo from the band and their replacement by the double bass and rhythm guitar separated it from its folklike roots. Duke Ellington helped to make it popular. (0489, 0495, 0524)

Tabby. On Sapelo Island and other Sea Islands, the buildings were often made of tabby. The name comes from the Spanish *tabia*, which means "mud" or "cement." Tabby was made by grinding burning oyster shells and lime and mixing them with sand, shells, and water. Whole oyster shells were added as a binder. (0057, 0060, 0072)

Take No More on Your Heels Than You Can Kick Off with Your Toes. In other words, don't be greedy. Always leave something for the other person. Moreover, don't profess to do more than you actually are able to do.

Tallow. The fat that is found in sheep and cattle. It was used for colds, in cooking, and by midwives to grease the vagina during delivery. *See* Rub Her Up. (0393)

Tansy. A strong-smelling plant with clusters of small yellow flowers used for medicinal purposes. It was once administered as a tea to aid expectant mothers in "holding" their babies until the appropriate time of delivery. Also, a mixture of tansy and mistletoe was taken by a mother who wanted to abort her fetus. (0393, 0414)

Tar Tea. Liquid tar was added to hot water and used for annoying coughs and colds. *See* Colds. (0390, 0395)

Teeth. A wide space between the front teeth indicated a liar, a person who could not keep a secret, a nagging person, or a person who would live far away from the home folks. (0383, 0407, 0409, 0423)

Teething. Fat hog meat was pressed with a spoon in a saucer along with drops of turpentine. The mixture was rubbed on the gums of the baby. Teething was believed to become more painful if a baby was held out of a window or allowed to see itself in a mirror. To ease teething pain, a necklace of alligator teeth was put around the child's neck, or a rabbit's ear was rubbed against the gums. **Asfeddity balls** were worn around the baby's neck to relieve the pain. Also, one should never put a man's hat on a baby before the baby had teethed. Teething was made a lot easier if a sheep bone was tied around the baby's neck so that the baby could chew on it. The powdered gizzard and liver of a skypoke helped many diseases. (0383, 0407, 0409, 0423)

Tennessee Folklore Society. Founded Tennessee Polytechnic Institute at Cookeville in 1934, the group elected J. A. Rickard its first president. It publishes the *Tennessee Folklore Society Bulletin.* (0165, 0230)

Terry, "Sonny" [Saunders Terrell], 1911–. Harmonica player. A Georgia native, he lost the sight in both eyes. As a child he sang in tent revivals. Moving to North Carolina, he teamed with **Blind Boy Fuller** in the 1930s and 1940s, offering such numbers as "I'm Gonna Get on My Feets Afterwhile." The Library of Congress asked him to record. He worked with Woodie Guthrie. Famous for his shout style, he played with **Leadbelly** on "Keep Your Hands Off Her." Forming a team with **Brownie McGhee**, he made such songs as "Pepper Headed Woman." He also fronted a washboard band. (0050, 0495, 0524)

Texas Folklore Society. Begun in 1909 at a state teachers' convention, the society was bolstered by early members John Lomax and Stith Thompson. The group published early collections of African American ballads. The University of Texas at Austin remained a center of the group's activities, with annual monographs being published by the university press. (0003, 0013)

Thunder. This was an indication that Satan was driving a chariot pulled by two black horses. It was a sure indication that the Lord was talking and everyone should remain silent. (1650, 1658)

Titi. Some interviewees from the Sea Islands revealed that some of the children of the Sea Islands used to refer to their mothers by this name.

Toby. This was used to rid people of a curse or to remove a fix that someone had put on them. Rusty nails, chicken's gizzards, a rooster's spur, powdered bluegrass, and pine resin made up the ingredients of the toby. This was tied in a cloth and worn around the ankle by the individual until the curse was removed. Red flannel inside a pecan hull often proved effective. *See* Conjure-Doctors; Protection. (1499, 1503, 1521)

Toothache. One quick method of relieving the pain of an ailing tooth was to combine a mixture of cornmeal and water. It was then placed in a piece of clean white cloth and placed next to the tooth. Smoke and buttermilk or red pepper mixed with biscuit dough helped relieve the pain. Many people were known to use or place a piece of dried walnut in or around the cavity for temporary relief. (0390)

Travel Alone, Travel Fast. As interpreted by an interviewee from Birmingham, people don't have to be with someone to go where they are going; nor do they have to have people around them to enjoy themselves.

Trees. Spanish moss was said to be the hair of a very old man who lived for ages after making a deal with the Devil. When he finally died, his hair was so long that it draped over the trees. The cottonwood tree was in the Garden of Gethsemane during the passing of Jesus. The Romans made the cross out of it, and it still trembles today because of Jesus' agony during the crucifixion. If one planted a cedar tree, one would die when it grew large enough to shade a grave. (0057)

Turner, "Big Joe" [Joseph Vernon], 1911–1985. Singer, billed as Boss of the Blues. A native of Jackson County, MO, he sang as a boy on the streets and in local church choirs in Kansas City. He traveled between Kansas City and New York in the 1930s, touring with various bands. During the 1940s, he toured and went abroad. When rock and roll developed in the mid-1950s, he was one of the founders, singing such songs as "Ooh-Wee Baby" and "Doggin' the Dog." His shout style of singing was influenced by **Bessie Smith**, and he influenced B. B. King. (0495)

Umbilical Cord. Commonly called the "navel string" by midwives, this, along with the afterbirth, was usually salted and wrapped with paper or some other type of material. In most instances, it was either buried or burned. Proper disposal of the cord was important because if it was not handled correctly, the mother could be prevented from ever having any more children. (0234, 0287, 0393)

Uncrossing a Conjure. If a person found a conjure or a fix in or around the house, he/she could dispose of it in a large body of water, which in turn would cause madness to the conjurer. *See* Dress or Dressing. (1503, 1515)

Unwanted Visitors. If someone comes to a house and stays too long, a broom should be put across the doorway where the person entered, and he or she will leave and not return, according to an interviewee from Alabama.

Urine. If a dog sniffed at someone's pants leg and urinated on it, it was a sure sign of good luck. Urine was used for several purposes. A few of our interviewees did confirm that there were some people who drank this occasionally as a cure for colds. It was placed in a bottle and left untouched for about three days. Afterward, it was administered in large dosages. Urine, or night water as it was sometimes called, was also used to relieve the pain of diaper rash. It was also applied to the face as a skin cleanser.

Vinegar Pie. Made from vinegar, sugar, butter, and flour, this dessert graced many tables in the South. (0392, 1247)

Virginia Folklore Society. C. Alphonso Smith of the University of Virginia was the first president of the group, founded in Richmond in 1913. The University of Virginia supported many efforts, including the collection of songs from the field. A bulletin was published between 1913 and 1924. (0237)

Visions. A strong religious element tinges many visions. Those who were prone to these visions often saw a ladder leading to heaven, like Jacob in the Bible. Jesus and white-robed figures were prominent in the visions. Heaven appeared as alabaster buildings that one entered through the pearly gates. To have the ability to see spirits if one wasn't born with the ability, one would break a rain crow's egg in water and wash his/her face with it. (0057, 0060)

Voodoo. Derived from the Dahomeian, *vodu*. First appeared in print in George Washington Cable's *Grandissimes* in 1880. Originated in the Ewe territory of West Africa as the worship of a snake god. Prevalent in Haiti, Cuba, and New Orleans. In Haiti, *voudon* designates the beliefs and practices of the cults. The deities are called Loa or Orisha. *See* Hoodoo. (1496, 1499)

Wakes. During a wake someone was always with the body, and the floor was never swept. Wakes usually lasted three days, but if the deceased had been a community figure, it sometimes went on longer. *See* Sitting Up. (0019, 0057, 0060, 0358)

Walker, "T-Bone" [Aaron Thibault], 1910–1975. Blues guitarist. Born in Linden, TX, he was influenced by such performers as **Blind Lemon Jefferson**. A self-taught player, he first recorded in 1929 and toured with a band through Texas and Oklahoma. He moved to the West Coast in the 1930s, where he became one of the first electric guitar players with the Les Hite orchestra. He first achieved national fame with "Stormy Monday" in 1947. He electrified the blues. (Obituary in *New York Times*, March 17, 1975, p. 32) (0489, 0495, 0531)

Warts. The removal of warts was done by tying a string around the wart for about a month. This process was also carried out by taking a strand of horse hair and cutting off the wart. They were also cured by stealing someone's dishrag and hiding it from them. (0390)

Washing Clothes. A Charleston interviewee said that to wash clothes on New Year's Day meant that you were washing away the life of one of your relatives.

Watch Night. Every December 24 and every December 31, many people of the Sea Islands had what was called a Christmas watch night meeting. The main purpose was to pray and give thanks to the Lord. Church services would begin around 8 P.M. and continue until the watchman said it was 12 midnight. This ceremony continues today in many African American churches across the South.

Water. *See* Pan of Water.

Waters, "Muddy" [McKinley Morganfield], 1915–1983. Guitar/harmonica player and singer. A self-taught harmonica player, he sang in church choirs as a boy. The Mississippi Delta native worked in **juke joints** and other venues until the early 1940s. He was an adult when he learned to play the guitar. Moving to Chicago in 1943 after working in a minstrel show, he joined **Sonny Boy Williamson** on the bill at the Plantation Club. Through no small effort on his part, the Chicago blues developed. After World War II he toured worldwide. He recorded for the Library of Congress. His songs included "Got My Mojo Working" and "Mule Kicking in My Stall." He was influenced by the early Delta bluesmen, and he influenced such performers as Jimi Hendrix. He was known as the Living Legend. (Obituary in *New York Times*, May 1, 1983, p. 44) (0489, 0495)

Waumpaus. Legendary creature. In eastern North Carolina, a monstrous creature was said to steal hogs at night. It left tracks that were like a dog's, but larger. Its cry ranged from soprano to bass, and it was tracked to the edge of a graveyard. (0136, 0137, 1711)

Wax from Your Ear. Several interviewees mentioned that it was suggested that one should apply a small amount of this on or between the toes to heal minor cuts or what was commonly referred to as fly toe. Bee stings could also be treated with ear wax.

Weak Kidneys. Peach tree leaves were brewed and administered as a tea for bed wetters. *See* Peach tree Leaves. (0380, 0389, 0390)

Wearing of Coins. One wore a penny or pennies, usually around the ankles, to prevent poisons from entering the body. If the coin turned green, it was an indication that something had been stepped in that could bring harm. As long as the coins were worn, there was protection from evil spells or conjures. (1515, 1521, 1522)

Wedding Rhyme. Mason Brewer recorded this rhyme, recited by the one who conducted the ceremony among slaves: (0025, 0026, 0268)

> *Dark an' stormy may come de wedder;*
> *I jines dis he-male and dis she-male togedder.*
> *Let none, bu Him dat makes de thunder.*
> *Put dis he-male and dis she-male asunder.*
> *I derefore 'nounce you befo' de same*
> *Be good, go 'long, an' keep up yo' name.*
> *De broomstick's jumped, de world not wide.*
> *She's now yo' own. Salute yo' bride!*

West Hell. Worst part of Hell. The foulest criminals and sinners get consigned to this place. When they die, their souls change into rubber, so that they will bounce rather than be carried, because even demons don't like to convey sinners there. (0061)

West Virginia Folklore Society. Founded in 1915, in conjunction with the University of West Virginia summer school, the group elected John H. Cox as its first president. Interest faded during the Depression, and the group ceased formal activities. Manuscript materials collected in the early years were deposited at the University of West Virginia in Morgantown. (0003, 0013)

Whangdoodle. Name for a spirit. In North Carolina, a ghost was referred to by this term. (0025, 0026)

What Goes Over the Devil's Back Will Come Under His Belly. An interviewee told us that if a person does wrong to others, eventually evil will come to that person.

Whooping Cough. One interviewee told us that a tea for whooping cough was made from a wad of a hornet's nest and was drunk until the person began to cough up phlegm.

Williams, "Big Joe" [Joe Lee], 1903–1982. Singer and player of accordion, guitar, harmonica, and kazoo. The son of a Cherokee Indian, he was born in the Mississippi Delta, one of 16 children. After learning music on a homemade guitar as a boy, he ran away from home and hoboed throughout the South. He worked for the Rabbit Foot Minstrels and in brothels before recording with the Birmingham Jug Band. He formed his own group, including **Muddy Waters**, and performed in the Delta area. He also appeared frequently in St. Louis, singing such songs as "Tell My Mother That Thing's in Town" and "Pretty Willie Done Me Wrong." (Obituary in *New York Times*, December 21, 1982, IV, p. 23) (0489, 0495)

Williamson, "Sonny Boy," 1899–1965. Singer, accompanying himself on drums, guitar, or harmonica. A product of the Mississippi Delta, he assumed his stepfather's name, Alex Miller. He called himself Little Boy Blue as he performed on the streets, playing the self-taught harmonica. After wandering during the depression, he appeared on the King Biscuit Time Show out of Helena, AR, and even worked the Grand Ole Opry. He frequently performed with **Howlin' Wolf** (his brother-in-law) and **Memphis Slim.** He influenced rockers Mike Bloomfield and Eric Clapton on such numbers as "Fattening Frogs for Snakes" and "She Got Next to Me." (0489, 0495)

Witches. Paper burned in the corners of a room deterred witches. Mustard seed strewn on the floor stopped a witch, since she must pick up each seed. (0055, 0127)

Woofing. Aimless talking. Much used in conversation between men and women, usually in wooing. Also heard in groups of young men talking idly to pass the time. (0141, 0160, 0165)

Work, John W., 1873–1925. Conductor, writer, composer, singer. He studied music at Fisk University in his native Nashville, TN. Studying classics at Harvard, he taught Latin and history at Fisk. After his 25-year teaching career at Fisk, he became president of Roger Williams University in Nashville. A scholar of note, he wrote *Folk Song of the American Negro* and contended that the Negro spiritual was America's only authentic folk music. He conducted the Jubilee Singers, in which his wife, Agnes Haynes Work, sang contralto. (0533, 0534, 0794)

Yellow Clay. This was eaten by many African American women in the South. Many of the women were pregnant at the time, while others just appeared to have a craving for it. One woman from Alabama told us that some of them were known to prepare their clay by baking it in the manner in which one would bake bread. Several of the women mentioned that some of their babies were born with dirt in their fingernails and hair as a result of their mothers having eaten yellow clay. *See* Dirt Eating.

Yellow Wasted. An interviewee explained that this term referred to mulattos or light-skinned African Americans who failed to use their skin color to their advantage to gain social and economic success.

Zar. Geographically, it was said to have been located on the other side of Far. There was little information about this place because only a few people ever came back to tell about it. (0001, 0019)

Zombie. (Afr.) Living dead. In voodoo, it was a person who had been killed and brought back to life by a sorcerer. A being without will, it performed absolutely any act commanded by the witch doctor. Not immortal, it did not die until it lived out its time "set by God." (1483, 1490)

Zydeco. African American counterpart of white Cajun music. It originated in southwest Louisiana, the name derived from French *les haricorts,* or "string beans." The accordion played in the style of the blues harmonica is the featured instrument, accompanied by a washboard, triangle, guitar, violin, and saxophone. Performers include Clifton Chenier and Queen Ida Guillory. (0585, 0623)

Menhaden Chanteymen—Beaufort, North Carolina, 1992. (Photograph by Deborah Luster.)

A Negro prayer meeting. (Courtesy of Sherman E. Pyatt.)

The Tabby Wall—Sea Islands, South Carolina, 1992. (Courtesy of Sherman E. Pyatt.)

Sweet grass baskets—Mt. Pleasant, South Carolina. (From the Joyce Coakley collection. Courtesy of Sherman E. Pyatt.)

Husband and wife with children on the porch of a log cabin—Alabama, 1930s. (From the photograph collections of the Birmingham Public Library, Birmingham, Alabama.)

Field workers—South Carolina, 1940s. (Courtesy of Sherman E. Pyatt.)

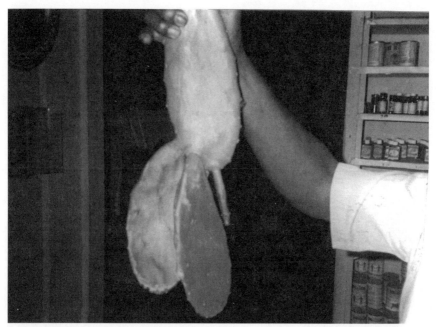

Prickly pear. (Courtesy of Sherman E. Pyatt.)

Aloe vera plant. (Courtesy of Sherman E. Pyatt.)

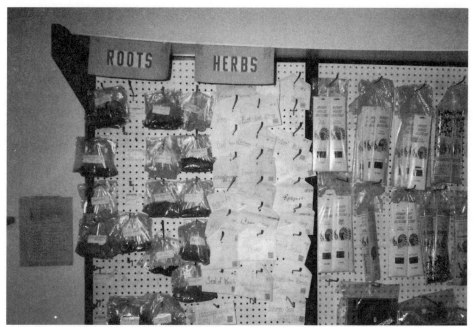

A display of various roots and herbal products, 1992. (Courtesy of Sherman E. Pyatt.)

A monkey jug. (Courtesy of Sherman E. Pyatt.)

Mr. Peter Russell, Master Netmaker—Wadmalaw Island, South Carolina, 1991. (Courtesy of Sherman E. Pyatt.)

Slave cabins—McLeod Plantation, James Island, South Carolina. (Courtesy of Sherman E. Pyatt.)

Mr. Vernon Sands, Numerologist and Herbologist—Jacksonville, Florida. (Courtesy of Sherman E. Pyatt.)

Mr. Phillip Simmons, Master Blacksmith—Charleston, South Carolina, 1991. (Courtesy of Sherman E. Pyatt.)

Ironwork by Philip Simmons—Charleston
airport, South Carolina, 1992. (Courtesy of
Sherman E. Pyatt.)

Iron gate by Philip Simmons—Charleston Welcoming Center, South Carolina,
1992. (Courtesy of Sherman E. Pyatt.)

Mrs. Leah Chase, Chef and co-owner of Dookey Chase restaurant—
New Orleans, Louisiana. (Courtesy of Sherman E. Pyatt.)

Ladies from the New Pilgrim Towers—Birmingham, Alabama. (Courtesy of Sherman
E. Pyatt.)

Corn crib—Alabama, 1930s. (From the photograph collections of the Birmingham Public Library, Birmingham, Alabama.)

Shotgun House—New Orleans, Louisiana. (Courtesy of Sherman E. Pyatt.)

Negro baptism—New Bern, North Carolina, 1910. (From the North Carolina Collection, University of N.C. Library at Chapel Hill.)

A modern-day baptism—Gee's Bend, Alabama, 1980. (From the photograph collections of the Birmingham Public Library, Birmingham, Alabama.)

A countryside wash-house with family servants—North Carolina, 1913. (From the North Carolina Collection, University of N.C. Library at Chapel Hill.)

1

General Works

0001 Abrahams, Roger D. *Afro-American Folktales: Stories from Black Traditions in the New World.* New York: Pantheon Books, 1985.

0002 Abrahams, Roger D. *Singing the Master: The Emergence of African-American Culture in the Plantation South.* New York: Pantheon Books, 1992. Bibliography on pp. 161–202.

0003 *Afro-American Life, History, and Culture.* Washington, DC: Collections and Development Branch, Library Programs Division, Office of Cultural Centers and Resources, Bureau of Educational and Cultural Affairs, U.S. Information Agency, 1985.

0004 Agee, G. W. *Alabama: A Guide to the Deep South.* New York: R. R. Smith, 1941.

0005 Allen-Olney, Mary. *The New Virginians.* 2 vols. Edinburgh, U.K.: Blackwood, 1880.

0006 Archbold, Annie, and Janice Morrill. *Georgia Folklife: A Pictorial Essay.* Atlanta: Georgia Folklife Program, State of Georgia, 1989.

0007 Archer, Jill. *Black American Folklore: A Bibliography.* Bloomington: Indiana University Press, 1968.

0008 Arkansas Writers' Project. *Arkansas, a Guide to the State—The WPA Guide to 1930s Arkansas.* Lawrence: University Press of Kansas, 1941.

0009 Asbury, Herbert. *The French Quarter: An Informal History of the New Orleans Underworld.* New York: Alfred A. Knopf, 1936.

0010 Aul, Billie. *An African-American Bibliography: The Arts: Selected Sources from the Collections of the New York State Library.* Albany: University of the State of New York, State Education Dept., New York State Library, 1990.

0011 Avirett, James B. *The Old Plantation.* New York: F. Tennyson Neely, 1901.

0012 Ballowe, Hewitt L. *The Lawd Sayin' the Same: Negro Folktales of the Creole Country*. Baton Rouge: Louisiana State University Press, 1947.

0013 Bartis, Peter. *Folklife Sourcebook: A Directory of Folklife Resources in the U.S. and Canada*. Washington, DC: American Folklife Center, Library of Congress, 1986.

0014 Belk Library Acquisitions Department. *Black American Culture Bibliography: List of Books and Periodicals on Black American Culture Located in the Belk Library, Appalachian State University*. Boone, NC: Appalachian State University Library, 1972.

0015 Bennett, Lerone, Jr. *The Negro Mood and Other Essays*. Chicago: Johnson, 1964.

0016 *Black Folklore*. Pittsburgh: University of Pittsburgh Department of Black Studies, 1971. Bibliography on pp. 73–77.

0017 Blackburn, M. J. *Folklore from Mammy Days*. Boston: Walter H. Baker Co., 1924.

0018 Boatright, Mody C. *Backwoods to Border*. Austin: Texas Folklore Society; Dallas University Press, Southern Methodist University, 1943.

0019 Botkin, Benjamin A., ed. *A Treasury of American Folklore: Stories, Ballads and Traditions of the People*. New York: Crown, 1944.

0020 Botkin, Benjamin A. *A Treasury of Mississippi River Folklore: Stories, Ballads, and Folkways of the Mid-American River Country*. New York: Crown, 1955.

0021 Botkin, Benjamin A. *A Treasury of Southern Folklore: Stories, Ballads, Traditions, and Folkways of the People of the South*. New York: Crown, 1949.

0022 Botume, Elizabeth H. *First Days Amongst the Contrabands*. Boston: Lee and Shepard, 1893.

0023 Boyd, Minnie C. *Alabama in the Fifties: A Social Study*. New York: Columbia University Press, 1931.

0024 Bradford, Roark. *John Henry*. New York: Literary Guild, 1931.

0025 Brewer, John M. *American Negro Folklore*. Chicago: Quadrangle Books, 1968.

0026 Brewer, John M. *Worser Days and Better Times: The Folklore of the North Carolina Negro*. Chicago: Quadrangle Books, 1965. Bibliography on pp. 17–18.

0027 Brookes, Stella B. *Joel Chandler Harris: Folklorist*. Athens: University of Georgia Press, 1950. Bibliography on pp. 166–176.

0028 Broussard, James F. *Louisiana Creole Dialect*. Baton Rouge: Louisiana State University Press, 1942.

0029 Brown, William W. *My Southern Home: Or, the South and Its People*. Boston: A. G. Brown and Co., 1880.

0030 Butcher, Margaret. *The Negro in American Culture, Based on Materials Left by Alain Locke*. New York: Knopf, 1972.

0031 Byrd, James W. *J. Mason Brewer: Negro Folklorist*. Austin: Steck-Vaughn Co., 1967.

0032 Cable, George W. *The Creoles of Louisiana*. New York: Charles Scribner's Sons, 1884.

0033 Cable, George W. *Strange True Stories of Louisiana*. New York: Charles Scribner's Sons, 1889.

0034 Calverton, Victor F., ed. *Anthology of American Negro Literature*. New York: Modern Library, 1929.

0035 Campbell, James E. *Echoes from the Cabin and Elsewhere*. Chicago: Donahue and Henneberry, 1895.

0036 Carawan, Guy. *Ain't You Got a Right to the Tree of Life? The People of Johns Island, South Carolina, Their Faces, Their Words, and Their Songs*. New York: Simon and Schuster, 1967.

0037 Carawan, Guy. *We Shall Overcome! Songs of the Southern Freedom Movement*. New York: Oak, 1963.

0038 Carmer, Carl. *Stars Fell on Alabama*. New York: Blue Ribbon Books, 1934.

0039 Carrothers, James D. *The Black Cat Club: Negro Humor and Folklore*. New York: Funk and Wagnalls, 1902.

0040 Carter, Wilmoth A. *The Urban Negro in the South*. New York: Vantage, 1962.

0041 Castellanos, Henry C. *New Orleans As It Was: Episodes of Louisiana Life*. New York: L. Graham & Son, 1895.

0042 Center for Southern Folklore. *American Folklore Films and Videotapes: A Catalog*. New York: Bowker, 1982.

0043 Child, David L. *The Despotism of Freedom*. Boston: Young Men's Anti-Slavery Society, 1833.

0044 Christensen, A. M. H. *Afro-American Folklore: Told Round Cabin Fires on the Sea Islands of South Carolina*. Westport, CT: Greenwood, 1973.

0045 Clarke, Lewis G. *Narratives of the Sufferings of Lewis and Milton Clarke . . . During a Captivity of More Than Twenty Years among the Slave-holders of Kentucky, One of the So-called Christian States of North America*. Boston: B. Marsh, 1846.

0046 Clinkscales, John G. *On the Old Plantation: Reminiscences of His Childhood*. Spartanburg, SC: Bond and White, 1916.

0047 Coe, Linda. *Folklife and the Federal Government: A Guide to Activities, Resources, Funds and Services*. Washington, DC: American Folklife Center, Library of Congress, 1977.

0048 Coffin, Tristram P. *An Analytical Index to the Journal of American Folklore*. Vols. 1–67, 68, 69, 70. Philadelphia: American Folklore Society, 1958.

0049 Cohen, Hennig, and Tristram P. Coffin, eds. *The Folklore of American Holidays*. 2nd ed. Detroit: Gale Research Co., 1991.

0050 Coleman, John W. *Slavery Times in Kentucky*. Chapel Hill: University of North Carolina Press, 1940.

0051 Conrad, Glenn R., ed. *The Cajuns: Essays on Their History and Culture*. Lafayette: Center for Louisiana Studies, University of Southwestern Louisiana, 1983.

0052 Cooley, Rossa B. *Homes of the Freed*. New York: New Republic, 1926.

0053   Cooley, Rossa B. *School Acres: An Adventure in Rural Education.* New Haven, CT: Yale University Press, 1930.

0054   Coughlan, Margaret N., comp. *Folklore from Africa to the United States: An Annotated Bibliography.* Washington, DC: Library of Congress, U.S. Government Printing Office, 1976.

0055   Council, William H. *Synopsis of Three Addresses: 1. Building the South, 2. The Children of the South, 3. Negro Religion and Character: No Apology.* Normal, AL: n.p., 1900.

0056   Courlander, Harold. *The Big Old World of Richard Creeks.* Philadelphia: Chilton, 1962.

0057   Courlander, Harold. *A Treasury of Afro-American Folklore: The Oral Literature, Recollections, Legends, Tales, Songs, and Humor of Peoples of African Descent in the Americas.* New York: Crown, 1988.

0058   Cousins, Paul M. *Joel Chandler Harris: A Bibliography.* Baton Rouge: Louisiana State University Press, 1968.

0059   Crammer, M. *Bibliography of American Folklore: Index to Material in Books on Select American Folk Characters.* Prince George County, VA: Prince George's County Memorial Library, 1975.

0060   Crum, Mason. *Gullah: Negro Life in the Carolina Sea Islands.* Durham: Duke University Press, 1940. Bibliography on pp. 345–351.

0061   David, Hilda. ''The African-American Women of Edisto Island, 1850–1920.'' Ph.D. dissertation, Emory University, 1989.

0062   Davis, Daniel W. *'Weh Down Souf.* Cleveland, OH: Helman-Taylor, 1897.

0063   Davis, Edwin Adams. *Plantation Life in the Florida Parishes of Louisiana, 1836–1846 as Reflected in the Diary of Bennet H. Barrow.* New York: Columbia University Press, 1943.

0064   Davis, John P., ed. *The American Negro Reference Book.* Englewood Cliffs, NJ: Prentice-Hall, 1966.

0065   Davis, Kenneth W., and Everett Gillis. *Black Cats, Hoot Owls, and Water Witches: Beliefs, Superstitions, and Sayings from Texas.* Denton: University of North Texas Press, 1989.

0066   Davis, Nathaniel. *Afro-American Reference: An Annotated Bibliography of Selected Resources.* Westport, CT: Greenwood Press, 1985.

0067   Davis, Sidney F. *Mississippi Folklore.* Jackson, TN: McCowat-Mercer, 1914.

0068   Davis, Sidney F. *Mississippi Negro Lore.* Jackson, TN: McCowat-Mercer, 1914.

0069   Diehl, Katherine S. *Religions, Mythologies, Folklores: An Annotated Bibliography.* New York: Scarecrow Press, 1962.

0070   Dobie, J. Frank, ed. *Follow De Drinkin' Gou'd.* Austin: Texas Folklore Society, 1928.

0071   Dollard, John. *Caste and Class in a Southern Town.* New Haven, CT: Yale University Press, 1937.

0072 Dorson, Richard M. *American Folklore.* Chicago: University of Chicago Press, 1959.

0073 Dorson, Richard M. *Handbook of American Folklore.* Bloomington: Indiana University Press, 1983.

0074 Doyle, Bertram W. *The Etiquette of Race Relations in the South: A Study in Social Control.* Chicago: University of Chicago Press, 1937.

0075 DuBois, W. E. B. *The Souls of Black Folks: Essays and Sketches.* Chicago: A. L. McClurg, 1903.

0076 Duke, Basil W. *Reminiscences of Basil W. Duke.* New York: Doubleday Page, 1911.

0077 Dunbar, Paul L. *Uncle Eph's Christmas.* N.p., n.d.

0078 Dundes, Alan, ed. *Mother Wit from the Laughing Barrel: Readings in the Interpretation of Afro-American Folklore.* Englewood Cliffs, NJ: Prentice-Hall, 1972.

0079 Edwards, Harry S. *The Two Runaways and Other Stories.* New York: Century, 1889.

0080 Emerson, William C. *Stories and Spirituals of the Negro Slave.* Boston: R. G. Badger, 1930.

0081 Eppse, Merl R. *The Negro, Too, in American History.* Nashville, TN: National Pub. Co., 1943.

0082 Federal Writers' Project. *These Are Our Lives.* 1939. Reprint, New York: Norton, 1975.

0083 Feldstein, Stanley. *Once a Slave: The Slave's View of Slavery.* New York: W. Morrow, 1971.

0084 Felton, Harold W. *John Henry and His Hammer.* New York: Knopf, 1950.

0085 Ferris, William, R., Jr. *Mississippi Black Folklore: A Research Bibliography and Discography.* Hattiesburg: University and College Press of Mississippi, 1971.

0086 Fisk University. Social Science Institute. *Unwritten History of Slavery: Autobiographical Accounts of Negro Ex-Slaves.* Nashville, TN: The Institute, 1945.

0087 Fisk University Library. *Fisk University Theses, 1917–1942.* Nashville, TN: The Library, 1942.

0088 Flanagan, Cathleen C., and John T. Flanagan. *American Folklore: A Bibliography, 1950–1974.* Metuchen, NJ: Scarecrow Press, 1977.

0089 *Folklore: A Dissertation Catalog.* Ann Arbor, MI: University Microfilms Intl., 1980.

0090 Franklin, John Hope. *From Slavery to Freedom: A History of American Negroes.* New York: Knopf, 1956.

0091 Friedland, William H., and Dorothy Nelkin. *Migrant: Agricultural Workers in America's Northeast.* New York: Holt, Rinehart and Winston, 1971.

0092 Fry, Gladys-Marie. *Night Riders in Black Folk History.* Knoxville: University of Tennessee Press, 1975.

0093 Gaines, Francis P. *The Southern Plantation: A Study in the Development and the Accuracy of a Tradition.* New York: Columbia University, 1925.

0094 Georgia Writers' Program Staff. *Drums and Shadows: Survival Studies Among the Georgia Coastal Negroes.* Westport, CT: Greenwood Press, 1973.

0095 Gilman, Caroline. *Recollections of a Southern Matron.* New York: Harper & Brothers, 1838.

0096 Gonzales, Ambrose E. *The Captain, Stories of the Black Border.* Columbia, SC: State Co., 1924.

0097 Gonzales, Ambrose E. *Laguerre, a Gascon of the Black Border.* Columbia, SC: State Co., 1924.

0098 Gordon, Taylor. *Born to Be.* Seattle: University of Washington Press, 1975.

0099 Grandy, Moses. *Narrative of the Life of Moses Grandy, Late a Slave in the United States of America.* Boston: O. Johnson, 1844.

0100 Gray, Pearl S. "African-American Folkloric Form and Function in Segregated One-room Schools." Ph.D. dissertation, Oregon State University, 1986.

0101 *Great Auction Sale of Slaves at Savannah, Georgia.* New York: American Anti-Slavery Society, 1859.

0102 Gregg, J. Chandler. *Life in the Army.* Philadelphia: Perkinpine and Higgins, 1866.

0103 Hampton Institute. *Twenty-Two Years Work of the Hampton Normal and Agricultural Institute.* Hampton, VA: Hampton Normal School Press, 1893.

0104 Harmon, Marion F. *Negro Wit and Humor: Also Containing Folk Lore, Folk Songs, Race Peculiarities, Race History.* Louisville, KY: Harmon, 1914.

0105 Harris, Joel Chandler. *Free Joe and Other Georgian Sketches.* New York: Charles Scribner's Sons, 1887.

0106 Harris, Joel Chandler. *The Tar-Baby, and Other Rhymes by Uncle Remus.* New York: D. Appleton, 1904.

0107 Harris, Joel Chandler. *Uncle Remus and His Friends: Old Plantation Stories, Songs, & Ballads with Sketches of Negro Character.* Boston, New York: Houghton Mifflin, 1892.

0108 Harris, Joel Chandler. *Uncle Remus, His Songs and Sayings: The Folk-lore of Old Plantation.* New York: D. Appleton, 1881.

0109 Harris, Middleton. *The Black Book.* New York: Random House, 1974.

0110 Haywood, Charles. *A Bibliography of North American Folklore and Folksong.* 2nd rev. ed. 2 vols. New York: Dover, 1961.

0111 Hearn, Lafcadio. *Creole Sketches.* Boston: Houghton Mifflin, 1924.

0112 Herskovits, Melville J. *The Myth of the Negro Past.* Boston: Beacon Press, 1958.

0113 Heyward, Du Bose. *The Half Pint Flask.* New York: Farrar and Rinehart, 1929.

0114 Heywood, Duncan C. *Seed from Madagascar.* Chapel Hill: University of North Carolina Press, 1937.

0115 Hirsch, Jerrold. *Folklore in the Making: B. A. Botkin.* N.p., n.d.

0116 *Historical Sketch Book and Guide to New Orleans and Environs with Map.* New York: Will H. Coleman, 1885.

0117 Hobson, Anne. *In Old Alabama, Being the Chronicles of Miss Mouse, the Little Black Merchant.* New York: Doubleday, Page, 1903.

0118 Holloway, Joseph E., ed. *Africanisms in American Culture.* Bloomington: Indiana University Press, 1991.

0119 Holmes, Isaac. *An Account of the United States of America, Derived from Actual Observation, During a Residence of Four Years in That Republic.* London: Caxton Press, 1823.

0120 Hudson, Arthur P. *Specimens of Mississippi Folk-Lore.* Anne Arbor, MI: Edwards Brothers, 1928.

0121 Hughes, Langston, ed. *The Book of Negro Humor.* New York: Dodd, Mead, 1966.

0122 Hughes, Langston, and Arna Bontemps, eds. *The Book of Negro Folklore.* New York: Dodd, Mead, 1958.

0123 Hundley, D. R. *Social Relations in Our Southern States.* New York: Henry B. Price, 1860.

0124 Hurston, Zora Neale. *Dust Tracks on a Road, an Autobiography.* Philadelphia: J. B. Lippincott, 1942.

0125 Hurston, Zora Neale. *Mules and Men.* 1935. Reprint, New York: Negro Universities Press, 1969.

0126 Ingraham, Joseph H. *The Southwest.* Vol. 2. New York: Harper's, 1835.

0127 Jackson, Bruce, ed. *The Negro and His Folklore in Nineteenth-century Periodicals.* Austin: University of Texas Press for the American Folklore Society, 1967.

0128 Jackson, Irene V., ed. *More than Dancing: Essays on Afro-American Music and Musicians.* Westport, CT: Greenwood Press, 1985.

0129 Jackson, Miles M. *A Bibliography of Negro History and Culture for Young Readers.* Pittsburgh: University of Pittsburgh Press for Atlanta University, 1969.

0130 Jagendorf, Moritz A. *Folk Stories of the South.* New York: Vanguard Press, 1972.

0131 Jahn, Janheinz. *A Bibliography of Neo-African Literature from Africa, America and the Caribbean.* New York: Praeger, 1965.

0132 Jahoda, Gloria. *The Other Florida.* New York: Charles Scribner's Sons, 1967.

0133 Johnson, Charles S. *Shadow of the Plantation.* Chicago: University of Chicago Press, 1934.

0134 Johnson, Clifton H. *What They Say in New England and Other American Folklore.* New York: Columbia University Press, 1963.

0135 Johnson, F. Roy. *The Fabled Doctor Jim Jordon: A Story of Conjure.* Murfreesboro, NC: Johnson, 1963.

0136 Johnson, F. Roy. *How and Why Stories in Carolina Folklore.* Murfreesboro, NC: Johnson, 1971.

0137 Johnson, F. Roy. *Tales from Old Carolina.* Murfreesboro, NC: Johnson, 1965.

0138 Johnson, Guion G. *A Social History of the Sea Islands with Special Reference to St. Helena Island, South Carolina.* Chapel Hill: University of North Carolina Press, 1930.

0139 Johnson, Guy B. *Folk Culture on Saint Helena Island.* Chapel Hill: University of North Carolina Press, 1930.

0140 Johnson, Guy B. *John Henry: Tracking Down a Negro Legend.* Chapel Hill: University of North Carolina Press, 1929.

0141 Jones, Bessie, and Bess L. Hawes. *Step It Down: Games, Plays, Songs, and Stories from the Afro-American Heritage.* Athens: University of Georgia Press, 1987. Bibliography on pp. 223–225; discography on pp. 227–228.

0142 Jones, Charles C. *Negro Myths from the Georgia Coast, Told in the Vernacular.* Boston: Houghton Mifflin, 1888.

0143 Jones, Lealon N. *Eve's Stepchildren.* Caldwell, ID: Caxton Printers, 1942.

0144 Joyner, Charles W. *Down by the Riverside: A South Carolina Slave Community.* Urbana: University of Illinois Press, 1984. Bibliography on pp. 244–344.

0145 Kane, Harnett P. *Deep Delta Country.* New York: Duell, Sloan and Pearce, 1944.

0146 Kearney, Belle. *A Slaveholder's Daughter.* New York: Abbey Press, 1900.

0147 Kemble, Frances A. *Journal of a Residence on a Georgian Plantation in 1838–1839.* New York: Harper & Brothers, 1863.

0148 Kennedy, John P. *Swallow Barn, or a Sojourn in the Old Dominion.* Philadelphia: Carey and Lea, 1832.

0149 Kennedy, Robert E. *Gritny People.* New York: Dodd, Mead & Co., 1927.

0150 Kennedy, Stetson. *Palmetto Country.* New York: Duell, Sloan & Pearce, 1942.

0151 Kerst, Catherine H. *Ethnic Folklife Dissertations from the United States and Canada, 1960–1980: A Selected Annotated Bibliography.* Washington, DC: Library of Congress American Folklife Center, 1986.

0152 Keyes, Frances P. *All This Is Louisiana.* New York: Harper, 1950.

0153 Killion, Ronald, and Charles Waller, eds. *Slavery Time When I Was Chillun Down on Marster's Plantation: Interviews with Georgia Slaves.* Savannah, GA: Beehive Press, 1973.

0154 Killion, Ronald, and Charles Waller, eds. *A Treasury of Georgia Folklore.* Atlanta: Cherokee, 1972.

0155 King, Edward. *The Great South.* Hartford, CT: American, 1875.

0156 Kirke, Edmund. *Among the Pines: Or, South in Secession Time.* New York: Gilmore, 1862.

0157 Kirke, Edmund. *My Southern Friends.* New York: Gilmore, 1863.

0158 Kunkel, Peter, and Sara S. Kennard. *Spout Spring: A Black Community.* New York: Holt, Rinehart and Winston, 1971.

0159 Latrobe, Benjamin H. *Impressions Respecting New Orleans.* New York: Columbia University Press, 1951.

0160 Leach, Maria, ed. *Funk & Wagnalls Standard Dictionary of Folklore, Mythology, and Legend.* New York: Funk & Wagnalls, 1949.

0161 LeConte, Joseph. *The Autobiography of Joseph LeConte.* New York: Appleton, 1903.

0162 Lehner, Ernst, and Johanna Lehner. *Folklore and Symbolism of Flowers, Plants, and Trees*. Detroit: Omnigraphics, 1990.

0163 Leigh, James W. *Other Days*. London: Unwin, 1921.

0164 Lester, Julius. *To Be a Slave*. New York: Dial Press, 1968. Bibliography on pp. 159–160.

0165 Levine, Lawrence. *Black Culture and Black Consciousness: Afro-American Folk Thought from Slavery to Freedom*. New York: Oxford University Press, 1977.

0166 Lewis, Hylan. *Blackways of Kent*. Chapel Hill: University of North Carolina Press, 1955.

0167 Livermore, Mary A. *The Story of My Life or the Sunshine and the Shadows of Seventy Years*. Hartford, CT: A. D. Worthington, 1897.

0168 Lomax, Alan. *The Rainbow Sign: A Southern Documentary*. New York: Duell, Sloan and Pearce, 1959.

0169 Louisiana Writers' Program. *Gumbo Ya-Ya*. Boston: Houghton Mifflin, 1945.

0170 Lowery, I. E. *Life on the Old Plantation in Ante-Bellum Days*. Columbia, SC: State Co., 1911.

0171 Lyell, Charles. *A Second Visit to the United States of North America*. 2 vols. London: J. Murray, 1849.

0172 McCarty, Mary W. *Flags of Five Nations*. Sea Island, GA: Cloister Hotel, n.d.

0173 McKim, J. Miller. *An Address Delivered by J. Miller McKim: The Freedmen of South Carolina*. Philadelphia: Willis P. Hazard, 1862.

0174 McTeer, J. E. *High Sheriff of the Low Country*. Beaufort, SC: Beaufort Book Co., 1970.

0175 Mackie, John M. *From Cape Cod to Dixie and the Tropics*. New York: Putnam, 1864.

0176 Malet, William W. *An Errand to the South in the Summer of 1862*. London: Richard Bentley, 1863.

0177 Mallard, R. Q. *Plantation Life Before Emancipation*. Richmond, VA: Whittet and Shepperson, 1892.

0178 Martin, Stephen H. *Alabama Folklife: Collected Essays*. Tuscaloosa: University of Alabama Press, 1989.

0179 Matthews, Essie C. *Aunt Phebe, Uncle Tom and Others: Character Sketches Among the Old Slaves of the South, Fifty Years After*. Columbus, OH: Champlin Press, 1915.

0180 Meier, August. *Negro Thought in America, 1880–1915: Racial Ideologies in the Age of Booker T. Washington*. Ann Arbor: University of Michigan Press, 1963.

0181 Mikell, I. Jenkins. *Rumbling of the Chariot Wheels*. Columbia, SC: State Co., 1923.

0182 Miller, Elizabeth W., comp. *The Negro in America: A Bibliography*. Cambridge, MA: Harvard University Press, 1970.

0183 Mott, Ed. *The Black Homer of Jimtown*. New York: Grosset and Dunlap, 1900.

0184 Murray, Albert. *South to a Very Old Place*. New York: McGraw-Hill, 1971.

0185 Newman, Richard, comp. *Black Access: A Bibliography of Afro-American Bibliographies*. Westport, CT: Greenwood Press, 1984.

0186 O'Donnell, E. P. *Delta Country*. New York: Duell, Sloan and Pearce, 1943.

0187 Olmstead, Frederick Law. *A Journey in the Seaboard Slave States: With Remarks on Their Own Economy*. New York: Dix and Edwards, 1856.

0188 Paine, Lewis W. *Six Years in a Georgia Prison*. New York: The Author, 1851.

0189 Parsons, Elsie. *Folk Lore of the Sea Islands, South Carolina*. Cambridge, MA: American Folklore Society, 1923.

0190 Pearson, Elizabeth W., ed. *Letters from Port Royal*. Boston: W. B. Clarke, 1906.

0191 Perdue, Charles L. "Movie Star Woman in the Land of Black Angries: Ethnography and Folklore of a Negro Community in Rural Virginia." Ph.D. dissertation, University of Pennsylvania, 1971.

0192 Peterkin, Julia, and Doris Ulmann. *Roll, Jordan, Roll*. New York: Robert O. Ballou, 1933.

0193 Pierson, Hamilton W. *In the Brush: Or, Old-Time Social, Political and Religious Life in the Southwest*. New York: Appleton, 1881.

0194 Pollard, Edward A. *Black Diamonds Gathered in the Darkey Homes of the South*. New York: Pudney and Russell, 1860.

0195 Porter, Dorothy B. *The Negro in the United States: A Selected Bibliography*. Washington, DC: Library of Congress, 1970.

0196 Postell, William D. *The Health of Slaves on Southern Plantations*. Baton Rouge: Louisiana State University Press, 1951.

0197 Poulos, Angela. *Negro Culture: A Selective Bibliography*. Bowling Green, OH: Bibliography Research Center, Bowling Green State University Libraries, 1968.

0198 Powdermaker, Hortense. *After Freedom: A Cultural Study in the Deep South*. New York: Viking, 1939.

0199 Pyrnelle, Louisa C. *Diddle, Dumps, and Tot; or Plantation Child-Life*. New York: Harper, 1898.

0200 Ravenel, Rose P. *Piazza Tales: A Charleston Memory*. Charleston, SC: Shaftesbury, 1952.

0201 Rawick, George P., ed. *The American Slave: A Composite Autobiography*. 19 vols. Westport, CT: Greenwood, 1972.

0202 Redpath, James. *The Roving Editor: Or Talks with Slaves*. New York: A. B. Burdick, 1859.

0203 Rice, James H. *Glories of the Carolina Coast*. Columbia, SC: R. L. Bryan, 1925.

0204 Rohrer, John H., and Munro S. Edmonson. *The Eighth Generation: Cultures and Personalities of New Orleans Negroes*. New York: Harper, 1960.

0205 Rousséve, Charles B. *The Negro in Louisiana; Aspects of His History and His Literature*. New Orleans: Xavier University Press, 1937.

0206 Rowell, Charles H. "Afro-American Literary Bibliographies: An Annotated List of Bibliographical Guides for the Study of Afro-American Literature, Folklore, and Related Areas." M.A. thesis, Ohio State University, 1972. Bibliography on lvs. 206–208.

0207   Russell, William H. *My Diary North and South.* New York: Harper, 1954.

0208   Rutledge, Archibald. *God's Children.* Indianapolis: Bobbs-Merrill, 1947.

0209   Sale, John B. *The Tree Named John.* Chapel Hill: University of North Carolina Press, 1929.

0210   Saxon, Lyle. *Fabulous New Orleans.* New York, London: Century, 1928.

0211   Saxon, Lyle. *Old Louisiana.* New York, London: Century, 1929.

0212   Scarborough, Dorothy. *From a Southern Porch.* New York: G. P. Putnam's Sons, 1919.

0213   Schoolcraft, Mrs. Henry R. *The Black Gauntlet: A Tale of Plantation Life in South Carolina.* Philadelphia: Lippincott, 1860.

0214   Sharps, Ronald L. "Happy Days and Sorrow Songs: Interpretations of Negro Folklore by Black Intellectuals." N.p., 1991.

0215   Smedes, Susan D. *Memorials of a Southern Planter.* Baltimore: Cushings and Bailey, 1887.

0216   Smetzer, Barbara. "An Annotated Collection of Negro Folktales from Harnett County, North Carolina." M.A. thesis, Indiana University, 1962.

0217   Smith, Michael P. *Spirit World: Pattern in the Expressive Folk Culture of Afro-American New Orleans: Photography & Journals.* New Orleans: New Orleans Urban Folklife Society, 1984.

0218   Smythe, Augustine T. *The Carolina Low Country.* New York: Macmillan, 1931.

0219   Soloman, Jack, and Olivia Soloman, comps. *Ghosts and Goosebumps: Ghost Stories, Tall Tales, and Superstitions from Alabama.* University: University of Alabama Press, 1981. Bibliography on pp. 187–198.

0220   South Carolina Writers' Program. *South Carolina Folk Tales: Stories of Animals and Supernatural Beings.* Columbia: University of South Carolina Press, 1941.

0221   Spalding, Henry D., comp. *Encyclopedia of Black Folklore and Humor.* Middle Village, NY: Jonathan David, 1972.

0222   Stearns, Charles. *The Black Man of the South, and the Rebels.* Boston: N. E. News, 1872.

0223   Sterling, Philip, ed. *Laughing on the Outside: The Intelligent White Reader's Guide to Negro Tales and Humor.* New York: Grosset and Dunlap, 1965.

0224   Street, Julian. *American Adventures: A Second Trip "Abroad at Home."* New York: Century, 1917.

0225   Szwed, John F., and Roger D. Abrahams. *Afro-American Folk Culture: An Annotated Bibliography of Materials from North, Central, and South America and the West Indies.* 2 vols. Philadelphia: Institute for the Study of Human Issues. Books on Demand, 1978.

0226   Tallant, Robert. *The Romantic New Orleaneans.* New York: E. P. Dutton, 1950.

0227   Tallman, Marjorie. *Dictionary of American Folklore.* New York: Philosophical Library, 1960.

0228 Taylor, Joe Gray. *Negro Slavery in Louisiana*. Baton Rouge: Louisiana Historical Association, 1963.

0229 Taylor, Rosser H. *Carolina Crossroads: A Study of Rural Life at the End of the Horse-and-Buggy Era*. Murfreesboro, NC: Johnson, 1966.

0230 Tennessee Writers' Project. *The WPA Guide to Tennessee*. Knoxville: University of Tennessee Press, 1986.

0231 Towne, Laura M. *Letters and Diary of Laura M. Towne Written from the Sea Islands of South Carolina, 1862–1884*. Cambridge, MA: Riverside, 1912.

0232 Tragle, Henry I. *The Southampton Slave Revolt of 1831: A Compilation of Source Material*. Amherst: University of Massachusetts Press, 1971.

0233 Turner, Frederick W. "Badmen, Black and White: The Continuity of American Folk Traditions." Ph.D. dissertation, University of Pennsylvania, 1965.

0234 Twining, Mary A. "An Examination of African Retentions in the Folk Culture of the South Carolina and Georgia Sea Islands." Ph.D. dissertation, Indiana University, 1977.

0235 Twining, Mary A., and E. Keith Baird, eds. *Sea Island Roots: African Presence in the Carolinas and Georgia*. Trenton, NJ: Africa World Press, 1991.

0236 Vanstory, Burnette. *Georgia's Land of the Golden Isles*. Athens: University of Georgia Press, 1956.

0237 Virginia Writers' Program. *The Negro in Virginia*. New Hastings, NY: Virginia State Writers' Program, WPA, 1940.

0238 Wade, Richard C. *Slavery in the Cities: The South, 1820–1860*. New York: Oxford University Press, 1964.

0239 Waters, Donald J. *Strange Ways and Sweet Dreams: Afro-American Folklore from the Hampton Institute*. Boston: G. K. Hall, 1983.

0240 Watkins, Floyd C., and Charles H. Watkins. *Yesterday in the Hills*. Chicago: Quadrangle Books, 1963.

0241 Wayne State University Folklore Archive. *Afro-American Folklore Collections*. Detroit: The Archive, 1977.

0242 Weeks, Linton. *Memphis: A Folk History*. Little Rock, AK: Parkhurst, 1982.

0243 Welsch, Erwin K. *The Negro in the United States: A Research Guide*. Bloomington: Indiana University Press, 1965.

0244 Whipple, Henry B. *Bishop Whipple's Southern Diary, 1843–1844*. Minneapolis: University of Minnesota Press, 1937.

0245 White, Newman I., ed. *The Frank C. Brown Collection of North Carolina Folklore: The Folklore at North Carolina*. 7 vols. Durham: Duke University Press, 1952–1964.

0246 Whiting, Helen A. J. *Negro Folk Tales for Pupils in the Primary Grades*. Washington, DC: Associated, 1967.

0247 Whitten, Norman E., Jr., and John F. Szwed, eds. *Afro-American Anthropology: Contemporary Perspectives*. New York: Free Press, 1970.

0248 Wightman, Orrin S., and Margaret D. Cate. *Early Days of Coastal Georgia.* St. Simons Island, GA: Fort Frederika Association, 1955.

0249 Woods, Frances J. *Marginality and Identity: A Colored Creole Family Through Ten Generations.* Baton Rouge: Louisiana State University Press, 1972.

0250 Woofter, T. F., Jr. *Black Yeomanry: Life on St. Helena Island.* New York: H. Holt and Co., 1930.

0251 Work, Monroe N. *A Bibliography of the Negro in Africa and America.* New York: Octagon Books, 1965.

0252 Wright, Richard. *Twelve Million Black Voices.* 1941. Reprint, New York: Thunder's Mouth Press, 1988.

0253 Wyatt, Emma O. "Negro Folklore from Alabama." M.A. thesis, University of Iowa, 1943.

0254 Wynar, Lubomyr R. *Guide to Ethnic Museums, Libraries, and Archives in the United States.* Kent, OH: Kent State University Press, 1978.

0255 Yader, Don. *Discovering American Folklife: Studies in Ethnic, Religious, and Regional Culture.* Ann Arbor: UMI Research Press, 1990.

ARTICLES

0256 Anderson, Solena. "Back in Dem Days: A Black Family Reminisces." *J Miss H* 36, no. 2 (1974): 179–185.

0257 Bacon, A. M. "Proposal For Folk-Lore Research at Hampton, VA." *JAFL* 6 (October–December 1893): 305–309.

0258 Bacon, A. M., and Elsie Parsons. "Folk-Lore from Elizabeth City County, Virginia." *JAFL* 35 (July–September 1922): 250–327.

0259 Baer, Florence E. "Sources and Analogues of the Uncle Remus Tales." *Ams* 25 (Fall 1984): 88.

0260 Banfield, Beryle. "Books on African American Themes: A Recommended Book List." *Inter BC* 16, no. 7 (1985): 4–8.

0261 Barker, Howard F. "Family Names of American Negroes." *AS* 14 (1939): 163–174.

0262 Barnett, Marguerite R. "Nostalgia as Nightmare: Blacks and American Popular Culture." *Crisis* 89, no. 2 (1982): 42–45.

0263 Batchelder, Ruth. "Beaufort, of the Real South." *Trav* 28 (February 1917): 28–31.

0264 Bergen, F. D. "Uncle Remus and Folklore." *OUTL* 48 (September 2, 1893): 427–428.

0265 Bradley, A. G. "North Carolina Negro Oral Narratives." *NCF* 9 (1961): 21–33.

0266 Bradley, A. G. "A Peep at the Southern Negro." *Mac* 39 (1878): 61–68.

0267 Bradley, A. G. "Some Plantation Memories." *Black Mag* 161 (1897): 331–341.

0268 Brewer, J. Mason. "Afro-American Folklore." *JAFL* 60 (1947): 377–382.

0269 Brewer, J. Mason. "American Negro Folklore." *Phyl* 6 (1945): 354–361.

0270 Brewer, J. Mason. "South Carolina Negro Folklore Guild." *JAFL* 59 (1946): 493–494.

0271 Brown, Sterling A. "The Muted South." *Phyl* 6 (1945): 22–34.

0272 Browne, Ray B. "Some Notes on the Southern 'Holler.' " *JAFL* 67 (1954): 73–77.

0273 Bryant, Margaret M. "Folklore from Edgefield County, South Carolina." *SFQ* 12 (1948): 197–209, 279–291; 13 (1949): 136–148.

0274 Buchanan, William J. "Legend of the Black Conquistador." *Man Q* 1, no. 5 (1968): 21–25, 93.

0275 Cable, George Washington. "Creole Slave Songs." *Cent* 31 (1886): 807–828.

0276 Cade, John B. "Out of the Mouth of Ex-Slaves." *JNH* 20 (1935): 294–337.

0277 Carawan, Guy. "The Living Heritage of the Sea Islands." *SQ* 14, no. 2 (1964): 29–32.

0278 Carew, Roy J. "New Orleans Recollection." *RC* (April 1943): 8–9; (May 1943): 10–11; (June 1943): 3–4; (September 1943): 3–4; (October 1943): 3–4; (November 1943): 3; (December 1943): 14–15; (January 1944): 3.

0279 Chamberlain, Alexander F. "Record of Negro Folk-lore." *JAFL* 16 (July–September 1903): 273–274; 17 (January–March 1904): 77–79; 18 (April–June 1905): 156; 18 (July–September 1905): 244; 19 (January–March 1906): 75–77; 21 (April–September 1908): 263–267; 22 (January–March 1909): 102–104.

0280 Clark, Kenneth. "Folklore of Negro Children in Greater Louisville Reflecting Attitudes Toward Race." *KFR* 10, no. 1 (1964): 1–11.

0281 Clark, Rogie. "What Is Negro Folklore?" *Negro Hist Bull* 27, no. 2 (1963): 40–41.

0282 Clayton, Ronnie W. "Federal Writers' Project in Louisiana." *LA Hist* 19, no. 34 (1978): 327–335.

0283 Cooke, Elizabeth J. "English Folktales in America." *JAFL* 12 (1899): 126–130.

0284 Cooley, Rossa B. "Aunt Jane and Her People: The Real Negroes of the Sea Island." *OUTL* 90 (1908): 424–432.

0285 Craig, Alberta R. "Old Wentworth Sketches." *NCHR* 11, no. 3 (1934): 185–204.

0286 Davis, Daniel W. "Echoes from a Plantation Party." *SW* 28 (1899): 54–59.

0287 Davis, H. C. "Negro Folklore in South Carolina." *JAFL* 27 (1914): 241–254.

0288 Davis, M. E. N. "Louisiana Folklore." *JAFL* 18 (1905): 251–252.

0289 Davis, Rebecca Harding. "Here and There in the South." *Harper's* 75 (1887): 431–443.

0290 Dickerson, Bruce D., Jr. "The 'John and Old Master' Stories and the World of Slavery: A Study in Folktales and History." *Phyl* 35, no. 4 (1974): 418–429.

0291 Dorson, Richard M. "American Folklore Bibliography." *Ams* 16, no. 1 (1977): 23–27.

0292 Dorson, Richard M. "Negro Tales from Bolivar County, Mississippi." *SFQ* 19 (1955): 104–116.

0293 Dowd, Jerome. "Art in Negro Homes." *SW* 30 (1901): 90–95.

0294 Ellison, Mary. "Black Perceptions and Red Images: Indian and Black Literary Links." *Phyl* 44, no. 1 (March 1983): 44–55.

0295 Fauset, A. H. "Negro Tales from the South (Alabama, Mississippi, Louisiana)." *JAFL* 40 (1927): 213–303.

0296 Fickling, Susan M. "Slave Conversion in South Carolina, 1830–1860." *Bull Univ SC* 146 (1924): 1–59.

0297 Fishwick, Marshall. "Uncle Remus vs. John Henry: Folk Tension." *WF* 20 (April 1961): 77–85.

0298 Fitchett, E. H. "Traditions of the Free Negro in Charleston, South Carolina." *JNH* 25 (1940): 139–152.

0299 Flanders, Ralph P. "Two Plantations and a County of Antebellum Georgia." *GHQ* 12 (1928): 1–37.

0300 "Folk-Lore and Ethnology." *SW* 23 (1894): 84–86.

0301 "Folk-Lore and Ethnology." *SW* 23 (1894): 209–210.

0302 "Folk-Lore and Ethnology." *SW* 28 (1899): 112–113.

0303 "Folklore from St. Helena, South Carolina." *JAFL* 38 (1925): 217–238.

0304 Forten, C. L. "Life on the Sea Islands." *Atl* 13 (1864): 487–596, 666–676.

0305 Funkhouser, Myrtle. "Folk-lore of the American Negro: A Bibliography. *Bul Bibliog* 16 (1937–1939): 28–29, 49–51, 72–73, 108–110, 136–137, 159–160.

0306 Garner, Thurman. "Black Ethos in Folktales." *J Black Stud* 15, no. 1 (1984): 53–66.

0307 Gehrke, William H. "Negro Slavery Among the Germans in North Carolina." *NCHR* 14, no. 4 (1937): 3027–324.

0308 Griska, Joseph M., Jr. "Uncle Remus Correspondence: The Development and Reception of Joel Chandler Harris' Writing, 1878–1885." *ALR* 14, no. 1 (Winter 1981): 26–37.

0309 Hampton, Bill R. "On Identification and Negro Tricksters." *SFQ* 31 (March 1967): 55–65.

0310 Haque, Abu S. Z. "A Bibliography of Mississippi Folklore." *Miss FR* 2 (1968): 43–48.

0311 Harn, Julia E. "Old Canoochee-Ogechee Chronicles." *GHQ* 15 (1931): 346–360; 16 (1932): 146–150, 232–240.

0312 Harrison, Lowell H. "The Folklore of Some Kentucky Slaves." *KFR* 17 (1971): 25–30, 53–60.

0313 Herskovits, Melville J. "Folklore After a Hundred Years: A Problem in Redefinition." *JAFL* 59 (1943): 89–100.

0314 Herskovits, Melville J. "Some Next Steps in the Study of Negro Folklore." *JAFL* 56 (1943): 1–7.

0315 Hirsch, Jerrold. "Folklore in the Making: B. A. Botkin." *JAFL* 100, no. 395 (1987): 3–38.

0316 Holsey, Albon L. "Learning How to Be Black." *Am Merc* 16 (1929): 421–425.

0317 Hurdle, Virginia J. "Folklore of a Negro Couple in Henry County." *FSB* 19 (1953): 71–78.

0318 Hurll, Margaret M. "Studies of Art in American Life IV: In Negro Cabins." *Brush & P* 7 (January 1901): 239–244.

0319 Hurston, Zora Neale. " 'High John De Conquerer': Negro Folklore Offers Solace to Sufferers." *Am Merc* 57 (October 1943): 450–458.

0320 Jackson, Margaret. "Folklore in Slave Narratives Before the Civil War." *NYFQ* 11 (1955): 5–19.

0321 Jaffe, Harry J. "American Negro Folklore: A Check List of Scarce Items." *SFQ* 36, no. 1 (March 1972): 68–70.

0322 James, Willis L. "The Romance of the Negro Folk Cry in America." *Phyl* 16 (Spring 1955): 15–30.

0323 Jones, J. Ralph. "Portraits of Georgia Slaves." *GR* 21 (1967): 126–132, 268–273, 407–411, 521–525; 22 (1968): 125–127, 254–257.

0324 Joyner, Charles W. "Southern Folklore as a Key to Southern Identity." *So HR* 1 (1967): 211–222.

0325 Law, Robert A. "Notes on Some Recent Treatments of Negro Folklore." *TFSB* 7 (1928): 140–144.

0326 Lesser, Alexander. "American Negro." In "Bibliography of American Folklore, 1915–1928." *JAFL* 41 (January–March 1928): 47–52.

0327 Light, Kathleen. "Uncle Remus and the Folklorists." *SLJ* 7, no. 2 (1975): 88–104.

0328 "Manner of Living of the Inhabitants of Virginia." *Am Mus J* 1 (March 1887): 214–216.

0329 Mason, Julia. "The South of Black Folk." *Miss Q* 34, no. 4 (Fall 1981): 472–476.

0330 Moore, Jack B. "The Voice in 12 Million Black Voices." *Miss Q* 42, no. 4 (Fall 1989): 415–424.

0331 Mullen, Patrick. "A Negro Street Performer: Tradition and Innovation." *WF* 29 (1970): 91–103.

0332 Nelson, Randy F. "George Black: A New Folk Hero." *NCF* 20, no. 1 (1972): 30–35.

0333 Nickels, Cameron C. "An Early Version of the 'Tar Baby' Story." *JAFL* 94, no. 373 (1981): 364–369.

0334 Oxrieder, Julia. "Folklife and Folklore from Amherst County, Virginia." *KFR* (1976): 47–51.

0335 Owens, William A. "Folklore of the Southern Negroes." *Lippinc* 20 (1877): 748–755.

0336 Park, Robert. "The Conflict of Fusion and Culture." *JNH* 4 (April 1919): 111–133.

0337 Parsons, Elsie C. "Folklore from Aiken, South Carolina." *JAFL* 34 (1921): 1–39.

0338 Parsons, Elsie C. "Folklore from Georgia." *JAFL* 47 (1934): 386–390.

0339 Parsons, Elsie C. "Folklore of the Cherokees of Robeson County, North Carolina." *JAFL* 32 (1919): 384–393.

0340 Parsons, Elsie C. "Notes on Folklore of Guilford County, North Carolina. *JAFL* 30 (1917): 201–208.

0341 Parsons, Mildred. "Negro Folklore from Fayette County." *TFSB* 19 (1953): 67–70.

0342 Peters, Paul. "Dockwallopers." *Am Merc* 20 (1930): 319–326.

0343 Peterson, Elizabeth, and Tom Rankin. "Free Hill: An Introduction." *TFSB* 50, no. 1 (1985): 1–9.

0344 Phillips, Ulrich B. "Plantations with Slave Labor and Free." *Am Hist Rev* 30 (1924–1925): 738–753.

0345 Piersen, William D. "An African Background for American Negro Folktales?" *JAFL* 84, no. 332 (1971): 204–214.

0346 Powe, Marilyn. "Black 'Isms.' " *Miss FR* 6 (1972): 76–82.

0347 Ravenel, H. W. "Recollections of Southern Plantation Life." *Yale R* (1936): 748–787.

0348 Read, Ira De A. "The John Canoe Festival." *Phyl*, 3 (1942): 349–370.

0349 Rowe, G. S. "The Negroes of the Sea Islands." *SW* 29 (1900): 709–715.

0350 Rowell, Charles H. "A Bibliography of Bibliographies for the Study of Black American Literature and Folklore." *Black Ex* 55 (June 1969): 95–111.

0351 Rubin, Louis D., Jr. "Uncle Remus and the Ubiquitous Rabbit." *SR* 10, no. 4 (1974): 787–804.

0352 "Schomburg Center Issue." *BRH* 84, no. 2 (Summer 1981).

0353 Scott, Patricia B. "Black Folklore in Tennessee: A Working Bibliography." *TFSB* 44, no. 3 (1978): 130–133.

0354 "The Sea Islands." *Harper's* 57 (1878): 839–861.

0355 Shaler, N. S. "African Element in America." *Ar* 2 (1890): 660–673.

0356 Not used.

0357 Showers, Susan. "Alabama Folk-Lore." *SW* 29 (1900): 179–180, 443–444.

0358 Showers, Susan. "A Weddin' and a Buryin' in the Black Belt." *New Eng Mag* 18 (1898): 478–483.

0359 Smiley, Portia. "Folk-lore from Virginia, South Carolina, Georgia, Alabama, and Florida." *JAFL* 32 (1913): 357–383.

0360 Smith, Grace P. "Scraps of Southern Lore." *SFQ* 9 (1945): 169–173.

0361 Smith, John D. "The Unveiling of Slave Folk Culture." *JAFL* 21, no. 1 (1984): 47–62.

0362 Snead, James A. "On Repetition in Black Culture." *BALF* 15, no. 4 (Winter 1981): 146–154.

0363 Spratling, William. "Cane River Portraits." *Scrib M* 83 (1928): 411–418.

0364 Szwed, John F. "Africa Lies Just Off Georgia: Sea Islands Preserve Origins of Afro-American Culture." *Afr Rep* 15, no. 7 (1970): 29–31.

0365 Thanet, Octave. "Folklore in Arkansas." *JAFL* 5 (1892): 121–125.

0366 Torian, Sarah, ed. "Ante-Bellum and War Memories of Mrs. Telfair Hodgson." *GHQ* 27 (1943): 350–356.

0367 Tullos, Allen, ed. "Long Journey Home: Folklife in the South." *South Exposure* 5, nos. 2–3 (1977).

0368 Twining, Mary A. "Sources in the Folklore and Folklife of the Sea Islands." *SFQ* 39, no. 2 (1975): 135–149.

0369 Walker, Barbara K. "Elmira and the Underground Railroad." *NYFQ* 17 (1961): 23–31.

0370 Waring, Martha G., ed. "Charles Seton Henry Hardee's Recollections of Old Savannah." *GHQ* 12 (1928): 353–389; 13 (1929): 13–48.

0371 Waring, Martha G., and Mary A. Waring. "Impressions of the Eighties upon a Child of Old Savannah." *GHQ* 17 (1933): 40–53.

0372 Webb, Walter Prescott. "Miscellany of Texas Folklore: Negro Songs and Stories." *PTFS* 2 (1923): 45–49.

0373 Webb, Walter Prescott. "Notes on Folk-lore of Texas." *JAFL* 28 (1915): 290–299.

0374 Wilson, William A. "Folklore and History: Fact amid the Legend." *Utah Hist Q* 41, no. 1 (1973): 40–58.

2

Folk Medicine

MONOGRAPHS

0375   Anderson, John Q. *Texas Folk Medicine*. Vol. 5. Austin, TX: Encino Press, 1970.

0376   Anderson, John Q. *Texas Folk Medicine: 1,333 Cures, Remedies, Preventives, and Health Practices*. Austin, TX: Encino Press, 1970.

0377   Andrews, Theodora. *Bibliography on Herbs, Herbal Medicine, "Natural" Foods, and Unconventional Medical Treatment*. Littleton, Co: Libraries Unlimited, 1982.

0378   Babb, Jewel. *Border Healing Woman: The Story of Jewel Babb*. Austin: University of Texas Press, 1981. Bibliography on pp. 131–134.

0379   Boyd, Eddie L. *Home Remedies and the Black Elderly: A Reference Manual for Health Care Providers*. Ann Arbor: Institute of Gerontology and College of Pharmacy, University of Michigan, 1984. Bibliography on pp. 23–25.

0380   Cameron, Vivian K. "Folk-Beliefs Pertaining to the Health of the Southern Negro." M.A. thesis, Northwestern University, 1930.

0381   Cochrane, P. *The Witch Doctors' Manual*. Santa Barbara, CA: Woodbridge Press, 1984.

0382   Dunbar, Lin. *Ferns of the Coastal Plain: Their Lore, Legends, and Uses*. Columbia: University of South Carolina Press, 1989.

0383   Fontenot, Wonda L. "Afro-American Folk Medicine and Practices in Rural Louisiana." M.A. thesis, University of California, Berkeley, 1987. Bibliography on lvs. 64–71.

0384   Jarvis, D. C. *Folk Medicine*. New York: Fawcett Book Group, 1985.

0385   Kirkland, James. *Herbal and Magical Medicine: Traditional Healing Today*. Durham: Duke University Press, 1992. Bibliography on pp. 197–233.

0386 Not used.

0387 *Medicine Without Doctors: Home Health Care in American History.* New York: Science History Publications, 1977.

0388 Meyer, Clarence. *American Folk Medicine.* Glenwood, IL: Meyerbooks, 1985. Bibliography on pp. 279–281.

0389 Mitchell, Faith. *Hoodoo Medicine: Sea Islands Herbal Remedies.* Berkeley, CA: Reed, Cannon and Johnson, 1978. Bibliography on pp. 95–97.

0390 Morton, J. *Folk Remedies of the Low Country.* Miami: E. A. Seemann, 1974.

0391 Scarborough, John. *Folklore and Folklore Medicine: The Reproduction and Practice of Healing.* Westport, CT: Greenwood, 1988.

0392 Solomon, Jack, and Olivia Solomon. *Cracklin Bread & Asfidity: Folk Recipes and Remedies.* Tuscaloosa: University of Alabama Press, 1977.

0393 Teaford, Ruth R. *Southern Homespun.* Huntsville, AL: Strode, 1980.

0394 Terrell, Suzanne J. *This Other Kind of Doctors: Traditional Medical Systems in Black Neighborhoods in Austin, Texas.* New York: AMS Press, 1990. Bibliography on pp. 96–104.

0395 *Water Cures and Other Remedies.* TN: Franklin County Historical Society, 1974.

0396 Watson, Wilbur H. *Black Folk Medicine: The Therapeutic Significance of Faith and Trust.* New Brunswick, NJ: Transaction Books, 1984. Bibliography on pp. 105–113.

ARTICLES

0397 "A Cure That's Worse than the Ailment." *Science News* 135 (January 28, 1989): 60.

0398 Bacon, A. M. "Conjuring and Conjure—Doctors in the Southern United States." *JAFL* 9 (1896): 143–147; 224–226.

0399 Baer, Hans A. "Toward a Systematic Typology of Black Folk Healers." *Phyl* 43 (1982): 327–343.

0400 Bass, Ruth. "Fern Seed—For Peace." *Folk-Say* 2 (1930): 145–156.

0401 Bergen, Fanny D. "Some Bits of Plant Lore." *JAFL* 5 (1892): 20–21.

0402 Borrois, Juli. "Herb Cures in an Isolated Black Community in the Florida Parishes." *LAFM* 3 (1970): 25–27.

0403 Brown, Marcie. "Notes on Classical and Renaissance Analog of Mississippi Negro Folklore." *Miss FR* 2 (1968): 37–41.

0404 Cadwallader, D. W. "Folklore Medicine Among Georgia's Piedmont Negroes After the Civil War." *GHQ* (1965): 217–227.

0405 Cole, Helen Rosemary. "Why Is Mistletoe?" *JAFL* 59 (1946): 528–529.

0406 Cooke, R. C. "Remedies." *TFSB* 42 (1976): 65–69.

0407 Fitchett, E. H. "Superstitions in South Carolina." *Crisis* 43 (1936): 360–361, 370.

0408 "Folk-Lore and Ethnology." *SW* 24 (1895): 49–50.

0409 Gibson, H. E. "Folk Medicine Among the Gullahs: African Legacy." *Negro D* 11 (August 1962): 77–80. (Reprinted from the *Charleston* [SC] *News and Courier*.)

0410 Gracy, David B., and Roger D. Abrahams. "Some Plantation Remedies and Recipes." *TFSB* 29 (1963): 29–34.

0411 Grayson, W. P. "The Folklore of a Medical Community." *LAFM* 5 (1981): 48–52.

0412 Hall, Ella R. "A Comparison of Selected Mississippi and North Carolina Remedies." *Miss FR* 5 (1971): 94–113.

0413 Harrison, Ira E. "Health Status and Healing Practices: Continuation from an African Past." *JASP* 2 (Winter 1975): 558.

0414 Hill, Carole E. "Black Healing Practices in the Rural South." *JPC* 6 (1973): 849–853.

0415 Hilliard, A. S. "What'll We Give the Baby-O?" *TFSB* 40 (1974): 41–46.

0416 Hough, Walter. "Folk Medicine." *JAFL* 15 (1902): 191.

0417 Hufford, David. "Customary Observances in Modern Medicine." *WF* 48 (April 1989): 129.

0418 Jones, F. A. "Some Medical Superstitions Among the Southern Negroes." *Journal of the American Medical Association* 50 (1908): 1207.

0419 Klaw, Spencer. "Belly-My-Grizzle." *American Heritage* 28 (1977): 96–105.

0420 La Mer, Nathaniel. "Creole Love Song." *Atl* 195, no. 6 (June 1955): 39–45.

0421 McLeod, W. C. "The Chewing of Tobacco in Southeastern North America." *AA* 32 (1930): 574–575.

0422 "The Negro Caesar's Cure for Poison." *Mass M* 4 (1792): 103–104.

0423 Packwood, L. H. C. "Cure for an Aching Tooth." *JAFL* 13 (1900): 66–67.

0424 Pedersen, D. "Healers, Deities, Saints and Doctors: Elements for the Analysis of Medical Systems." *Social Science & Medicine* 29 (August 15, 1989): 487.

0425 Stewart, Horace. "Kindling of Hope in the Disadvantaged: A Study of the Afro-American Healer." *Ment Hyg* 35, no. 1 (1971): 96–100.

0426 Stewart-Baxter, Derrick. "Blues and Views," *JJ* 27, no. 4 (1974): 24–25.

0427 Trahant, Y. L. "The Oral Tradition of the Physician." *LAFM* 5 (1981): 38–47.

0428 Waller, Tom, and Gene Killian. "Georgia Folk Medicine." *GFM* 36 (1972): 71–92.

3

Folk Music

MONOGRAPHS

0429 Allen, William F., C. P. Ware, and L. M. Garrison. *Slave Songs of the United States*. New York: Peter Smith, 1929.

0430 Armstrong, Louis. *Satchmo: My Life in New Orleans*. New York: Prentice-Hall, 1954.

0431 Armstrong, Louis. *Swing That Music*. New York: Longmans, Green and Co., 1936.

0432 Armstrong, M. F. *Hampton and Its Students*. New York: G. P. Putnam's Sons, 1874. Songs on pp. 175–255.

0433 Arnold, Byron. *Folk Songs of Alabama*. University: University of Alabama Press, 1950. Bibliography on p. 187.

0434 Asch, Moses, and Alan Lomax, eds. *The Leadbelly Songbook: The Ballads, Blues, and Folk Songs of Huddie Ledbetter*. New York: Oak, 1962. Discography on pp. 96–97.

0435 Backus, Rob. *Fire Music: A Political History of Jazz*. Chicago: Vanguard Books, 1976.

0436 Baker, Houston A., Jr. *Blues, Ideology, and Afro-American Literature: A Vernacular Theory*. Chicago: University of Chicago Press, 1984.

0437 Ballanta-Taylor, Nicholas George Julius. *St. Helena Island Spirituals*. New York: G. Schirmer, 1925.

0438 Balliett, Whitney. *Such Sweet Thunder: Forty-nine Pieces on Jazz*. Indianapolis: Bobbs-Merrill, 1966.

0439 Barker, Edward, and Willa A. Townsend. "Way Down Yonder in New Orleans." In *Hear Me Talkin' to Ya*, ed. Nat Shapiro and Nat Hentoff. New York: Dover, 1955.

0440   Barlow, William. *"Looking Up at Down": The Emergence of Blues Culture.* Philadelphia: Temple University Press, 1989. Bibliography on pp. 349–382.

0441   Barret, Eugene H. "Negro Popular Music, 1945–53." M.A. thesis, University of California, Los Angeles, 1967.

0442   Barrett, Harris. *Negro Folk Songs.* Hampton, VA: Hampton Institute Press, 1912.

0443   Barton, W. E. *Old Plantation Hymns.* Boston: Lamson, Wolffe, 1899.

0444   Bastin, Bruce. *Crying for the Carolines.* London: Studio Vista, 1971.

0445   Bechet, Sidney. *Treat It Gentle.* New York: Hill and Wang, 1960.

0446   Benedict, Helen Dymond. *Belair Plantation Melodies.* Cincinnati: Willis Music Co., 1924.

0447   Blackstone, Orin. *Index to Jazz: Jazz Recordings, 1917–1944.* Westport, CT: Greenwood Press, 1978. Reprint.

0448   Blades, William C. *Negro Poems, Melodies, Plantation Pieces, Camp Meeting Songs, etc.* Boston: R. G. Badger, 1921.

0449   Boatner, Edward, and William A. Townsend. *Spirituals Triumphant, Old and New.* Nashville, TN: Sunday School Publishing Board, National.

0450   Bogaert, Karel. *Blues Lexicon: Blues, Cajun, Boogie Woogie, Gospel.* Antwerp: Standard, 1971. Bibliography on pp. 421–422.

0451   Bolton, Dorothy G., ed. *Old Songs Hymnal.* New York: Century, 1929.

0452   Bond, Carrie Jacobs, comp. *Old Melodies of the South.* Chicago: Bond Shop, 1918.

0453   Botkin, B. A., and Alvin F. Harlow. *A Treasury of Railroad Folklore.* New York: Crown, 1953.

0454   Botsford, Florence Hudson. *Botsford Collection of Folk Songs.* 3 vols. New York: G. Schirmerine [1930–1933].

0455   Broonzy, William, and Yannick Bruynoghe. *Big Bill Blues: William Broonzy's Story.* New York: Oak, 1964. Discography on pp. 153–173.

0456   Broucek, Jack W. "Eighteenth-Century Music in Savannah, Georgia." Ed.D. dissertation, Florida State University, 1963. Bibliography on lvs. 243–251.

0457   Broughton, Viv. *Black Gospel: An Illustrated History of the Gospel Sound.* New York: Sterling, 1985.

0458   Broun, Lawrence. *Spirituals.* London: Schott, 1923.

0459   Broven, John. *Walking to New Orleans: The Story of New Orleans Rhythm and Blues.* Bexhill, UK: Blues Unlimited, 1974.

0460   Brown, William W. *My Southern Home: or, the South and Its People.* Boston: A. G. Brown, 1880.

0461   Buchanan, Annabel Morris. *American Folk Music: Native Folk Music Found in America.* Ithaca, NY: National Federation of Music Clubs, 1939. Chapters 4 and 5 concern black music.

0462   Buerkle, Jack V., and Danny Barker. *Bourbon Street Black: The New Orleans Black Jazzman.* New York: Oxford University Press, 1973.

0463 Burlin, Natalie Curtis. *Hampton Series of Negro Folk-Songs*. 4 vols. New York: G. Schirmer, 1918–1919.

0464 Calloway, Cab. *Cab Calloway's Cat-ologue*. New York: Mills Artists, 1938.

0465 Carawan, Guy, and Candie Carawan. *Ain't You Got a Right to the Tree of Life? The People of Johns Island, South Carolina—Their Faces, Their Words, and Their Songs*. Rev. and expanded ed. Athens: University of Georgia Press, 1989. Bibliography on pp. 237–239.

0466 Carawan, Guy, and Candie Carawan. *Freedom Is a Constant Struggle: Songs of the Freedom Movement*. New York: Oak, 1968.

0467 Carr, Ian. *Jazz: The Essential Companion*. New York: Prentice-Hall, 1988.

0468 Carter, Albert E. "The Louisiana Negro and His Music." M.M. thesis, Northwestern University, 1947.

0469 Case, Brian, and Stan Britt. *The Illustrated Encyclopedia of Jazz*. London, New York: Harmony Books, 1978.

0470 Charters, Samuel B. *The Bluesmen*. New York: Oak, 1967.

0471 Charters, Samuel B. *The Country Blues*. New York: Rinehart, 1959.

0472 Charters, Samuel B. *Jazz, New Orleans, 1885–1963: An Index to the Negro Musicians of New Orleans*. 1963. Reprint, New York: Da Capo Press, 1983. Discography on pp. 130–154.

0473 Charters, Samuel B. *The Legacy of the Blues: A Glimpse into the Art and Lives of Twelve Great Bluesmen*. New York: Da Capo, 1977. Bibliography on pp. 187–188; discography on pp. 189–192.

0474 Charters, Samuel B. *Robert Johnson*. New York: Oak, 1973.

0475 Charters, Samuel B. *The Roots of the Blues: An African Search*. New York: Putnam, 1982.

0476 Chase, Gilbert. *America's Music from the Pilgrims to the Present*. 3d ed. Urbana: University of Illinois Press, 1987. Bibliography on pp. 647–688.

0477 Chilton, John. *A Jazz Nursery: The Story of the Jenkins Orphanage Bands of Charleston, South Carolina*. London: Bloomsbury Book Shop, 1980. Bibliography on p. 51.

0478 Chilton, John. *Who's Who of Jazz: Storyville to Swing Street*. 4th ed. New York: Da Capo Press, 1985. Bibliography on p. 374.

0479 Christy, Edwin P. *Christy's Plantation Melodies*. New York: Fisher & Bros., 1851.

0480 Cohen, Lily Young. *Lost Spirituals*. New York: W. Neale, 1928.

0481 Coleman, J. Winston. *Slavery Times in Kentucky*. Chapel Hill: University of North Carolina Press, 1940. Bibliography on pp. 327–332.

0482 Coleman, Z. A. *The Jubilee Singers, a Collection of Plantation Melodies*. Cincinnati: John Church, 1883.

0483 Coleridge-Taylor, Samuel. *Twenty-four Negro Melodies . . .* Boston: Ditson, 1905.

0484 Cone, James H. *The Spirituals and the Blues: An Interpretation*. c. 1972. Reprint, Westport, CT: Greenwood Press, 1980.

0485 Conway, Eugenia C. "The Afro-American Traditions of the Folk Banjo." Ph.D. dissertation, University of North Carolina, 1980.

0486 Cooper, David E. *International Bibliography of Discographies: Classical Music and Jazz and Blues, 1962–1972: A Reference Book for Record Collectors, Dealers, and Libraries.* Littleton, CO: Libraries Unlimited, 1975.

0487 Courlander, Harold. *Negro Folk Music, U.S.A.* New York: Columbia University Press, 1963. Bibliography on pp. 229–301; discography on pp. 302–308.

0488 Cox, John H. *Folk Songs of the South.* Cambridge, MA: Harvard University Press, 1925.

0489 Cuney-Hare, Maud. *Negro Musicians and Their Music.* Washington, DC: Associated, 1936. Annotated list of spirituals and slave songs on pp. 413–418; bibliography on pp. 419–423.

0490 Cuney-Hare, Maud. *Six Creole Folk-songs with Original Creole and Translated English Text.* New York: Carl Fischer, 1921.

0491 Cushing, Helen Grant. *Children's Song Index: An Index to More than 22,000 Songs in 189 Collections Comprising 222 Volumes.* New York: H. W. Wilson, 1936.

0492 Dahl, Linda. *Stormy Weather: The Music and Lives of a Century of Jazzwomen.* New York: Limelight, 1989. Bibliography on pp. 355–359; discography on pp. 307–354.

0493 Davis, Arthur Kyle, Jr. *Folk-songs of Virginia: A Descriptive Index and Classification of Material Collected Under the Auspices of the Virginia Folklore Society.* Durham, NC: Duke University Press, 1949. Section 16, pp. 311–323, has African American songs found in Virginia.

0494 De Lerma, Dominique-René. *Bibliography of Black Music.* Vol, 2, *Afro-American Indians.* Westport, CT: Greenwood Press, 1981.

0495 De Lerma, Dominique-René, and Marsha J. Reisser. *Black Music and Musicians in the New Grove Dictionary of American Music and the New Harvard Dictionary of Music.* Chicago: Center for Black Music Research, Columbia College, Chicago, 1989.

0496 Delaunay, Charles. *New Hot Discography: The Standard Directory of Recorded Jazz,* ed. Walter E. Schaap and George Avakian. New York: Criterion, 1948.

0497 Deming, Clarence. *By-ways of Nature and Life.* New York: Putnam's, 1884. Songs and hymns on pp. 370–383.

0498 Dennison, Tim. *The American Negro and His Amazing Music.* New York: Vantage, 1963.

0499 Dett, R. Nathaniel. *The Dett Collections of Negro Spirituals.* 4 vols. Chicago: Hall and McCreary, 1936.

0500 Dett, R. Nathaniel. *Negro Spirituals.* 3 vols. Cincinnati: John Church, 1919.

0501 Dett, R. Nathaniel, ed. *Religious Folk-Songs of the Negro as Sung at Hampton Institute.* Hampton, VA: Hampton Institute Press, 1927.

0502 Dexter, Dave, Jr. *The Jazz Story: From the 90s to the 60s.* Englewood Cliffs, NJ:

Prentice-Hall, 1964. Modern jazz bibliography on pp. 161–164; discography on pp. 165–167.

0503 Diton, Carl. *Thirty-six South Carolina Spirituals.* New York: G. Schirmer, 1928.

0504 Divers, Jessica P. *The African Methodist Episcopal Church and Its Hymnal.* M.M. thesis, Northwestern University, 1944. Bibliography on lvs. 57–59.

0505 Dixon, Christa. *Negro Spirituals: From Bible to Folk Song.* Philadelphia: Fortress Press, 1976.

0506 Dixon, Robert M. W., and John Godrich. *Blues & Gospel Records, 1902–1943.* 3d rev. ed. Essex, UK: Storyville, 1982.

0507 Dixon, Robert M. W., and John Godrich. *Recording the Blues.* New York: Stein and Day, 1970.

0508 Dixon, Willie. *I Am the Blues: The Willie Dixon Story.* New York: Da Capo Press, 1990.

0509 DjeDje, Jacqueline C. *American Black Spiritual and Gospel Songs from Southeast Georgia: A Comparative Study.* Los Angeles: Center for Afro-American Studies, University of California, 1978.

0510 Dobie, J. Frank. *Guide to Life and Literature of the Southwest.* Dallas: Southern Methodist University Press, 1952. Bibliographical essay on pp. 176–177; chapter 31 includes black songs and tales.

0511 Dodds, Baby. *The Baby Dodds Story* (as told to Larry Gara). Los Angeles: Contemporary Press, 1959.

0512 Doerflinger, William M. *Songs of the Sailor and Lumberman.* Rev. ed. New York: Macmillan, 1972.

0513 Driggs, Franklin S. "Kansas City and the Southwest." *In Jazz,* ed. Nat Hentoff and Albert J. McCarthy. New York: Rinehart, 1959, 191–230, 365–366.

0514 Emerson, William Canfield, ed. *Stories and Spirituals of the Negro Slave.* Boston: R. G. Badger, 1930.

0515 Emery, Lynne Fauley. *Black Dance in the United States from 1619 to 1970.* Palo Alto, CA: National Press Books, 1972.

0516 Epstein, Dena. "Myths About Black Folk Music." In *Folk Music and Modern Sound,* ed. William Ferris and Mary L. Hart. Jackson: University Press of Mississippi, 1982.

0517 Epstein, Dena. *Sinful Tunes & Spirituals: Black Folk Music to the Civil War.* Champaign: University of Illinois Press, 1981. Bibliography on pp. 374–415.

0518 Evans, David. *Big Road Blues: Tradition and Creativity in the Folk Blues.* New York: Da Capo Press, 1987. Bibliography on pp. 351–364.

0519 Evans, David. *Charlie Patton.* Knutsford, UK: Blues World Booklet, no. 2, 1969.

0520 Evans, David. *Tommy Johnson.* London: Studio Vista, 1971. Life of a Mississippi bluesman with a study of his musical style, bibliography.

0521 Evans, David, and Richard M. Raichelson. *Tennessee Blues and Gospel: From Jug Band to Jublee*; Smithsonian Institution, National Park Service, June 25–29/

July 2–6; 50–55. In *1986 Festival of American Folklife*, ed. Thomas Vennum, Jr. Washington, DC: Smithsonian Institution, 1986.

0522 Fahey, John. *Charley Patton*. London: Studio Vista, 1970.

0523 Fairbairn, Ann. *Call Him George*. New York: Crown, 1969.

0524 Feather, Leonard. *The Encyclopedia of Jazz*. New York: Horizon Press, 1960. Bibliography on pp. 524–527; Discography on pp. 500–504.

0525 Fenner, Thomas. *Religious Folk Songs of the Negro*. Hampton, VA: Hampton Institute Press, 1916.

0526 Fenner, Thomas, comp, *Cabin and Plantation Songs, as Sung by the Hampton Students*. Hampton, VA: Hampton Institute, 1874.

0527 Ferlingere, Robert D. *A Discography of Rhythm & Blues and Rock n' Roll Vocal Groups, 1945 to 1970*. Pittsburg, CA: California Trade School, 1976.

0528 Ferris, William. *Blues from the Delta*. 1978. New York: Da Capo, 1984. Bibliography on pp. 195–204; discography on pp. 205–220; filmography on pp. 221–222.

0529 Ferris, William. *Mississippi Folk Voices*. Memphis: Center for Southern Folklore, 1976.

0530 Finkelstein, Sidney. *Jazz: A People's Music*. New York: Citadel Press, 1948.

0531 Finn, Julio. *The Bluesmen: The Musical Heritage of Black Men and Women in the Americas*. London, New York: Quartet Books, 1986. Bibliography on pp. 239–246.

0532 Fisher, Miles Mark. *Negro Slave Songs in the United States*. Ithaca, NY: Cornell University Press, 1953. Bibliography on pp. 192–213.

0533 Fisher, William Arms. *Ten Negro Spirituals*. Boston: Oliver Ditson, 1925.

0534 Fisher, William Arms, ed. *Seventy Negro Spirituals*. Boston: Oliver Ditson, 1926.

0535 Floyd, Samuel A., and Marsha J. Reisser. *Black Music in the United States: An Annotated Bibliography of Selected Reference and Research Materials*. Millwood, NY: Kraus International Publications, 1983.

0536 *Folk Blues*. New York: Arc Music, 1965.

0537 Forten, Charlotte L. *The Journal of Charlotte L. Forten*, ed. Ray Allen Billington. New York: Dryden Press, 1953.

0538 Foster, William P. "The Influence of the Negro on Music in America." M.A. thesis, Wayne State University, 1950. Bibliography on lvs. 126–128.

0539 Frey, Hugo. *A Collection of 25 Celebrated American Negro Spirituals*. New York: Robbins-Engel, 1926.

0540 Garon, Paul. *The Devil's Son in Law: The Story of Peetie Wheatstraw and His Songs*. London: Studio Vista, 1971.

0541 Garvin, Richard M., and Edmond G. Addeo. *The Midnight Special: The Legend of Leadbelly*. New York: Bernard Geis, 1971.

0542 Garwood, Donald. *Masters of Instrumental Blues Guitar*. New York: Oak, 1968.

0543 Gellert, Lawrence, comp. *Me and My Captain: Chain-Gang Songs*. New York: Hours Press, 1939.

0544 George, Zelma W. "A Guide to Negro Music: An Annotated Bibliography of Negro Folk Music, and Art Music by Negro Composers or Based on Negro Thematic Material." Ed.D. dissertation, New York University, 1953. Bibliography on lvs. 253–277.

0545 Gillis, Frank, and Alan P. Merriam. *Ethnomusicology and Folk Music: An International Bibliography of Dissertations and Theses.* Middletown, CT: Wesleyan University Press, 1966.

0546 Glover, Tony I. *Blues Harp: An Instruction Method for Playing the Blues Harmonica.* New York: Oak, 1965.

0547 Gonzalez, Fernando L. *The Discographical Catalogue of American Rock & Roll and Rhythm & Blues.* Flushing, NY: F. L. Gonzalez, 1974.

0548 Gordon, Robert W. "The Negro Spiritual." In *The Carolina Low County*, ed. Augustin Smythe. New York: Macmillan, 1931, 192–222.

0549 Greenberg, Alan, and Stanley Crouch. *Love in Vain: The Life and Legend of Robert Johnson.* New York: Doubleday (Dolphin), 1983.

0550 Greenway, John. *American Folk Songs of Protest.* Philadelphia: University of Pennsylvania Press, 1953.

0551 Grissom, Mary Allen. *The Negro Sings a New Heaven.* Chapel Hill: University of North Carolina Press, 1930.

0552 Groom, Bob. *Blind Lemon Jefferson.* Knutsford, UK: Blues World Booklet, no. 1, 1969.

0553 Grossman, Stefan. *The Country Blues Guitar.* New York: Oak, 1968.

0554 Grossman, Stefan. *Delta Blues Guitar.* New York: Oak, 1969.

0555 Grossman, Stefan. *Ragtime Blues Guitarists.* New York: Oak, 1970.

0556 Grossman, William L., and Jack W. Farrell. *The Heart of Jazz.* New York: New York University Press, 1956.

0557 Guion, David. *Darkey Spirituals.* New York: Witmark, 1918.

0558 Guralnick, Peter. *Feel like Going Home: Portraits in Blues and Rock n' Roll.* New York: Outerbridge and Dienstfrey, 1971.

0559 Guralnick, Peter. *The Listener's Guide to the Blues.* New York: Facts on File, 1982.

0560 Heilbut, Anthony. *The Gospel Sound: Good News and Bad Times.* 1975. Reprint, New York: Limelight, 1985. Discography on pp. 335–353.

0561 Hallowell, Emily, ed. *Calhoun Plantation Songs.* 2d ed. Boston: C. W. Thompson, 1907.

0562 Hammond, Stella L. "Contribution of the American Indian and Negro to the Folk-Music of America." M.A. thesis, Wayne State University, 1963.

0563 Handy, William C., ed. *Blues: An Anthology.* New York: A. & C. Boni, 1926.

0564 Handy, William C., ed. *Father of the Blues.* New York: Collier Books, 1970.

0565 Handy, William C., ed. *W. C. Handy's Collection of Negro Spirituals.* 2 vols. New York: Handy Bros. Music, 1938.

0566 Hansen, Chadwick C. "The Ages of Jazz: A Study of Jazz in Its Cultural Context." Ph.D. dissertation, University of Minnesota, 1956.

0567 Haralambos, Michael. *Right On: From Blues to Soul in Black America*. New York: Drake, 1975.

0568 Hare, Maud Cuney. "Folk Music of the Creoles." In *Negro Anthology*, ed. Nancy Cunard. London: Wishart, 1934, 396–400.

0569 Hare, Maud Cuney. *Negro Musicians and Their Music*. Washington, DC: Associated, 1936.

0570 Hare, Maud Cuney. *Six Creole Folk Songs*. New York: Fischer, 1921.

0571 Harris, Joel Chandler. *Uncle Remus and His Friends: Old Plantation Stories, Songs, and Ballads With Sketches of Negro Character*. New York: Houghton Mifflin, 1892.

0572 Harris, Sheldon. *Blues Who's Who*. New Rochelle: Arlington House, 1979. Reprint, New York: Da Capo Press, 1980. Bibliography on pp. 599–609.

0573 Harris, Steve. *Jazz on Compact Disc: A Critical Guide to the Best Recordings*. New York: Harmony Books, 1987.

0574 Harrison, Daphne D. *Black Pearls: Blues Queens of the 1920s*. New Brunswick, NJ: Rutgers University Press, 1990. Bibliography on pp. 285–289.

0575 Harrison, Max. "Boogie-Woogie." In *Jazz*, ed. Nat Hentoff and Albert J. McCarthy. New York: Rinehart, 1959, 107–135, 360–362.

0576 Harrison, Max. *The Essential Jazz Records*. Vol. 1. London: Mansell, 1984. Reprint, New York: Da Capo Press, 1988. Bibliography on pp. 561–566.

0577 Hart, Mary L., Eagles, Brenda M., Howorth, Lisa N., Ferris, William, and Ronald A. Bailey. *The Blues: A Bibliographical Guide*. New York: Garland, 1989.

0578 Hays, Roland. *My Songs: Aframerican Religious Folk Songs*. Boston: Little, Brown, 1948.

0579 Haywood, Charles. *A Bibliography of North American Folklore and Folksong*. Vol 1. New York: Dover, 1961. Part 3, pp. 429–560, covers African American folklore and music.

0580 Hefele, Bernhard. *Jazz Bibliography: International Literature on Jazz, Blues, Spirituals, Gospel, and Ragtime Music with a Selected List of Works on the Social and Cultural Background from the Beginning to the Present*. New York: Saur, 1981.

0581 Heilbut, Anthony. "The Secularization of Black Gospel Music." In *Folk Music and Modern Sound*, ed. William Ferris and Mary L. Hart. Jackson: University Press of Mississippi, 1982.

0582 Henry, Mellinger Edward. *A Bibliography for the Study of American Folk-songs with Many Titles of Folk-songs (and Titles That Have to Do with Folk Songs) from Other Lands*. London: Mitre Press, 1937.

0583 Hentoff, Nat, and Albert J. McCarthy, eds. *Jazz*. New York: Rinehart, 1959. Discography on pp. 343–371.

0584 Higginson, Thomas Wentworth. *Army Life in a Black Regiment*. Boston: Fields, Osgood & Co., 1870. Chapter 9 is on Negro spirituals.

0585 Hitchcock, H. Wiley, and Stanley Sadie, eds. *The New Grove Dictionary of American Music*. New York: Grove's Dictionaries of Music, 1986.

0586 Hobson, Anne. *In Old Alabama, Being the Chronicles of Miss Mouse, the Little Black Merchant*. New York: Doubleday, Page, 1903. Spirituals and plantation songs lyrics on pp. 157–237.

0587 Hobson, Wilder. *American Jazz Music*. New York: W. W. Norton, 1939. Annotated discography of 30 records on pp. 177–217.

0588 Hodeir, Andre. *Jazz, Its Evolution and Essence*. New York: Grove Press, 1979. Discography on pp. 267–274.

0589 Horn, David. *The Literature of American Music in Books and Folk Music Collections: A Fully Annotated Bibliography*. Metuchen, NJ: Scarecrow Press, 1988.

0590 Howard, John Tasker. *Our American Music: Three Hundred Years of It*. New York: Thomas Y. Crowell, 1931. Bibliography of African American music on pp. 649–652.

0591 Howard, John Tasker, and George Kent Bellows. *A Short History of Music in America*. New York: Thomas Crowell, 1957.

0592 Hoyt, Charles A. "Jazz and Its Origin." B.A. thesis, Wesleyan University, 1953.

0593 Hungerford, James. *The Old Plantation, and What I Gathered There in an Autumn Month*. New York: Harper & Bros., 1859.

0594 Huntley, Fred H. *The National Collection of Spirituals*. Vol. 1. Chicago: Franklin Earl Hathaway, 1935.

0595 Hurston, Zora Neale. *Mules and Men*. Philadelphia: Lippincott, 1935. Songs with music on pp. 309–331.

0596 Hurston, Zora Neale. "Spirituals and Neo-Spirituals." *In Negro Anthology*, ed. Nancy Cunard. London: Wishart, 1934, 359–361.

0597 Hutson, Katherine C., Josephine Pinckney, and Caroline Rutledge. "Some Songs the Negro Sang." In *The Carolina Low County*, ed. Augustin Smythe. New York: Macmillan, 1931, 225–327.

0598 Indiana University, Folklore Institute, Archives of Traditional Music Staff. *A Catalog of Phonorecording of Music and Oral Data Held by the Archives of Traditional Music*. Boston: G. K. Hall, 1975.

0599 Jackson, Bruce. "The Glory Songs of the Lord." In *Our Living Traditions*, ed. Tristram P. Coffin. New York: Basic Books, 1968, 103–110.

0600 Jackson, Bruce. *Wake Up Dead Man: Afro-American Work Songs from Texas Prisons*. Cambridge, MA: Harvard University Press, 1972. Bibliography and discography on pp. 317–320.

0601 Jackson, Clyde Owen. *The Songs of Our Years: A Study of Negro Folk Music*. New York: Exposition Press, 1968. Bibliography on pp. 53–54.

0602 Jackson, Eileen S. *The Use of Negro Folk Songs in Symphonic Form*. M.A. thesis, University of Chicago, 1941. Bibliography on lvs. 41–42.

0603 Jackson, George Fullen. *White and Negro Spirituals*. New York: J. J. Augustin, 1943.

0604 Jackson, George Fullen. *White Spirituals of the Southern Uplands*. Chapel Hill: University of North Carolina Press, 1933.

0605 Jackson, I. *Afro-American Religious Music: A Bibliography and a Catalogue of Gospel Music*. Westport, CT: Greenwood Press, 1979.

0606 Jackson, I. *More Than Dancing: Essays on Afro-American Music and Musicians*. Westport, CT: Greenwood Press, 1985.

0607 Jackson, J. *The Colored Sacred Harp*. Ozark, AL: J. Jackson, 1931.

0608 Jackson, Joyce M. "The Performing Black Sacred Quartet: An Expression of Cultural Values and Aesthetics." Ph.D. dissertation, Indiana University, 1988.

0609 Jackson, Mahalia. *Movin' On Up*. New York: Hawthorn Books, 1966. Discography on pp. 215, 218–219.

0610 Jahn, Janheinz. *Negro Spirituals*. Frankfurt: Fischer, 1962.

0611 Jahn, Janheinz, and Alfons M. Dauer. *Blues und Worksongs*. Frankfurt am Main: Fischer Bucherei, 1964.

0612 Johnson, Guy B. *Folk Culture on St. Helena Island, South Carolina*. Chapel Hill: University of North Carolina Press, 1930. Reprint, Hatboro, PA: Folklore Associates, 1968. Bibliography on dialect and song on pp. 174–179.

0613 Johnson, Guy B. "Negro Folk Songs in the South." *In Culture in the South*, ed. W. T. Couch. Chapel Hill: University of North Carolina Press, 1934.

0614 Johnson, Hall. *The Green Pastures Spirituals*. New York: Farrar and Rinehart, 1930.

0615 Johnson, Hall. *Thirty Negro Spirituals*. New York: G. Schirmer, 1949.

0616 Johnson, James Weldon, and J. R. Johnson, eds. *The Books of American Negro Spirituals*. 2 vols. 1926. Reprint, New York: Da Capo Press, 1977.

0617 Johnson, John R. *Rolling Along in Song: A Chronological Survey of American Negro Music, with Eighty-seven Arrangements of Negro Songs, Including Ring Shouts, Spirituals, Work Songs, Plantation Ballads, Chain-Gang, Jail-House, and Minstrel Songs, Street Cries, and Blues*. New York: Viking, 1937.

0618 Jones, Max, and Albert McCarthy. *A Tribute to Huddie Ledbetter*. London: Jazz Music Books, 1946.

0619 Joyner, Charles W. *Folk Song in South Carolina*. Columbia: University of South Carolina Press, 1971.

0620 Katz, Bernard, ed. *The Social Implications of Early Negro Music in the United States: With Over 150 of the Songs, Many of Them with Their Music*. New York: Arno Press and The New York Times, 1969. Selected bibliography on pp. 141–143.

0621 Kaufman, Frederick. *The African Roots of Jazz*. Sherman Oaks, CA: Alfred, 1979. Bibliography on pp. 134–137; discography on pp. 138–139.

0622 Kayser, Erhard. *Mahalia Jackson*. Wetzlar, Germany: Pegasus, 1962.

0623 Keepnews, Orrin, and Bill Grauer, Jr. *A Pictorial History of Jazz: People and Places from New Orleans to the Sixties*. 2d ed. New York: Bonanza Books; dist. by Crown Publishers, 1981.

0624 Kemble, Frances Anne. *Journal of a Residence on a Georgian Plantation in 1838–1839*. New York: Harper & Brothers, 1863.

0625 Kennedy, Robert Emmet. *Black Cameos*. New York: A. & C. Boni, 1924.

0626 Kennedy, Robert Emmet. *Mellows: A Chronicle of Unknown Singers*. New York: A. & C. Boni, 1925.

0627 Kennedy, Robert Emmet. *More Mellows*. New York: Dodd, Mead, 1931.

0628 Kennington, Donald. *The Literature of Jazz: A Critical Guide*. Chicago: American Library Association, 1980.

0629 Kerlin, Robert Thomas. *Negro Poets and Their Poems*. Washington, DC: Associated, 1923.

0630 Kernfeld, Barry, ed. *The New Grove Dictionary of Jazz*. New York: Grove's Dictionaries of Music, 1988. Bibliography and discography on pp. 661–681.

0631 Kerr, Thomas Henderson. "A Critical Survey of Printed Vocal Arrangements of Afro-American Religious Folk Songs." M.M. thesis, Eastman School of Music, University of Rochester, 1939. Bibliography on lvs. 126–130.

0632 Killion, Ronald, and Charles Waller, eds. *Slavery Time When I Was Chillun Down on Marster's Plantation: Interviews with Georgia Slaves*. Savannah: Beehive Press, 1973. Bibliography on pp. 165–166.

0633 Kinscella, Hazel G. "Songs of the American Negro and Their Influence on Composed Music." M.A. thesis, Columbia University, 1934.

0634 Kmen, Henry A. *Music in New Orleans: The Formative Years, 1791–1841*. Baton Rouge: Louisiana State University Press, 1966.

0635 Krehbiel, H. E. *Afro-American Folk Songs: A Study in Racial and National Music*. New York: G. Schirmer, 1914.

0636 Kriss, Eric. *Six Blues-Root Pianists*. New York: Oak, 1973. Bibliography on pp. 96–97; discography on pp. 98–104.

0637 Lamkin, Marjorie, and Wendell Hall. *Southern Songs and Spirituals*. Chicago: Forster Music, 1926.

0638 Lang, Iain. *Jazz in Perspective: The Background of the Blues*. New York: Hutchinson, 1947. Bibliography on pp. 153–170.

0639 Lawless, Ray M. *Folksingers and Folksongs in America*. 2d rev. ed. New York: Duell, Sloan, & Pearce, 1965.

0640 Laws, G. Malcolm, Jr. *Native American Balladry: A Descriptive Study and a Bibliographic Syllabus*. Philadelphia: American Folklore Society, 1950. Chapter 7 on African American ballads. See detailed account of 19 ballads on pp. 23–443; bibliography on pp. 267–270.

0641 Leadbitter, Mike. *Crowley, Louisiana Blues*. Oxford, UK: Blues Unlimited, 1968.

0642 Leadbitter, Mike. *Delta Country Blues*. Oxford, UK: Blues Unlimited, n.d.

0643 Leadbitter, Mike. *Nothing but the Blues: An Illustrated Documentary*. London: Hanover Books, 1971.

0644 Leadbitter, Mike, and Eddie Shuler. *From the Bayou*. Oxford, UK: Blues Unlimited, 1967.

0645 Leadbitter, Mike, and Neil Slaven. *Blues Records, 1943–1970: A Selective Discography.* Vol. 1, A–K. Milford, NH: Big Nickel, 1987.

0646 Lee, George W. *Beale Street: Where the Blues Began.* New York: R. O. Ballou, 1934.

0647 *Legacy: The Documenting of Louisiana Traditions and Folklife.* New Orleans: Xavier University of Louisiana Legacy Programs, 1979.

0648 Leichter, Albert. *A Discography of Rhythm & Blues and Rock & Roll Circa 1946–1964.* Staunton, VA: A. Leichter, 1975.

0649 Leiding, Harriet Kershaw. *Street Cries of an Old Southern City.* Charleston, SC: Daggett, 1910.

0650 Lester, Julius. *The Folksinger's Guide to the 12-String Guitar as Played by Leadbelly.* New York: Oak, 1965.

0651 Lieb, Sandra R. *Mother of the Blues: A Study of Ma Rainey.* Amherst: University of Massachusetts Press, 1981.

0652 Locke, Alain, ed. *The New Negro.* New York: A. & C. Boni, 1925.

0653 Logan, William A., and Allen M. Garrett. *Road to Heaven.* University: University of Alabama Press, 1955.

0654 Lomax, Alan. *American Ballads and Folk Songs.* New York: Macmillan, 1934.

0655 Lomax, Alan. *The Folk Songs of North America in the English Language.* Garden City, NY: Doubleday, 1960.

0656 Lomax, Alan. *Mister Jelly Roll.* New York: Duell, Sloan and Pearce, 1950.

0657 Lomax, Alan. *75 Years of Freedom.* Washington, DC: Library of Congress, 1943. See section on reels and work songs.

0658 Lomax, Alan, and John A. Lomax. *Negro Folk Songs as Sung by Lead Belly.* New York: Macmillan, 1936.

0659 Lomax, John A., and Alan Lomax. *Folk Song U.S.A.* New York: Duell, Sloan and Pearce, 1947.

0660 Lomax, John A., and Alan Lomax. *Our Singing Country.* New York: Macmillan, 1949.

0661 Long, Norman G. "The Theology and Psychology of the Negroes' Religion Prior to 1860 as Shown Particularly in the Spirituals." M.A. thesis, Oberlin College, 1936.

0662 Lornell, Kip. *Virginia's Blues, Gospel, & Country Records, 1902–1943.* Lexington: University of Kentucky Press, 1989. Bibliography on pp. 159–164.

0663 Lovell, John. *Black Song: The Forge and the Flame: The Story of How the Afro-American Spiritual Was Hammered Out.* New York: Macmillan, 1972.

0664 Lucas, John S. "Rhythms of Negro Music and Negro Poetry." M.S. thesis, University of Minnesota, 1945.

0665 Ludlow, Helen W. *Tuskegee Normal and Industrial School for Training Colored Teachers at Tuskegee, Alabama: Its Story and Its Songs.* Hampton, VA: Normal School Press, 1884.

0666 Mann, Woody. *Six Black Blues Guitarists.* New York: Oak, 1973.

0667 Marsh, J. B. T. *The Story of the Jubilee Singers with Their Songs.* Boston: Houghton Mifflin, 1880.

0668 Maultsby, P. "Afro-American Religious Music, 1619–1861." Ph.D. dissertation, University of Wisconsin, 1974. Bibliography on lvs. 338–355.

0669 McAdams, Nettie F. "The Folksongs of the American Negro: A Collection of Unprinted Texts Preceded by a General Survey of the Traits of the Negro Song." M.A. thesis, University of California, 1923. Bibliography on lvs. 139–149.

0670 McCarthy, Albert, comp. *Jazz on Record: A Critical Guide to the First 50 Years: 1917–1967.* London: Hanover, 1968.

0671 McGhee, Brownie, and Happy Traum. *Guitar Styles of Brownie McGhee.* New York: Oak, 1971.

0672 McIlhenny, Edward A. *Befo' de War Spirituals and Melodies.* New York: AMS Press, 1973.

0673 McIlwaine, Shields. *Memphis: Down in Dixie.* New York: E. P. Dutton, 1948.

0674 McKee, Margaret, and Fred Chisenhall. *Beale Black & Blue: Life and Music on Black America's Main Street.* Baton Rouge: Louisiana State University Press, 1981.

0675 McNeilly, James H. *Religion and Slavery: A Vindication of the Southern Churches.* Nashville: Publishing House of the M.E. Church, South, 1911.

0676 Macy, James C. *Jubilee and Plantation Songs.* Boston: Ditson, 1887.

0677 Mann, Woody. *Six Black Blues Guitarists.* New York: Oak, 1973.

0678 Marquis, Donald M. *In Search of Buddy Bolden: First Man of Jazz.* Baton Rouge: Louisiana State University Press, 1978. Bibliography on pp. 153–170.

0679 Marsh, J. B. T. *The Story of the Jubilee Singers.* Boston: Houghton Mifflin, 1880.

0680 Martinez, Raymond J. *Portraits of New Orleans Jazz.* Jefferson, LA: Hope, 1971.

0681 Mead, Whitman. *Travels in North America . . .* New York: C. S. Van Winkle, 1820.

0682 Meadows, Eddie S. *Jazz Reference and Research Materials: A Bibliography.* New York: Garland, 1981.

0683 Megill, Donald D. *Introduction to Jazz History.* 2nd ed. Englewood Cliffs, NJ: Prentice-Hall, 1989. Bibliography on pp. 271–272; discography on pp. 273–279.

0684 Melnick, Mimi Clar. "I Can Step Through Muddy Water and Spy Dry Land: Boasts in the Blues." In *Folklore International*, ed. D. K. Wilgus. Hatboro, PA: Folklore Associates, 1967.

0685 Merriam, Alan P. "Instruments and Instrumental Usages in the History of Jazz." M.M. thesis, Northwestern University, 1948.

0686 Merriam, Alan P., and Robert J. Benford. *A Bibliography of Jazz.* New York: Da Capo Press, 1970.

0687 Merritt, Nancy G. "Negro Spirituals in American Collections: A Handbook for Students Studying Negro Spirituals." M.A. thesis, Howard University, 1940. Bibliography on lvs. 39–46.

0688 Meryman, Richard. *Louis Armstrong—A Self-Portrait*. Millerton, NY: Eakins Press, 1971.

0689 Miller, James W. *Sing with Africa: Negro Spirituals Taken from Plantation Melodies*. Chicago: Rodeheaver, 1906.

0690 Miller, Louise. "Folk Music in Louisiana." M.M. thesis, Northwestern University, 1940.

0691 Miller, Paul E., ed. *Esquire's 1945 Jazz Book*. New York: A. S. Barnes, 1945.

0692 Mitchell, George. *Blow My Blues Away*. New York: Da Capo Press, 1984.

0693 Monroe, Mina, and Kurt Schindler. *Bayou Ballads: Twelve Folksongs from Louisiana*. New York: G. Schirmer, 1921.

0694 Montague, J. Harold. "A Historical Survey of Negro Music and Musicians and Their Influence on Twentieth Century Music." M.A. thesis, Syracuse University, 1929.

0695 Moore, Carman. *Somebody's Angel Child: The Story of Bessie Smith*. New York: Thomas Y. Crowell, 1969.

0696 Moore, M. C. "Multicultural Music Education: An Analysis of Afro-American and Native American Folk Songs in Selected Elementary Music Textbooks of the Periods 1928–1955 and 1965–1975." Ph.D. dissertation, University of Michigan, 1977. Bibliography on lvs. 261–275.

0697 Mott, Abigail. *Biographical Sketches and Interesting Anecdotes of Persons of Color* . . . New York: M. Day, 1839.

0698 Napier, Simon. *Back Woods Blues*. Bexhill-on-Sea, England: Blues Unlimited, 1968.

0699 Newton, Francis (E. J. Hobsbawn). *The Jazz Scene*. London: MacGibbon and Kee, 1959.

0700 Nickerson, Camille L. "Africo-Creole Music in Louisiana: A Thesis on the Plantation Songs Created by the Creole Negroes of Louisiana." M.A. thesis, Oberlin College, 1932. Bibliography on lvs. 85–86.

0701 Niles, J. J. *Singing Soldiers*. New York: Scribner's, 1927.

0702 Noble, Gilford C. *The Most Popular Plantation Songs*. New York: Hines, Noble and Eldridge, 1911.

0703 Odum, Howard W. *Negro Workaday Songs*. Chapel Hill: University of North Carolina Press, 1926. Selected bibliography of early material on pp. 265–270.

0704 Odum, Howard W., and Guy B. Johnson. *The Negro and His Songs: A Study of Typical Negro Songs in the South*. Chapel Hill: University of North Carolina Press, 1925. Reprint, New York: Negro Universities Press, 1968. Pages 297–300 list fifteen early books and periodical collections of songs.

0705 Oliver, Paul. *Aspects of the Blues Tradition*. New York: Oak, 1970. (Originally published as *Screening the Blues: Aspects of the Blues Tradition*. London: Cassell, 1968.)

0706 Oliver, Paul, ed. *Bessie Smith*. New York: A. S. Barnes & Co., 1959. Selected bibliography on pp. 73–74; selected discography on pp. 75–82.

0707 Oliver, Paul, ed. *The Blackwell Guide to Blues Records*. Cambridge, MA: Blackwell Reference, 1989. Bibliographical references, pp. 321–323.

0708 Oliver, Paul, ed. *The Meaning of the Blues*. New York: Collier Books, 1960. Originally titled *Blues Fell This Morning*. Selected bibliography on pp. 376–378; discography on pp. 339–369.

0709 Oliver, Paul, ed. *Savannah Syncopators: African Retentions in the Blues*. New York: Stein and Day, 1970.

0710 Oliver, Paul, ed. *Songsters and Saints: Vocal Traditions on Race Records*. New York: Cambridge University Press, 1984. Bibliography on pp. 309–313; discography on pp. 314–317.

0711 Oliver, Paul, and Mike Leadbitter. *Muddy Waters*. Collectors Classic 1. Oxford, UK: Blues Unlimited, 1964.

0712 Olsson, Bengt. *Memphis Blues and Jug Bands*. London: Studio Vista, 1970. Bibliography on pp. 107–109; discography on pp. 110–112.

0713 Osborne, Jerry. *Popular and Rock Records, 1948–1978*. Phoenix: O'Sullivan, Woodside, 1978.

0714 Osgood, Henry O. *So This Is Jazz*. Boston: Little, Brown, 1926.

0715 Owens, William A. *Texas Folk Songs*. 2d ed. Dallas: Southern Methodist University Press, 1976. Bibliography on pp. 183–186.

0716 Parrish, Lydia. *Slave Songs of the Georgia Sea Islands*. New York: Creative Age Press, 1942. Selected bibliography on work songs and slave songs on pp. 253–256.

0717 Pearson, Barry L. *Sounds So Good to Me: The Bluesman's Story*. Philadelphia: University of Pennsylvania Press, 1984. Bibliography on pp. 165–170.

0718 Pearson, Barry L. *Virginia Piedmont Blues: The Lives and Art of Two Virginia Bluesmen*. Philadelphia: University of Pennsylvania Press, 1990. Bibliography on pp. 283–285; discography on pp. 274–280.

0719 Pearson, Elizabeth Ware, ed. *Letters from Port Royal, Written at the Time of the Civil War*. Boston: W. B. Clarke, 1906.

0720 Peterson, Clara G. *Creole Songs from New Orleans*. New Orleans: L. Grunewald, 1902.

0721 Pinkston, Alfred A. "Lined Hymns, Spirituals, and the Associated Lifestyle of Rural Black People in the United States." M.A. thesis, University of Miami, 1975.

0722 Pleasant, Joe, and Harriet J. Ottenheimer. *Cousin Joe: Blues from New Orleans*. Chicago: University of Chicago Press, 1987. Bibliography on pp. 197–199; discography on pp. 201–224.

0723 Pollard, Edward A. *Black Diamonds Gathered in the Darkey Homes of the South*. New York: Pudney & Russell, 1859.

0724 Pyke, Launcelot A., II. "Jazz, 1920 to 1927: An Analytical Study." 2 vols. Ph.D. dissertation, Iowa State University, 1963. Bibliography on lvs. 109–115.

0725 Raichelson, Richard M. "Black Religious Folksong: A Study in Generic and

Social Change: A Dissertation in Folklore, Folk Life.'' M.A. thesis, University of Pennsylvania, 1975. Bibliography on lvs. xxxv–xcix; discography on lvs. c–cii.

0726 Ramsey, Frederic, Jr., and Charles E. Smith. *Jazzmen.* New York: Harcourt & Brace, 1939. Reprint, New York: Limelight, 1985.

0727 Redd, Lawrence. *Rock Is Rhythm and Blues: The Impact of Mass Media.* East Lansing: Michigan State University Press, 1974.

0728 *Rhythm & Blues: BMI, 1943–1975.* New York: Broadcast Music, 1976.

0729 Ricks, George R. *Some Aspects of the Religious Music of the United States Negro: An Ethnomusicological Study with Special Emphasis on the Gospel Tradition.* New York: Arno Press, 1977. Bibliography on pp. 400–414.

0730 Roberts, John S. *Black Music of Two Worlds.* New York: Holt, Rinehart and Winston, 1972.

0731 Robinson, Mabel L. ''American Negro Folk Music: The Evolution of Its Structure and Technique.'' M.A. thesis, Boston University, 1940.

0732 Rockmore, Noel. *Preservation Hall Portraits.* Baton Rouge: Louisiana State University Press, 1968.

0733 Rodeheaver, Homer A. *Plantation Melodies.* Chicago: Rodeheaver, 1918.

0734 Rodeheaver, Homer A. *Rodeheaver's Negro Spirituals.* Chicago: Rodeheaver, 1923.

0735 Rooney, James. *Bossmen: Bill Monroe and Muddy Waters.* New York: Dial Press, 1971.

0736 Rose, Al. *Storyville, New Orleans: Being an Authentic, Illustrated Account of the Notorious Red-Light District.* University: University of Alabama Press, 1974. Bibliography on pp. 216–217.

0737 Rose, Al, and Edmund Souchon. *New Orleans Jazz: A Family Album.* 3d ed. Baton Rouge: Louisiana State University Press, 1984.

0738 Rublowsky, John. *Black Music in America.* New York: Basic Books, 1971.

0739 Russell, Ross. *Jazz Style in Kansas City and the Southwest.* Berkeley: University of California Press, 1971.

0740 Sackheim, Eric, and Jonathan Shahn. *The Blues Line: A Collection of Blues Lyrics.* New York: Schirmer Books, 1969.

0741 Sadler, Cora. ''Creole Songs.'' M.A. thesis, University of Michigan, 1939.

0742 Sandburg, Carl. *The American Songbag.* New York: Harcourt, Brace, 1927.

0743 Scarborough, Dorothy. *On the Trail of the Negro Folk Songs.* Cambridge, MA: Harvard University Press, 1925.

0744 Schafer, W. J., and R. B. Allen. *Brass Bands and New Orleans Jazz.* Baton Rouge: Louisiana State University Press, 1977. Bibliography on pp. 100–102; discography on pp. 102–105.

0745 Schuller, Gunther. *Early Jazz: Its Roots and Musical Development.* New York: Oxford University Press, 1986. Discography on pp. 385–389.

0746 Sergeant, Winthrop. *Jazz: Hot and Hybrid.* New York: E. P. Dutton, 1946.

0747   Seward, Theodore F. *Jubilee Songs: Complete as Sung by the Jubilee Singers of Fisk University.* New York: Bigelow and Main, 1872.

0748   Shapiro, Nat, comp. *Hear Me Talkin' to Ya: The Story of Jazz as Told by the Men Who Made It.* New York: Dover, 1955.

0749   Shaw, Arnold. *Dictionary of American Pop/Rock.* New York: Schirmer Books, 1982.

0750   Shaw, Arnold. *The World of Soul: Black America's Contribution to the Pop Music Scene.* New York: Cowles, 1970.

0751   Sheppard, E. (Marth Young). *Plantation Songs for My Lady's Banjo and Other Negro Lyrics and Monologues.* New York: R. H. Russell, 1901.

0752   Shockett, Bernard I. "Stylistic Study of the Blues, 1917–1931, as Practiced by Jazz Instrumentalists." Ph.D. dissertation, New York University, 1964.

0753   Silverman, Jerry. *Folk Blues: 101 American Folk Blues.* New York: Macmillan, 1971.

0754   Skowronski, JoAnn. *Black Music In America: A Bibliography.* New Jersey: Scarecrow Press, 1981.

0755   Small, Katherine L. "The Influence of the Gospel Song on the Negro Church." M.A. thesis, Ohio State University, 1945. Bibliography on lvs. 50–51.

0756   Smith, Charles Edward. "New Orleans and Traditions in Jazz." In *Jazz,* ed. Nat Hentoff and Albert J. McCarthy. New York: Rinehart, 1959.

0757   Smith, N. Clark. *New Plantation Melodies as Sung by the Tuskegee Students.* Tuskegee, AL: Tuskegee Press, 1909.

0758   Smith, Reed. *South Carolina Ballads.* Cambridge, MA: Harvard University Press, 1928.

0759   Smythe, A. T., et al. *The Carolina Low-Country.* New York: Macmillan, 1932.

0760   Soloman, Jack, and Olivia Soloman. *"Honey in the Rock": The Ruby Pickens Tartt Collection of Religious Folk Songs from Sumter County, Alabama.* Macon, GA: Mercer University Press, 1992.

0761   Southern, Eileen. *Biographical Dictionary of Afro-American and African Musicians.* Westport, CT: Greenwood Press, 1982. Bibliography on pp. 447–452.

0762   Southern, Eileen. *The Music of Black Americans: A History.* New York: W. W. Norton, 1971.

0763   Southern, Eileen, and Wright, Josephine. *African-American Traditions in Song, Sermon, Tale and Dance, 1600s–1920: An Annotated Bibliography of Literature, Collections, and Artworks.* New York: Greenwood Press, 1990.

0764   Stewart-Baxter, Derrick. *Ma Rainey and the Classic Blues Singers.* New York: Stein and Day, 1970.

0765   Swan, Alfred Julius, ed. *Eight Negro Songs from Bedford County, Virginia,* collected by Francis H. Abbot. New York: Enoch & Sons, 1923.

0766   Swenson, John. *The Rolling Stone Jazz Record Guide.* New York: Random House, 1985. Bibliography on pp. 215–219.

0767   Taft, Michael. *Blues Lyric Poetry: A Concordance.* New York: Garland, 1984.

0768 Talley, Thomas W. *Negro Folk Rhymes: Wise & Otherwise*. New York: Macmillan, 1922.

0769 Thomas, Will H. *Some Current Folk-songs of the Negro*. Austin, TX: Texas Folklore Society, 1936.

0770 Thorpe, Earl E. *African Americans and the Sacred: Spirituals, Slave Religion, and Symbolism*. Durham, NC: Harrington, 1982.

0771 Thrower, Sarah S. "The Spiritual of the Gullah Negro in South Carolina." M.M. thesis, College Music of Cincinnati, 1954. Bibliography on lvs. 65–67.

0772 Thurman, Howard. *Deep River*. Port Washington, NY: Kennikat Press, 1969.

0773 Tinsley, Vallie. "Some Negro Songs Heard on the Hills of North Louisiana." M.A. thesis, Louisiana State University, 1928.

0774 Titon, Jeff T. *Downhome Blues Lyrics: An Anthology from the Post–World War II Era*. 2d ed. Urbana: University of Illinois Press, 1990. Bibliography on pp. 169–170.

0075 Titon, Jeff T. *Early Downhome Blues: A Musical and Cultural Analysis*. Champaign: University of Illinois Press, 1979. Bibliography on pp. 279–289.

0776 Tocus, Clarence S. "The Negro Idiom in American Musical Composition." M.A. thesis, University of Southern California, 1942.

0777 Townley, Eric. *Tell Your Story: A Dictionary of Jazz and Blues Recordings, 1917–1950*. Chigwell, UK: Storyville Publications, 1976.

0778 Townsend, A. O. "The American Folk-Song and Its Influence on the Works of American Composers." M.A. thesis, University of Southern California, 1938. `

0779 Trantham, Carrie P. "An Investigation of the Unpublished Negro Folk Songs of Dorothy Scarborough." M.A. thesis, Baylor University, 1941.

0780 Traum, Happy. *Guitar Styles of Brownie McGhee*. New York: Oak, 1971.

0781 Tulane University. William Ransom Hogan Jazz Archive. *Catalog of the William Ransom Hogan Jazz Archive: The Collection of 78 rpm Phonograph Recordings*. Boston: G. K. Hall, 1984.

0782 Von Haupt, Lois. "Jazz: An Historical and Analytical Study." M.A. thesis, New York University, 1945.

0783 Walden, Jean E. "The History, Development, and Contribution of the Negro Folk Song." M.M. thesis, Northwestern University, 1945. Bibliography on lvs. 76–78.

0784 Watson, Jack M. "Negro Folk Music in Eastern South Carolina." M.A. thesis, University of South Carolina, 1940. Bibliography on lvs. 82–85.

0785 Wheeler, Mary. *Steamboatin' Days: Folk Songs of the River Packet Era*. Baton Rouge: Louisiana State University Press, 1944.

0786 Whitburn, Joel C. *Top Rhythm & Blues Records: 1949–1971*. Menomonee Falls, WI: Record Research, 1973.

0787 White, Lillian O. "The Folksongs of the American Negro and Their Value Today." M.A. thesis, University of Idaho, 1925.

0788 White, Newman I. *American Negro Folk-songs*. Cambridge, MA: Harvard University Press, 1928. Bibliography on pp. 469–480.

0789   Williams, Martin T. *Jazz Masters of New Orleans*. New York: Macmillan, 1967.

0790   Williams, Thelma A. "Origin and Analysis of Negro Folk-Song." M.A. thesis, Wayne State University, 1938.

0791   Williford, Doxie K. "A Discography of Mississippi Negro Vocal Blues, Gospel, and Folk Music." M.A. thesis, University of Mississippi, 1968. Selective bibliography on pp. 75–76.

0792   Wolfe, Richard J. *Secular Music in America, 1801–1825: A Bibliography*. 3 vols. New York: New York Public Library, 1964.

0793   Work, Frederick J. *New Jubilee Songs, as Sung by the Fisk Jubilee Singers of Fisk University*. Nashville, TN: Fisk University, 1902.

0794   Work, John W. *Folk Song of the American Negro*. Nashville, TN: Work Bros., 1907.

ARTICLES

0795   Abrahams, Roger D. "Folklore on Records." *MF* 10 (1960): 147–151.

0796   Adams, Edward, C. L. "A South Carolina Folksong." *SW* 54 (1925): 568.

0797   Adins, George. "Sleepy John Estes." *JJ* 16, no. 8 (1963): 8–11.

0798   Allen, G. "Negro's Contribution to American Music." *Curr Hist* 26 (May 1927): 245–249.

0799   "American Negro Music." *IRM* 15 (1926): 748–753.

0800   Ames, Russell. "Art in Negro Folk Song." *JAFL* 56 (1943): 241–255.

0801   Arnold, Byron. "Some Historical Folk Songs from Alabama." *JIFMC* 6 (1954): 45–47.

0802   Arrowood, M. D., and T. H. Hamilton. "Nine Negro Spirituals, 1850–1861, from Lower South Carolina." *JAFL* 41 (1928): 579–585.

0803   Ashbury, Samuel E., and Henry E. Meyer. "Old-Time White Camp-Meeting Spiritual." *PTFS* 10 (1932): 169–185.

0804   Backus, E. M. "Christmas Carols from Georgia." *JAFL* 12 (1899): 272.

0805   Backus, E. M. "Cradle-Songs of Negroes in North Carolina." *JAFL* 7 (1894): 310.

0806   Backus, E. M. "Negro Songs from Georgia." *JAFL* 10 (1897): 116, 202, 216, 264; 11 (1898): 22, 60.

0807   Backus, E. M. "Negro Songs from North Carolina." *JAFL* 11 (1898): 60.

0808   Bacon, Margaret Hope. "Lucky McKim Garrison: Pioneer in Folk Music." *Penn Hist* 54, no. 1 (1987): 1–16.

0809   Baer, Hans A. "Black Spiritual Israelites in a Small Southern City." *SQ* 23 (Spring 1984): 103–124.

0810   Bales, Mary V. "Some Negro Folk-Songs of Texas." *PTFS* 7 (1928): 85–112.

0811   Bales, Mary V. "Some Texas Spirituals." *PTFS* 26 (1954): 167–174.

0812   Banes, Ruth A., David A. Bealmear, and Kent Kaster. "Florida Bound Blues." *Pop Mus & Soc* 12 (Winter 1988): 43–58.

0813   Barker, Danny. "A Memory of King Bolden." *ER* 37 (September 1965): 66–74.

0814   Barrett, W. A. "Negro Hymnology." *MT* 15 (1871–1872): 559–561.

0815   Barrow, David G. "A Georgia Corn-Shucking." *Cent* 24 (1883): 873–878.

0816   Barton, W. E. "Hymns of Negroes." *N Eng Mag* 19 (1898): 669, 707.

0817   Barton, W. E. "Hymns of the Slave and the Freedman." *N Eng Mag* 19 (1899): 609–624.

0818   Bass, Robert Duncan. "Negro Songs from Peedee Country." *JAFL* 44 (1931): 418–437.

0819   Bass, W. H. "McDonald Craig's Blues: Black and White Traditions in Contest." *TFSB* 48 (Fall 1982): 46–61.

0820   Bastin, Bruce. "From the Medicine Show to the Stage: Some Influences upon the Development of a Blues Tradition in the Southeastern United States." *Am Mu* 2 (1984): 29–42.

0821   Batchelder, Ruth. "Beaufort, of the Real South." *Trav* 28 (February 1917): 28–31.

0822   Bentley, John. "Origin of the Blues." *Mus Mem* 3, no. 4 (1963): 4–5.

0823   Berry, R. E. "Home of the Blues." *NYTM*, May 5, 1940, 21.

0824   "Birmingham Blues—The Story of Robert McCoy." *Mus Mem* 3, no. 2 (1963): 13–14.

0825   Black, Elizabeth. "A Show at the Quarter." *Theatre Arts Monthly* 16 (June 1932): 493–500.

0826   Blesh, Rudi. "The Guitar—The Blues' Other Voice." *BB* (17 August 1968): Sect. 2, 22–26.

0827   Blues Archive Interview: B. B. King. *Liv Blues* 68 (1986): 12–14.

0828   Borneman, Ernest. "Creole Echoes." *Jazz R* 2, no. 8 (1959): 13–15; 2, no. 10 (1959): 26–27.

0829   Botkin, B. A. "Self-Portraiture and Social Criticism in Negro Folksong." *OPP* 5 (February 1927): 38–42.

0830   Boyd, Joe Dan. "Ballad of the Black Sharecropper." *Farm J* (January 1969): 39.

0831   Boyd, Joe Dan. "Judge Jackson: Black Giant of White Spirituals." *JAFL* 83 (1970): 446–451.

0832   Brawley, Benjamin. "Singing of Spirituals." *SW* 63 (1934): 209–213.

0833   Brown, Edwin L. ". . . To Make a Man Feel Good: John Henry Mealing, Railroad Caller." *Lab Hist* 27 (Spring 1986): 257–264.

0834   Brown, J. M. "Songs of the Slave." *Lippinc* 2 (1869): 617–623.

0835   Brown, Sterling A. "The Blues." *Phyl* 13, no. 4 (1952): 286–292.

0836   Browne, Ray B. "The Alabama 'Holler' and Street Cries." *JAFL* 70 (1957): 363.

0837   Buehler, Richard E. "Stacker Lee: A Partial Investigation into the History of a Negro Murder Ballad." *KFQ* 12 (1967): 187–191.

0838 Burlin, Natalie Curtis. "Again the Negro." *Poet* 11 (1917): 147–151.

0839 Cable, George Washington. "Creole Slave Songs." *Cent* 31: 807–828.

0840 "Canning Negro Melodies." *Lit Dig* 52 (1916): 1156–1559.

0841 Carawan, Guy. "Spiritual Singing in the South Carolina Sea Islands." *Car* 20 (1960): 20–25.

0842 Carew, Roy J. "Of This and That and Jelly Roll." *JJ* 10, no. 12 (1957): 10–12.

0843 Carew, Roy J., and Don E. Fowler. "Scott Joplin: Overlooked Genius." *RC* (September 1944): 12–14, 59; (October 1944): 10–12, 65; (December 1944): 10–11, 48.

0844 Carlyle, N. T. "Old-time Darky Plantation Melodies." *TFSB* 5 (1921): 137–143.

0845 Carner, Gary. "A Bibliography of Jazz and Blues Biographical Literature." *BALF* 20 (Spring–Summer 1986): 161–202.

0846 Charters, Samuel B. "The Mississippi Delta Blues." *Hoot* 1, no. 2 (March 1964): 51, 72–73.

0847 Charters, Samuel B., and Walter C. Adams. "The Jug Bands of Memphis." *JM* 4, no. 12 (1959): 2–5, 31.

0848 Chase, Gilbert. "A Note on Negro Spirituals." *CWH* 4, no. 3 (1958): 261–267.

0849 Chase, Kathleen. "Syncopated Dirges, Ragtime Parades." *Am S* 16, no. 3 (1964): 16–20.

0850 Christensen, Abigail M. "Spirituals and Shouts of Southern Negroes." *JAFL* 7 (1894): 154–155.

0851 Clar, Mimi. "Folk Belief and Custom in the Blues." *WF* 19, no. 3 (1960): 173–189.

0852 Clarke, Mary Olmstead. "Song Games of Negro Children in Virginia." *JAFL* 3 (1890): 288–290.

0853 Clothier, Agnes E. "Two Negro Spirituals from Georgia." *JAFL* 55 (1942): 98.

0854 Cohen, Hennig. "Caroline Gilman and Negro Boatmen's Songs." *SFQ* 20 (1956): 116–117.

0855 Cohen, Norman. "Blues, Pre-Blues, and Gospel Reissues." *JAFL* 99 (1986): 241–247.

0856 Cohen, Norman. "Railroad Folk-Songs on Record—A Survey." *NYFQ* 26 (1970): 91–113.

0857 Coleback, David. "Louis Jordan Discography." *Blues* 143 (Autumn-Winter 1982): 14–18.

0858 Corritore, Bob, Bill Ferris, and Jim O'Neal. "Willi Dixon, I & II." *Liv Blues* 19 (July-August 1935): 16–25.

0859 Cowley, John. "Really the 'Walking Blues': Son House, Muddy Waters, Robert Johnson and the Development of a Traditional Blues." *Pop Mus & Soc* 1 (1981): 57–72.

0860 Cox, John Harrington. "John Hardy." *JAFL* 32 (1919): 505–520.

0861 Cox, John Harrington. "Negro Music: Recent Recordings." *JAFL* 82 (1970): 403–405.

0862 Cureau, Rebecca T. "Black Folklore, Musicology and Willis Laurence James." *Negro Hist Bull* 43, no. 1 (1980): 16–20.

0863 D., C. W. "Contraband Singing." *DJM* 19 (1861): 182.

0864 Damon, S. Foster. "The Negro in Early American Songsters." *Pap Bibl Soc Am* 28 (1934): 132–163.

0865 Danberg, A. R. "The American Minstrel Theatre on Phonograph Records, 1894–1929." *RR* 22 (1959): 3–5; 24 (1959): 7–9; 25 (1959): 11; 27 (1960): 9; 30 (1960): 10; 32 (1961): 11; 33 (1961): 11, 24; 34 (1961): 24.

0866 Darby, L. "Ring Game from Georgia." *JAFL* 30 (1917): 218–221.

0867 Darch, Robert R. "Blind Boone." *The Ragtimer* 6, no. 5/6 (1967): 9–13.

0868 "Delving into the Genealogy of Jazz." *Cur Opinion* 67 (August 1919): 97–99.

0869 "Done Yo' See de Chariot Ridin' on de Clouds?" *JAFL* 9 (1896): 210.

0870 Engel, Carl. "Negro Spirituals." *MQ* 12 (1926): 299–314.

0871 Engel, Carl. "Views and Reviews." *MQ* 23 (1937): 388–395.

0872 Epstein, Dena J. "Slave Music in the United States Before 1860: A Survey of Sources." *MLAN* 20 (1963): 195–212, 377–390.

0873 Evans, David. "Afro-American One-stringed Instruments." *WF* 29 (1970): 229–246.

0874 Evans, David. "Afro-American Traditions." *JAFL* 95 (1982): 104–109.

0875 Evans, David. "The Art of Country Blues Singing." *BU* 67 (November 1969): 8–9.

0876 Evans, David. "Black Fife and Drum Music in Mississippi." *Miss FR* 6 (1972): 94–107.

0877 Evans, David. "Black Religious Music." *JAFL* 84 (1971): 472–480.

0878 Evans, David. "Black Religious Music." *JAFL* 86 (1973): 82–86.

0879 Evans, David. "Blues on Dockery's Plantation." *BU* (1968): 14–15.

0880 Evans, David. "Charles Patton's Life and Music." *CG* 5, no. 2 (1945): 76–83.

0881 Evans, David. "Charles Patton's Life and Music." *BW* 23 (1969): 3–7.

0882 Evans, David. "Folk Elements in American Dance Music, Ragtime, and Jazz." *JAFL* 92 (1979): 365–369.

0883 Evans, David. "Techniques of Blues Composition Among Black Folksingers." *JAFL* 87 (1974): 240–249.

0884 Ferris, William. "Blues from the Delta: A Photoessay." *NJ Folk* 7 (Spring 1982): 34–38.

0885 Ferris, William. "Lee Kizart Recalls the Delta Blues." *BU* 72 (May 1970): 9–10.

0886 Ferris, William. "Racial Repertoires Among Blues Performers." *Ethmus* 14, no. 3 (September 1970): 439–449.

0887   Ferris, William. "Railroad Chants, Form and Function." *Miss FR* 4 (1970): 1–14.

0888   Ferris, William. "Records and the Delta Blues Tradition." *KFQ* 14 (1969): 158–165.

0889   "Folklore from St. Helena, South Carolina." *JAFL* 38 (1925): 217–238.

0890   Foster, Barry. "Mississippi Fred McDowell." *JPC* 5 (1981): 446–451.

0891   Garon, Paul. "Blues and the Church: Revolt and Resignation." *Liv Blues* 1, no. 1 (Spring 1970): 18–23.

0892   Gaul, Harvey B. "Negro Spirituals." *N Music R* 17 (1918): 147–151.

0893   Glyn, Thomas. "Hear the Music Ringing." *NS* 23, no. 3 (1968): 37–46.

0894   Goffin, Robert. "Big Eye Louis Nelson." *JR* (June 1946): 7–9.

0895   Goines, Leonard. "Early Afro-American Music in the United States—Sacred and Secular." *All* (1971): 11, 15.

0896   Gombosi, Otto. "The Pedigree of the Blues." *Volumes of Proceedings of the Music Teachers National Association*, 40th ser., 70th year, 1946, 382–389.

0897   Gordon, Robert W. "Folk Songs of America: Negro 'Shouts.' " *NYTM*, April 24, 1927, 4, 22.

0898   Gordon, Robert. "Folk Songs of America: Work Chanteys." *NYTM*, January 16, 1927, 7, 19.

0899   Gordon, Robert W. "Lyrics Collected from the Folk-Songs of Georgia Negroes." *GBM* 8 (August 1928): 194–196.

0900   Gordon, Robert W. "Palmettos: Folk-Songs of Georgia Negroes." *GBM* 9 (May 1929): 76–77.

0901   Govenar, Allan. "Alex Moore: More Piano Players in North Dallas than Anywhere—I Could Call Them All." *Liv Blues* 19 (November-December 1988): 26–28.

0902   Graham, Alice. "Original Plantation Melodies as One Rarely Hears Them." *Ethmus* (1922): 40.

0903   Grant, Frances. "Negro Patriotism and Negro Music." *OUTL* 121 (1919): 343–347.

0904   Greene, Charles Richard. "Three Florida Negro Tunes and Works." *SFQ* 9 (1945): 103–105.

0905   Greene, Maude. "The Background of the Beale Street Blues." *TFSB* 7 (1941): 1–11.

0906   Griffin, George H. "The Slave Music of the South." *AM* 36 (1882): 70–72.

0907   Griffith, Benjamin W. "A Longer Version of 'Guinea Negro Song': From a Georgia Frontier Songster." *SFQ* 28 (1964): 116–118.

0908   Groom, Bob. "The Blues Archive at Ole Miss." *Liv Blues* 68 (1986): 14–19.

0909   Groom, Bob. "The Library of Congress Blues and Gospel Recordings." *BW* 38 (Spring 1971): 8–11.

0910   Gruver, Rod. "The Funny Blues: Cryin' Just to Keep from Laughin'." *BW* 33 (Autumn 1970): 19–20; 34 (September 1970): 19–21; 35 (October 1970): 20–21.

0911   Gruver, Rod. "Sex, Sound, Cows and the Blues." *JEMFQ* 7, no. 21 (1971): 37–39.

0912   Gunn, Larry. "Three Negro Folk Songs from the Northern Mississippi Delta." *Miss FR* 3, no. 3 (1969): 89–94.

0913   Guralnick, Peter. "Blues as History." *BW* 22 (December 1968): 5–13.

0914   Guralnik, Peter. "Searching for Robert Johnon." *Liv Blu* 52 (Summer–Autumn 1982): 27–41.

0915   Hall, Frederick. "The Negro Spiritual." *Lit Dig* 98, no. 12 (1928): 34.

0916   Handy, William C. "Negro Roustabout Songs." *TFSB* 13 (1947): 86–88.

0917   Not used.

0918   Harrison, R. C. "The Negro as Interpreter of His Own Folk Songs." *TFSB* 5 (1939): 144–153.

0919   Haskell, M.A. "Negro Spirituals." *Cent* 36 (1899): 577–581.

0920   Hatch, Dave, and John Williams. "The Country Blues: A Musical Analysis." *BU* (April 1965): 8.

0921   Hatfield, James Taft. "Some Nineteenth Century Shanties." *JAFL* 59 (1946): 108–113.

0922   Hay, Fred J. "The Sacred/Profane Dialectic in Delta Blues: The Life and Lyrics of Sonny Boy Williamson." *Phyl* 48 (Winter 1987): 317–326.

0923   Heaton, C. P. "The 5-String Banjo in North Carolina." *SFQ* 35 (1971): 62–82.

0924   Hechman, Don. "Five Decades of Rhythm and Blues." *BMI The Many Worlds of Music* (Summer 1969): 4–31.

0925   Henry, Mellinger E. "More Songs from the Southern Highlands." *JAFL* 44 (1931): 61.

0926   Henry, Mellinger E. "Negro Songs from Georgia." *JAFL* 44 (1931): 437–447.

0927   Henry, Mellinger E. "Nursery Songs and Game-Songs from Georgia." *JAFL* 47 (1934): 335–340.

0928   Higginson, Thomas W. "Negro Spirituals." *AM* 19 (1867): 685–694.

0929   Hinson, Glenn Douglas. "When the Words Roll and the Fire Flows: Spirit, Style and Experience." *J Am Stud* 17 (August 1983): 251–263.

0930   Hoefer, George. "History of the Drum in Jazz." *Jazz* 10 (1965): 11–15.

0931   Hoffman, Daniel G. "The Folk Art of Jazz." *Antioch Review* 5 (1945): 110–120.

0932   Hoffman, Daniel G. "From Blues to Jazz: Recent Bibliographies and Discographies." *MF* 5, no. 2 (Summer 1955): 107–114.

0933   Holzknecht, R. J. "Some Negro Song Variants from Louisville, Kentucky." *JAFL* 41 (1928): 558–578.

0934   Not used.

0935   House, Son. "I Can Make My Own Song." *SQ* 15, no. 3 (1965): 38–45.

0936 Howse, R. W. "The Negro and His Songs." *SW* 51 (n.d.): 381–383.

0937 Howse, Ruth Whitener. "Folk Music of West Tennessee." *TFSB* 13 (1947): 77–78.

0938 Hubbell, Jay. B. "Negro Boatmen's Songs." *SFQ* 18 (1954): 244–245.

0939 Hudson, Arthur Palmer. "Ballads and Songs from Mississippi." *JAFL* 39 (1926): 93–124.

0940 Hughes, Langston. "Songs Called the Blues." *Phyl* 2 (1941): 143–145.

0941 "In the Driftway." *Nat* 131 (Sept. 3, 1930): 245.

0942 Jackson, Bruce. "The Personal Blues of Skip James." *SQ* 15, no. 6 (1966): 26–30.

0943 Jackson, Bruce. "Prison Worksongs: The Composer in Negatives." *WF* 16 (1967): 245–268.

0944 Jackson, Bruce. "Stagolee Stories: A Badman Goes Gentle." *SFQ* 29 (1965): 228–233.

0945 Jackson, Bruce. "What Happened to Jody?" *JAFL* 80 (1967): 387–396.

0946 Jackson, George P. "The Genesis of the Negro Spiritual." *Am Merc* 26 (1932): 243–248.

0947 Johnson, Eldridge R., III. "Crescent City Blues." *LAFM* 3, no. 2 (1971): 53–55.

0948 Johnson, Guy B. "Double Meaning in the Popular Negro Blues." *JASP* 22, no. 1 (April–June 1927): 12–20.

0949 Johnson, Guy B. "Recent Contributions to the Study of American Negro Songs." *Social Forc* 4 (1926): 788–792.

0950 Kay, George W. "William Christopher Handy, Father of the Blues—A History of Published Blues." *JJ* 24, no. 3 (1971): 10–12.

0951 Kempf, Paul, Jr. "Striking the Blue Note in Music." *Musc* 34 (1929): 29.

0952 Kennedy, Phillip Houston. "An Unusual Work-Song Found in North Carolina." *NCF* 15, no. 1 (1967): 30–34.

0953 Kerlin, Robert Thomas. " 'Canticles of Love and Woe': Negro Spirituals." *SW* 50 (1921): 62–64.

0954 Kingsley, Walter. "Enigmatic Folk Songs of the Southern Underworld." *Cur Opinion* 67, no. 3 (September 1919): 165.

0955 Kirby, Percival R. "A Study of Negro Harmony." *MQ* 16 (1900): 404–441.

0956 Kittredge, George Lyman. "Note on the Song of 'Mary Blane.' " *JAFL* 39 (1926): 200–207.

0957 Kmen, Henry A. "Old Corn Meal: A Forgotten Urban Negro Folksinger." *JAFL* 75 (1962): 29–34.

0958 Krehbiel, Henry E. "Folk-Music Studies: Slave Songs in America." *New York Tribune*, September 10, 1899, 1–11.

0959 Kunstadt, Len. "Mamie Smith—The First Lady of the Blues." *RR* 57 (1964): 3–12.

0960 Kustner, Axel. "Living Country Blues." *Blues* 142 (Summer 1982): 30–35.

0961 Laubenstein, Paul F. "Race Values in Afro-American Music." *MQ* 16 (1930): 378–403.

0962 Laughton, Bob, and Cedric Hayes. "Mahalia Jackson: Recordings to 1959." *BU* 144 (Spring 1983): 37–42.

0963 Laughton, Bob, and Cedric Hayes. "Post-War Gospel Records." *BU* 142 (Summer 1982): 36–38.

0964 Leach, MacEdward, and Horace P. Beck. "Songs from Rappahannock County, Virginia." *JAFL* 63 (1950): 257–284.

0965 Lee, Hector. "Leadbelly's 'Frankie and Albert.' " *JAFL* 64 (1951): 314–317.

0966 Lee, Hector. "Some Notes on Leadbelly." *JAFL* 76 (1963): 135–140.

0967 Lejeune, Emilie. "Creole Folk Songs." *LA Hist* 2 (1919): 454–462.

0968 Lemmerman, Karl. "Improvised Negro Songs." *New Rep* 13 (December 22, 1917): 214–215.

0969 Lester, Julius. "Country Blues Come to Town: The View from the Other Side of the Tracks." *SQ* 14 (1964): 37–39.

0970 Lindemann, Bill. "Black Gospel Music." *Liv Blues*, no. 6 (Autumn 1971): 21–22.

0971 Linneman, Russell J. "The Historian and the Country Blues." *Griot* 3 (Winter 1984): 27–40.

0972 Locke, Don. "The Importance of Jelly Roll Morton." *JJ* 12, no. 6 (1959): 2–4.

0973 Locke, Don. "Jelly Roll Morton—The Library of Congress Recordings." *JJ* 13, no. 1 (1960): 15–18.

0974 Lomax, Alan. "I Got the Blues." *CG* 8, no. 4 (1948): 38–52.

0975 Lomax, Alan. "The Passing of a Great Singer—Vera Hall." *SQ* 14, no. 3 (1964): 30–31.

0976 Lomax, John A. "Self-Pity in Negro Folk Songs." *Nat* 105 (1892): 141–145.

0977 Lomax, John A. "Sinful Songs of the Southern Negroes." *MQ* 20 (1934): 177–187.

0978 Lomax, John A. "Some Types of American Folk Songs." *JAFL* 28 (1915): 1–17.

0979 Not used.

0980 Lovell, John, Jr. "Reflections on the Origin of the Negro Spiritual." *NALF* 3, no. 3 (1969): 91–97.

0981 Not used.

0982 Lovell, John, Jr. "The Social Implications of the Negro Spiritual." *JNE* 8 (1939): 4–8, 634–643.

0983 McCormick, Mack. "A Conversation with Lightnin' Hopkins." *JJ* 14, no. 1 (1961): 16–18; no. 2, 18–19.

0984 McCormick, Mack. "The Midnight Special." *Jazz R* 3, no. 5 (1960); 11–14. (Reprinted from *Caravan*, no. 19 [1960]: 10–21.)

0985 McCormick, Mack. "Sam 'Lightnin' Hopkins—A Description." *SQ* 10, no. 3 (1960): 4–8.

0986 Mangurian, David. "Big Joe Williams." *JJ* 16, no. 6 (1963): 14–17.

0987 Martin, John. "Inquiry into Boogie Woogie." *NYTM*, July 16, 1944, 18, 45–46.

0988 May, Earl C. "Where Jazz Comes From." *Pop Mech* 44 (January 1926): 97–102.

0989 Meikleham, R. "Negro Ballad." *JAFL* 6 (1893): 300–301.

0990 Mellinger, E. Henry. "Negro Songs from Georgia." *JAFL* 44 (1931): 437–447.

0991 Merriam, Alan P. "Jelly Roll Morton: A Review Article." *MF* 8 (1958): 217–221.

0992 Milling, Chapman J. "Delta Holmes—A Neglected Negro Ballad." *SFQ* 1, no. 4 (1937): 3–9.

0993 Minton, John. " 'Our Goodman' in Blackface and 'The Maid' at the Sookey Jump: Two Afro-American Variants of Child Ballads on Commercial Disc." *JEMFQ* 18, no. 65–66 (1982): 31–40.

0994 Moore, John H. "A Hymn of Freedom—South Carolina, 1813." *JNH* 50 (1965): 50–53.

0995 Moton, R. R. "Universal Language." *SW* 56 (1927): 349–351.

0996 Murphey, Edward F. "The Negro Spiritual." *Lit Dig* 98, no. 12 (1928): 34.

0997 Murphy, Jeannette R. "Gawd Bless Dem Yankees." *Cent* 56 (1898): 797–798.

0998 Nathan, Hans. "The First Negro Minstrel Band and Its Origin." *SFQ* 16 (1942): 132–144.

0999 "A Negro Explains Jazz." *Lit Dig* 61 (1919): 28–29.

1000 "A Negro Spiritual Contest in Columbus." *Playground* 20 (1926): 90–92.

1001 Neuffer, Claude Henry. "The Bottle Alley Song." *SFQ* 29 (1965): 234–238.

1002 Niles, Abbe. "Ballads, Songs, and Snatches: Columbia Race Records." *Bk* 67 (June 1928): 422–424.

1003 Niles, John J. "In Defense of Backwoods." *Scrib M* 83 (1928): 738–745.

1004 Niles, John J. "Shout, Coon, Shout!" *MQ* 16 (1930): 516–530.

1005 Noblett, Richard A. "Stavin' Chain: A Study of a Folk Hero, IV." *Blues* 142 (Summer 1982): 24–26.

1006 Odum, Anna K. "Negro Folk Songs from Tennessee." *JAFL* 27 (1914): 255–265.

1007 Odum, Howard W. "Folk-Song and Folk-Poetry as Found in the Secular Songs of the Southern Negroes." *JAFL* 24 (July–September 1911): 255–294; (October–December 1911): 351–396.

1008 Okeke-Ezigbo, E. "The Alleged Self-Pity in Afro-American Folk Songs." *Western Journal of Black Studies* 6 (Summer 1982): 108–115.

1009 Oliver, Paul. "Bill Williams." *JB* 1 (August–September 1971): 10–11.

1010 Oliver, Paul. "Blind Lemon Jefferson." *Jazz R* 2, no. 7 (1959): 9–12.

1011 Oliver, Paul. "Can't Even Write: The Blues and Ethnic Literature." *MELUS* 10 (Spring 1983): 7–14.

1012 Oliver, Paul. "Gutter Man Blues—Champion Jack Dupree." *JM* 5, no. 9 (January 1960): 4–8.

1013 Oliver, Paul. "Key to the Highway." *JM* 4, no. 6 (1958): 2–5, 31.

1014 Oliver, Paul. "Kokomo Arnold." *JM* 8, no. 3 (1962): 10–15.

1015 Oliver, Paul. "Special Agents: An Introduction to the Recording of Folk Blues in the Twenties." *Jazz R* 2, no. 2 (February 1959): 20–25.

1016 Oliver, Paul. "Too Tight: Bill Williams in Person." *JB* 1, no. 8 (1971): 37–38.

1017 Olmstead, Charles H. "Savannah in the '40's." *GHQ* 1 (1917): 243–253.

1018 O'Neal, Jim. "Kentucky Blues." *Liv Blues* 51 (Summer 1981): 25–36.

1019 O'Neal, Jim, and Amy O'Neal. "Muddy Waters." *Liv Blues* 64 (March–April 1985): 15–40.

1020 Oster, Harry. "Negro French Spirituals of Louisiana." *JIFMC* 14 (1962).

1021 Otto, John Solomon, and Augustus M. Burns. " 'Tough Times': Downhome Blues Recordings as Folk History." *SQ* 21 (Spring 1983): 27–43.

1022 Otto, John Solomon, and Augustus M. Burns. " 'Welfare Store Blues': Blues Recordings and the Great Depression." *Pop Mus & Soc* 7 (1980): 95–102.

1023 Owen, M. W. "Negro Spirituals: Their Origin, Development, and Place in American Folksong." *Mu Ob* 19, no. 12: 12–13.

1024 Pack, Howery. "The Blues Had a Baby: A Partial List of Blues Songs Copied by Rock, Soul, and Pop Artists." *Liv Blues* 76 (1987): 34–37.

1025 Parson, Barry Lee. " 'Good Times When Times Were Bad': Recollections of Rural House Parties in Virginia." *Folk F Va* 3 (1984): 45–55.

1026 Parsons, Elsie Clews. "From 'Spiritual' to Vaudeville." *JAFL* 35 (1922): 331.

1027 Patterson, Dan. "A Sheaf of North Carolina Folksongs." *NCF* 4, no. 1 (1956): 23–31.

1028 Peabody, Charles. "Notes on Negro Music." *JAFL* 16 (1903): 148–152. (Reprinted in *SW* 33 [1904]: 305–309.)

1029 Perkins, A. E. "Negro Spirituals from the Far South." *JAFL* 35 (1922): 223–249.

1030 Perrow, E. C. "Songs and Rhymes from the South." *JAFL* 25 (1912): 137–155; 26 (1913): 123–173; 28 (1915): 129–190.

1031 Peters, Erskine. "The Poetics of the Afro-American Spiritual." *BALF* 23, no. 3 (Fall 1989): 559.

1032 "Plantation Songs." *SW* 30 (1901): 88, 196, 294, 406, 510, 558, 590.

1033 "Plantation Songs." *SW* 31 (1902): 122, 339, 617, 678.

1034 "Plantation Songs." *SW* 32 (1903): 35, 102, 228a, 410, 461, 592.

1035 "Plantation Songs." *SW* 32 (1904): 161.

1036 "Plantation Songs." *SW* 35 (1906): 163, 528, 655.

1037 "Plantation Songs." *SW* 36 (1907): 144, 207, 394b, 689.

1038   "Plantation Songs." *SW* 37 (1908): 272, 400.

1039   "Plantation Songs." *SW* 41 (1912): 208.

1040   "Plantation Songs." *SW* 42 (1913): 48, 704.

1041   "Plantation Songs." *SW* 45 (1916): 88, 336, 413, 646.

1042   "Plantation Songs." *SW* 46 (1917): 126.

1043   "Plantation Songs." *SW* 49 (1920): 88, 340, 435.

1044   "Plantation Songs." *SW* 50 (1921): 560.

1045   Pound, L. "The Ancestry of a 'Negro Spiritual.' " *MLN* 33 (1918): 442–444.

1046   Powers, Luke A. "The Art of Meditation in Afro-American Folksong: Roy Dunn's Holy Blues." *NC FL* 34 (Winter-Spring 1987): 38–51.

1047   Ramsey, Frederic, Jr. "Leadbelly: A Great Long Time." *SQ* 15, no. 1 (1965): 7–11, 13–24.

1048   Ramsey, Frederic, Jr. "Lines from Buckner's Alley." *Sat R* 40 (September 14, 1957): 61, 63–64.

1049   Ramsey, Frederic, Jr. "A Photographic Documentary of Jazz and Folk Backgrounds." *RC* 12, no. 7–8 (July–August 1953): 23–47.

1050   Reddihough, John. "Country Brass Bands and New Orleans Jazz." *JM* 2, no. 6 (1956): 7–8.

1051   Redfearn, Susan Fort. "Songs from Georgia." *JAFL* 34 (1921): 121–124.

1052   Reinders, Robert C. "Sound of the Mournful Dirge." *Jazz: A Quarterly of American Music* 4 (1959): 296–298.

1053   Reitz, Rosetta. "Mean Mothers: Independent Women's Blues." *Harvard Educational Review* 3 (1980): 57–60.

1054   Robinson, Norborne T. N., Jr. "Blind Tom, Musical Prodigy." *GHQ* 51 (1967): 336–358.

1055   Rogers, Charles P. "Delta Jazzmen." *Jazz Forum* 1 (1946): 11–12.

1056   Rush, Ralph. "Muddy Waters: Father of Rhythm and Blues." *SI* 29 (July–September 1983): 38–42.

1057   Russell, Michele. "Slave Codes and Liner Notes." *Harvard Educational Review* 3 (1980): 52–56.

1058   Saerchinger, C. "Folk Elements in American Music." *Art of Music* 4 (1915): 277–330.

1059   Sanders, Lynn Moss. " 'Black Ulysses Singing': Odom's Folkloristic Trilogy." *SLJ* 22, no. 1 (Fall 1989): 107–116.

1060   Not used.

1061   Scarborough, Dorothy. "The 'Blues' as Folksongs." *PTFS* 2 (1923): 52–66.

1062   Schaefer, William J. "Further Thoughts on Jazz Historiography: That Robert Charles Song." *JJ* 5, no. 1 (1978): 19–27.

1063   Schrodt, Helen, and Bailey Wilkinson. "Sam Lindsey and Milton Roby: Memphis Blues Musicians." *TFSB* 30 (1964): 52–56.

1064 Seale, Lea, and Marianna Seale. "Easter Rock: A Louisiana Negro Ceremony." *JAFL* 55 (1942): 212–218.

1065 Skipper, James K., Jr., and Paul L. Leslie. "Nicknames & Blues Singers, I: Frequency of Use, 1890–1977." *Pop Mus & Soc* 12 (Spring 1988): 37–47.

1066 Smith, Joseph H. "Folk-Songs of the American Negro." *Sew R* 32 (1992): 206.

1067 Smith, Joseph H. "Six Negro Folk Songs." *TFSB* 7 (1928): 113–119.

1068 "Son House—Delta Bluesman." *Sat R* 28 (September 1968): 68–69.

1069 Speers, M. W. F. "Negro Songs and Folk Lore." *JAFL* 23 (1910): 435–439.

1070 Spence, M. E. "The Jubilee of Jubilees at Fisk University." *So Work* 51 (1922): 73–80.

1071 Spencer, Jon M. "The Hymnody of the African Methodist Episcopal Church." *Am Mu* 8, no. 3 (Fall 1990): 274.

1072 Spencer, Onah L. "First Blues Disc Was Made by Minnie Smith." *DBT* (June 1941): 8.

1073 "Stale Bread's Sadness Gave Jazz to the World." *Lit Dig* 61 (April 26, 1919): 47–48.

1074 Standish, Tony. "Joseph Robichaux—Those Early Days." *JJ* 12, no. 4 (1959): 10–12.

1075 Steinberg, Richard U. "See That My Grave Is Kept Clean." *Liv Blues* 19 (November-December 1988): 24–25.

1076 Subor, Charles. "Jazz and the New Orleans Press." *DBT* 36, no. 12 (1969): 18–19.

1077 Szwed, John F. "Musical Adaptation Among Afro-Americans." *JAFL* 82 (1969): 112–121.

1078 Terrel, Clemmi S. "Spirituals from Alabama." *JAFL* 43 (1930): 322–324.

1079 Thanet, Octave. "Cradle Songs of Negroes in North Carolina." *JAFL* 7 (1895): 310.

1080 Thomas, Gates. "Six Negro Songs from the Colorado Valley." *PTFS* 26 (1945): 162–166.

1081 Thomas, Gates. "South Texas Negro Work Songs." *PTFS* 5 (1926): 154–180.

1082 Thomas, Lorenzo. "For Bluesman Sonny Boy Williamson, Pass the Biscuits One More Time." *BU* 135–136 (1979): 34–38.

1083 Titon, Jeff Todd. "African American Religious Music." *JAFL* 96 (1983): 111–113.

1084 Titon, Jeff Todd. "African American Traditions." *JAFL* 98 (1985): 495–501.

1085 Titon, Jeff Todd. "Thematic Pattern in Downhome Blues Lyrics: The Evidence on Commercial Phonograph Records Since World War II." *JAFL* 90 (1977): 316–330.

1086 Titon, Jeff Todd. "Zydeco: A Musical Hybrid." *JAFL* 95 (1982): 403–405.

1087 Tonsor, Johann. "Negro Music." *MUSC* 11 (1892–1893): 119–122.

1088 Tupper, V. G. "Plantation Echoes: A Negro Folk Music-Drama, as Given Each Year in Charleston, South Carolina." *Etude* 55 (1937): 153.

1089 Turner, Lucile Price. "Negro Spirituals in the Making." *MQ* 17 (1931): 480–485.

1090 Uzzel, Robert L. "Music Rooted in the Texas Soil: Blind Lemon Jefferson." *Liv Blues* 19 (November–December 1988): 22–23.

1091 Van Valen, Leigh. "Talking Drums and Similar African Tonal Communication." *SFQ* 19, no. 4 (1955): 252–256.

1092 Van Vechten, Carl. "The Black Blues." *VF* 24, no. 6 (August 1925): 57, 86, 92.

1093 Walser, Richard. "His Worship the John Kuner." *NCF* 19, no. 4 (1971): 160–172.

1094 Weinstock, Ron. "Big Joe Turner, 1911–1985." *Liv Blues* 69 (1986): 11–12.

1095 Welding, Pete. "I Sing for the People." *DBT* 34, no. 25 (1967): 20–23.

1096 Welding, Pete. "Stringin' the Blues!" *DBT* 32, no. 19 (1965): 22–24, 56.

1097 West, Steve. "The Devil Visits the Delta: A View of His Role in the Blues." *Miss FR* 19 (Spring 1985): 11–23.

1098 Whalum, Wendell P. "James Weldon Johnson's Theories and Performance Practices of Afro-American Folksong." *Phyl* 32, no. 4 (1971): 383–395.

1099 White, N. I. "Racial Traits of the Negro Song." *Sew R* 28 (1919): 396–404.

1100 Wilgus, D. K. "Afro-American Tradition." *JAFL* 84 (1971): 265–271.

1101 Wilgus, D. K. "Cajun and Zydeco Music." *JAFL* 81 (1968): 274–276.

1102 Wilgus, D. K. "Cajun Music." *JAFL* 80 (1967): 205–206.

1103 Wilgus, D. K. "Folksongs of Kentucky, East and West." *KFR* 3 (1957): 89–118.

1104 Wilgus, D. K. "From the Record Review Editor." *JAFL* 78 (1965): 183–191.

1105 Wilgus, D. K. "Negro Music." *JAFL* 81 (1968): 89–94.

1106 Wilgus, D. K. "Negro Music." *JAFL* 80 (1967): 105–109.

1107 Wilgus, D. K. "Negro Secular Music." *JAFL* 79 (1966): 404–408.

1108 Wilgus, D. K., and Lynwood Montell. "Clure and Joe Williams: Legend and Blues Ballad." *JAFL* 81 (1968): 295–315.

1109 Williams, John. "The Country Blues: A Musical Analysis." *Blues* 21 (April 1965): 8.

1110 Williams, John. "Gospel." *SQ* 16, no. 6 (1967): 23.

1111 Williams, John. " 'Mister White, Take a Break': An Interview with Booker (Bukka) White." *SQ* 18, no. 4 (1968): 4–15, 18–19, 23, 67.

1112 Winans, Robert B. "The Folk, the Stage, and the Five-string Banjo in the Nineteenth Century." *JAFL* 89 (1976): 407–437.

1113 Windham, Wyolene. "Huddie 'Leadbelly' Ledbetter: Some Reminiscences of His Cousin, Blanche love." *NLHAJ* 7, no. 3 (1976): 96–100.

1114 Wolffe, D. Leon. "The Blues Are Dead!" *MR* 12, no. 7 (January 1942): 8, 50.

1115 Work, John W. "Changing Patterns in Negro Folk Songs." *JAFL* 62 (1949): 136–144.

1116   Work, Monroe N. "Some Parallelisms in the Development of Africans and Other Races." *So Work* 36 (1907): 106–111.

1117   Work, Monroe N. "The Spirit of Negro Poetry." *So Work* 37 (1908): 73–77.

1118   Yale, Andrew. "Our Place Was Beale Street." *South Exposure* 6, no. 3 (1978): 26–38.

RECORDINGS

1119   *Alligator Stomp*. Rhino R4 70740. 1991. Cassette. [Clifton Chenier, Terrence Simien and the Mallet Playboys, Balfa Brothers, Fats Domino, Doug Kershaw, Rusty Kershaw, Boozoo Chavis, Beausoleil, Buckwheat Zydeco, Rockin' Dopsie, Belton Richard, Jim Delafose]

1120   Armstrong, Louis. *Louis Armstrong Plays the Blues*. Riverside RLP 1001. 1954. LP.

1121   Armstrong, Louis. *Louis Armstrong Plays W. C. Handy*. Columbia CK 40242. 1986. CD.

1122   Bechet, Sidney. *The Legendary Sidney Bechet*. RCA/Bluebird 6590-4-RB. 1988. Cassette.

1123   *The Best of the Blues Singers*. LRC CDC-8530. 1989. CD. [Joe Lee Williams, Charles Ray, Little Parker, Jr., Muddy Waters, T-Bone Walker, Joe Turner, Memphis Slim]

1124   Blake, Blind. *Blind Blake: Ragtime Guitar's Foremost Fingerpicker*. Yazoo 1068. 1988. Cassette.

1125   *Blues Came Down From Memphis*. Charly CD 67. 1987. CD. [Isiah Ross, James Cotton, Willie Nix, Rufus Thomas, Jimmy DeBarry, Sammy Lewis, Milton Campbell, Willie Johnson]

1126   *Bless My Bones: Memphis Gospel Radio, the Fifties*. Rounder 2063. 1988. LP.

1127   Carr, Leroy. *Blues Before Sunrise*. Portrait Masters RK 44122. 1988. CD.

1128   Charters, Samuel. *An Introduction to Gospel Song*. Booklet included with RBF LP record RF 5.

1129   *Classic Jazz*. CBS Records RD 033; DIDP 071436; A5 19477; A 19478. 1987. CD. [Scott Joplin, Jelly Roll Morton, W. C. Handy, Bessie Smith, King Oliver, Clarence Williams, Sidney Bechet, James P. Johnson, Louis Armstrong, Lil Hardin Armstrong, Earl Hines, Carmen Lombardo, Harold Arlen, Jimmy McHugh, Frank Trumbauer, Hoagy Carmichael, Byron Gay, Jimmie Noone]

1130   Cox, Ida. *Wild Women Don't Have the Blues*. Rosetta RR 1304. 1981. LP.

1131   Dodds, Johnny. *Blue Clarinet Stomp*. Bluebird 2293-2-RB. 1990. CD.

1132   *Early and Rare: Classic Jazz*. Riverside RLP 12–134. 1960. LP. [Meade Lewis, Ma Rainey, Tommy Ladnier, Cripple Clarence Lofton, Big Bill Broonzy, Scott Joplin, Jelly Roll Morton, Fats Waller, Blind Lemon Jefferson, Ike Rodgers, Joe Smith, Trixie Smith, Turner Parrish]

1133   Fisk Jubilee Singers. *Ezekiel Saw De Wheel*. Columbia A3370. 1921. 78.

1134   Fisk Jubilee Singers. *The Fisk Jubilee Singers*. Word W 4007. LP.

1135   Fisk Jubilee Singers. *The Gold and Blue Album*. Scholastic Records. 1955. LP.

1136   Fisk Jubilee Singers. *Were You There?* Columbia A3919. 1921. 78.

1137   Fuller, Blind Boy. *East Coast Piedmont Style*. Columbia Legacy CK 46777. 1991. CD.

1138   Golden Eagles. *Lightning and Thunder*. Rounder C-2073. 1988. CD.

1139   Gospel Warriors. *Spirit Feel*. SF 1003. 1987 LP. [Rosetta Tharpe, Georgia Peach, Mary Johnson Davis, Clara Ward, Marion Williams, Bessie Griffin, Jessie May Renfro, Frances Steadman]

1140   Grauer, Bill J.; Orrin Keepnews; and Charles Edward Smith. *History of Classic Jazz*. Booklet included with Riverside LP record set SOP-11.

1141   Hampton Institute Choir. *Music of Dett and Carter*. Richsound Records. RSSW02091. 1970. LP.

1142   Hampton Quartette. *Spirituals and Folk Songs*. Indiana University, Bloomington. Archives of Traditional Music. 1917. Cylinders.

1143   Holliday, Billie. *Lady Sings the Blues*. Verve 833 770–2. 1990. CD.

1144   Hopkins, Lightnin'. *How Many Years I Got?* Fantasy FCD-24725-2. 1989. CD.

1145   House, Son. *The Complete Library of Congress Sessions, 1941–1942*. Travelin' Man (UK) TM CD 02. 1990. CD.

1146   Howlin' Wolf. *Message to the Young*. Chess CH 50002. 1979. LP.

1147   Hurt, Mississippi John. *The Immortal Mississippi John Hurt*. Vanguard Records VMD 79248. 1990. CD.

1148   Jackson, Mahalia. *Gospels, Spirituals, and Hymns*. Sony Music Entertainment CK 47084-CK 47085. 1991. CD.

1149   *Jailhouse Blues: 1936 & 1939*. Rosetta Records RC 1316. 1987. Cassette. [Recorded at the Women's Camp, Mississippi State Penal Farm, Parchman, by John H. Lomax and Herbert Halpert for the Library of Congress]

1150   Jefferson, Blind Lemon. *Early Blues*. Olympic Records OL 7134. 1974. LP.

1151   Johnson, Bunk. *Bunk & Lu*. Good Times Jazz GTCD-12024-2. 1990. CD.

1152   Johnson, James Price. *Carolina Shout*. Biograph BDC 105. 1988. CD.

1153   Johnson, Lonnie. *Blues and Ballads*. Prestige/Bluesville Records OBCCD-531-2. 1990. CD.

1154   Johnson, Robert. *The Complete Recordings*. Columbia C2K 46222. 1990. CD.

1155   Jordon, Louis. *The Best of Louis Jordon*. MCA MCAD-4079. 1989. CD.

1156   Leadbelly. *Alabama Bound*. RCA 9600-4-R. 1989. Cassette.

1157   Lofton, Cripple Clarence. *In De Mornin': Early Blues*. Session 10–006. 1944. 78.

1158   Lofton, Cripple Clarence. *Lofton/Noble '35–'36*. Magpie PY 4409. 1979. LP.

1159   Lomax, Alan. *Georgia Sea Islands. Vols. 1, 2*. Booklet included with Prestige LP record Int 25001, 25002.

1160   Lomax, Alan. *Negro Church Music*. Booklet included with Atlantic LP record 1351.

1161 Lomax, Alan. *Negro Prison Songs from the Mississippi State Penitentiary*. Booklet included with Tradition LP record TLP 1020.

1162 Lomax, Alan. *Negro Sinful Songs Sung by Leadbelly*. Booklet included with Musicraft 78 rpm. record album no. 31.

1163 Lomax, Alan. *Roots of the Blues*. Booklet included with Atlantic LP record 1348.

1164 Lomax, Alan. *Sounds of the South*. Booklet included with Atlantic LP record 1346.

1165 Lomax, Alan. *Yazoo Delta Blues and Spirituals*. Booklet included with Prestige LP record Int 25010.

1166 Martin, Sara. *Sara Martin*. Best of Blues BoB 19. 1989. LP.

1167 McCormick, Mack. *Mance Lipscomb: Texas Sharecropper and Songster*. Booklet included with Aroolie LP record F 1001.

1168 McCormick, Mack. *Robert Shaw: Texas Barrelhouse Piano*. Booklet included with Almanac LP record 10.

1169 McCormick, Mack. *A Treasury of Field Recordings, Vol. 2: Regional and Personalized Song*. Booklet included with 77 LP record LA 12/3.

1170 Memphis Jug Band. *Memphis Jug Band*. Yazoo L-1067. 1987. LP.

1171 Memphis Slim. *Memphis Slim*. Sonet SNTCD 647. 1988. CD.

1172 *National Downhome Blues Festival*. Southland SLP-21-24. 1986. 4 LPs. [Lonnie Pitchford, Precious Bryant, Thomas Burt, Jessie Mae Hemphill, Junior Kimbrough and the Soul Blues Boys, Sunnyland Slim, Frank Edwards, John Cephas, Phil Wiggins, John Jackson, Albert Macon, Robert Thomas, Robert Junior Lockwood, Snooky Pryor, Homesick James, Piano Red, Eddie Kirkland, Doctor Ross, Booker T. Laury, Son Thomas, Henry Townsend, Vernell Townsend, Larry Johnson, and Hezekiah and the Houserockers]

1173 Nicholas, Joe. *Wooden Joe's New Orleans Band*. Storyville SLP 204. LP.

1174 Noone, Jimmy. *Jazz*. Trip JT-11. LP.

1175 *OJL's Georgia—1927–1936: The Black Country Music of Georgia*. Origin Jazz Library OJL-25. 1980. LP. [Tampa Red, Lillie Mae, Bumble Bee Slim, Georgia Tom, Barbecue Bob, Buddy Moss, Sam Montgomery, Sylvester Weaver, Charlie Lincoln, Rufus Quinlan, Ben Quinlan, Rufus Head, Kokomo Arnold, Sara Martin, Luther Magby, J. M. Gates]

1176 Oliver, King. *King Oliver, Volume 1*. Classic Jazz Masters [Sweden] CJM 19. 1980. LP.

1177 Ory, Kid. *Kid Ory: The Great New Orleans Trombonist*. Columbia CL-835. 1956. LP.

1178 Oster, Harry. *Angola Prison Spirituals Recorded at Louisiana State Penitentiary in Angola*. Record notes to Folk-Lyric LP record LSF A6.

1179 Oster, Harry. *Angola Prison Worksongs*. Booklet included with Folk-Lyric LP record LFS A5.

1180 Oster, Harry. *Country Negro Jam Sessions*. Booklet included with Folk-Lyric LP record FL 111.

1181 Page, Hot Lips. *After Hours in Harlem*. Onyx 207. LP.

1182 Patton, Charley. *Charley Patton, Founder of the Delta Blues*. Yazoo 1020. 1989. CD.

1183 Rainey, Ma. *Ma Rainey's Black Bottom*. Yazoo L-1071. 1970. LP.

1184 Rainey, Ma. *The Paramounts [1923–1924], vol. 1*. Black Swan Records WCH-12001. 1986. LP.

1185 Rainey, Ma. *Queen of the Blues: 1923–1924*. Biograph BLP-12032. 1970. LP.

1186 Ramsey, Frederic, Jr. *Music from the South, vol. 1: Country Brass Bands*. Booklet included with Folkways LP record 650.

1187 Ramsey, Frederic, Jr. *Music from the South, vols. 2, 3, 4: Horace Sprott*. Booklet included with Folkways LP records 651, 652, 653.

1188 Ramsey, Frederic, Jr. *Music from the South, vol. 5: Songs, Play and Dance*. Booklet included with Folkways LP record 654.

1189 Ramsey, Frederic, Jr. *Music from the South, vols. 6, 7: Elder Songster*. Booklet included with Folkways LP records 655, 656.

1190 Ramsey, Frederic, Jr. *Music from the South, vols. 8, 9: Young Songsters; Song and Worship*. Booklet included with Folkways LP records 657, 658.

1191 Rinzler, Ralph. *Traditional Music at Newport, Part I*. Booklet included with Vanguard LP record VRS 9182.

1192 *Say Amen, Somebody*. DRG Records SB2L 12584. 1983. LP. [Soundtrack from the motion picture of the same name. Performers include Thomas A. Dorsey, Willie Mae Ford Smith, Mahalia Jackson, Sallie Martin, O'Neal Twins, Interfaith Choir, Barrett Sisters, Zella Jackson Price, Delois Barrett Campbell, and Kansas City Kitty]

1193 Seeger, Peter. *Negro Prison Camp Work Songs*. Booklet included with Folkways LP record 475.

1194 Smith, Bessie. *Bessie Smith, the Collection*. Columbia CK 44441. 1989. CD.

1195 Smith, Charles Edward. *Down Home: A Portrait of a People*. Booklet included with Folkways LP record set 2691.

1196 Smith, Charles Edward. *Folk Music, U.S.A.* Booklet included with Folkways LP record set FE 4530.

1197 Smith, Charles Edward. *Jazz Begins: Sounds of New Orleans Streets—Funeral and Parade Music by the Young Tuxedo Brass Band*. Record notes to Atlantic LP record 1297.

1198 Smith, Clara. *Complete Recordings in Chronological Order*. Document DLP-566-567. 1989. LP.

1199 Smith, Mamie. *Crazy Blues*. Official 6037. 1989. LP.

1200 *Songs We Taught Your Mother*. Prestige/Bluesville BV 1052. 1987. LP. [Alberta Hunter, Lucille Hegamin, Victoria Spivey]

1201 *Sorry But I Can't Take You: Women's Railroad Blues*. Rosetta Records RR 1301. 1980. LP. [Trixie Smith, Clara Smith, Bessie Smith, Bertha Chippie Hill, Ada

Brown, Sippie Wallace, Martha Copeland, Lucille Bogan, Blue Lou Barker, Rosetta Tharpe, Nora Lee King]

1202 *Super Sisters*. Rosetta RC 1308. 1985. Cassette. [Ida Cox, Bertha Idaho, Helen Humes, Sara Martin, Mildred Bailey, Sweet Peas Spivey, Lil Johnson, Trixie Smith, Susie Edwards, Lucille Bogan, Cleo Gibson, Martha Copeland, Edith Johnson, Albennie Jones, Lizzie Miles, Ella Fitzgerald]

1203 Turk, Roy. *Aggravatin' Papa: Don't You Try to Two-time Me*. Cameo 275-B. 1923. 78.

1204 Wallace, Sippy. *Sippy Wallace Sings the Blues*. Storyville SLP-4017. 1967. LP.

1205 Waters, Muddy. *Hard Again*. Columbia ZK 34449. 1987. CD.

1206 *When Women Sang the Blues*. Blues Classics BC 26. 1970. LP. [Lillian Glinn, Bobby Cadillac, Emma Wright, Chippie Hill, Bessie Tucker, Bessie Jackson, Georgia White, Willie B. Huff]

1207 White, Bukka, Skip James, and Blind Willie McTell. *Three Shades of Blues*. Biography BCD 107. 1988. CD.

1208 Williams, Big Joe. *Nine String Guitar Blues*. Delmark DD-627. 1990. CD.

1209 Williamson, Sonny Boy. *Bummer Road*. Chess CHD-9324. 1991. CD.

1210 Wilson, Edith. *He May Be Your Man—But He Comes to See Me Sometimes*. Delmark DS-637. 1976.

4

Folk Material

MONOGRAPHS

1211 Alexander, Wade. *God's Greatest Hits.* New York: Random House, 1970.

1212 Archbold, Annie, and Janice Morrill, eds. *Georgia Folklife: A Pictorial Essay.* Atlanta: Georgia Folklife Program, State of Georgia, 1989.

1213 Armstrong, Orland K. *Old Massa's People: The Old Slaves Tell Their Story.* Indianapolis: Bobbs-Merrill, 1931.

1214 Atwater, Wilbur, O., and Charles D. Woods. *Dietary Studies with Reference to the Food of the Negroes in Alabama in 1895 and 1896.* Washington, DC: U.S. Government Printing Office, 1897. U.S. Department of Agriculture Bulletin no. 38.

1215 Barlow, Gale J. "Black Craftsmen in North Carolina Before 1850." M.A. thesis, University of North Carolina at Greensboro, 1979.

1216 Bastide, Roger. *African Civilizations in the New World.* New York: Harper & Row, 1971.

1217 Beardsley, John, and Jane Livingstone. *Black American Folk Art 1930–1980.* Washington, DC: Corcoran Gallery, 1982. Bibliography on pp. 179–185.

1218 Bishop, Robert. *American Folk Sculpture.* New York: Dutton, 1974. Bibliography on pp. 388–389.

1219 *Black Artists in Historical Perspective.* Black Dimensions in Art, 1976.

1220 Black, Mary, and Jean Lipman. *American Folk Painting.* New York: Crown, 1987. Bibliography on pp. 233–240.

1221 Blasingame, John W. *Black New Orleans, 1860–1880.* Chicago: University of Chicago Press, 1973. Bibliography on pp. 275–292.

1222 Blasingame, John W. *The Slave Community: Plantation Life in the Antebellum South.* New York: Oxford University Press, 1979. Bibliography on pp. 383–402.

1223 Blasingame, John W. ed. *Slave Testimony: Two Centuries of Letters, Speeches, Interviews, and Autobiographies.* Baton Rouge: Louisiana State University Press, 1977.

1224 Brawley, Benjamin G. *The Negro in Literature and Art in the United States.* New York: Duffield, 1921.

1225 Brewer, J. Mason. *Humorous Folk Tales of the South Carolina Negro.* Orangeburg: South Carolina Folklore Guild, 1945.

1226 Brewer, James H. *The Confederate Negro: Virginia's Craftsmen and Military Laborers 1861–1865.* Durham, NC: Duke University Press, 1969. Bibliography on pp. 201–204.

1227 Bridenbaugh, Carl. *The Colonial Craftsman.* 1950. Reprint, New York: Dover, 1990.

1228 Bronner, Simon J. *American Folk Art: A Guide to Sources.* Vol. 464. New York: Garland, 1984. Garland Reference Library of the Humanities.

1229 Brown, William W. *My Southern Home: Or, the South and Its People.* Boston: Brown and Co., 1880.

1230 Butcher, Margaret J. *The Negro in American Culture, Based on Materials Left by Alain Locke.* 2d ed. New York: Knopf, 1973.

1231 Cederholm, Theresa D. *Afro-American Artists: A Bio-Bibliographical Directory.* Boston: Boston Public Library, 1973.

1232 Chase, Judith W. *Afro-American Art and Craft.* New York: Van Nostrand Reinhold, 1971. Bibliography on pp. 138–139.

1233 Chase, Leah. *The Dooky Chase Cookbook.* Gretna, LA: Pelican, 1990.

1234 Christensen, Erwin O. *The Index of American Design.* New York: Macmillan, 1950.

1235 Christian, Marcus. *Negro Ironworkers of Louisiana 1718–1900.* Gretna, LA: Pelican, 1972. Bibliography on pp. 37–43.

1236 Clinton, Anita, and Lynn Lofton. *Pioneer Places of Lawrence County, Mississippi.* Monticello, MS: Lawrence County Historical Society, 1981.

1237 Coleman, William H. *La Cuisine Créole: A Collection of Culinary Recipes.* New York: Coleman, 1885.

1238 Combes, John. "Ethnography, Archeology, and Burial Practices among South Carolina Blacks." In *Conference of Historic Site Archeology Papers 7,* ed. Stanley South. Columbia, SC: Institute of Archeology and Anthropology, 1972.

1239 Cook, Sterling. *Two Black Folk Artists: Clementine Hunter and Nellie Mae Rowe.* Coral Gables, FL: Miami University Art Museum, 1986.

1240 Cooley, Rossa B. *Homes of the Freed.* New York: New Republic, Inc., 1926.

1241 Cooper, Virginia M. *Creole Kitchen Cook Book.* San Antonio, TX: Naylor, 1941.

1242 Courlander, Harold. *The Drum and the Hoe: Life & Love of the Haitanian People.* Berkeley: University of California Press, 1985. Bibliography and discography on pp. 363–366.

1243 Craig, James H. *The Arts and Crafts in North Carolina, 1699–1840.* Winston-Salem, NC: Museum of Early Southern Decorative Arts, 1965.

1244 Crum, Mason. *Gullah: Negro Life in the Carolina Sea Islands.* Durham, NC: Duke University Press, 1940. Bibliography on pp. 347–351.

1245 Dabbs, Edith M. *Face of an Island: Leigh Richmond Miner's Photographs of Saint Helena Island.* New York: Grossman, 1971.

1246 David, Hilda B. "The African-American Women of Edisto Island, 1850–1920." Ph.D. dissertation, Emory University, 1990. Bibliography on lvs. 262–280.

1247 Davis, Gerald. "Afro-American Coil Basketry in Charleston County, South Carolina." In *American Folklife*, ed. Don Yoder. Austin: University of Texas Press, 1976, 151–184.

1248 Dew, Charles B. *Ironmaker to the Confederacy: Joseph R. Anderson and the Tredegar Iron Works.* 1966. Reprint, Wilmington, NC: Broadfoot, 1987. Bibliography on pp. 327–334.

1249 Dover, Cedric. *America Negro Art.* Greenwich, CT: New York Graphic Society, 1960. Bibliography on pp. 57–60.

1250 Driskell, David C. *Two Centuries of Black American Art.* New York: Knopf, 1976. Bibliography on pp. 206–219.

1251 Du Bois, W. E. B. *The Negro American Artisan.* Atlanta: Atlanta University Press, 1912. Atlanta University publications, no. 17.

1252 Du Bois, W. E. B. *The Negro American Family.* Atlanta: Atlanta University Press, 1908. Atlanta University publications, no. 13.

1253 Du Bois, W. E. B., and Augustus G. Dill. *The Negro American Artisan.* Atlanta: Atlanta University Press, 1912. Atlanta University publications, no. 17.

1254 Farlow, Gale J. "Black Craftsmen in North Carolina Before 1850." M.A. thesis, University of North Carolina at Greensboro, 1979. Bibliography on lvs. 113–121.

1255 Ferrell, Stephen T., and T. M. Ferrell. *Early Decorated Stoneware of the Edgefield District, South Carolina.* Greenville, SC: Greenville County Museum of Art, 1976.

1256 Ferris, William R., Jr., ed. *Afro-American Folk Art and Crafts.* Jackson: University Press of Mississippi, 1983. Bibliography on pp. 356–397.

1257 Ferris, William R., Jr., ed. *Local Color: A Sense of Place in Folk Art.* New York: McGraw-Hill, 1982. Bibliography on pp. 229–234.

1258 Ferris, William R., Jr., ed. *Mississippi Black Folklore: A Research Bibliography and Discography.* Hattiesburg: University and College Press of Mississippi, 1971.

1259 Ferris, William R., Jr., ed. *Mississippi Folk Architecture.* Washington, DC: Smithsonian Institution, 1973.

1260 Ferris, William R. Jr., ed. *"You Live and Learn. Then You Die and Forget It All." Ray Lum's Tales of Horses, Mules, and Men.* New York: Anchor Books, 1992.

1261 Fine, Elsa H. *The Afro-American Artist.* New York: Hooker Art Books, 1982. Bibliography on pp. 288–300.

1262 Fleischhauer, Carl, and Howard W. Marshall. *Sketches of South Georgia Folklife.* Washington, DC: Library of Congress, 1977.

1263 Fogel, Robert W., and Stanley L. Engerman. *Time on the Cross: The Economics of American Negro Slavery.* Boston: Little, Brown, 1974.

1264 Folly, Dennis W. "You Preach Your Funeral While You're Living: Death in Afro-American Folklore." M.A. thesis, University of California, Berkeley, 1980. Bibliography on lvs. 100–107.

1265 Foner, Phillip, and Ronald S. Lewis, eds. *The Black Worker: A Documentary History from Colonial Times to the Present.* Philadelphia: Temple University Press, 1978–1984.

1266 Franklin, John H. *The Free Negro in North Carolina, 1790–1860.* Chapel Hill: University of North Carolina Press, 1943.

1267 Fraser, Douglas, ed. *The Many Faces of Primitive Art: A Critical Anthology.* Englewood Cliffs, NJ: Prentice-Hall, 1966.

1268 Frazier, E. Franklin. *The Negro Family in the United States.* Chicago: University of Chicago Press, 1966. Repr. of 1939 ed.

1269 Freeman, Roland. "Folkroots: Images of Mississippi Black Folklife." In *Long Journey Home: Folklife in the South*, ed. Allen Tullos. Chapel Hill, NC: Southern Exposure, 1977, 29–35.

1270 Frissell, Hollis B., and Isabel Brevier. *Dietary Studies of Negroes in Eastern Virginia.* Washington, DC: U.S. Government Printing Office, 1899. U.S. Department of Agriculture Bulletin no. 71.

1271 Fry, Gladys-Marie. "Harriet Powers: Portrait of a Black Quilter." In *Missing Pieces: Georgia Folk Art 1770–1976,* ed. Anna Wadsworth. Atlanta: Georgia Council for the Arts and Humanities, 1976, 16–23.

1272 Gayden, Donna M. *Black Folk Art: A Bibliography.* n.p.: The Author, 1984.

1273 Glassie, Henry. *Folk Housing in Middle Virginia: A Structural Analysis of Historic Artifacts.* Knoxville: University of Tennessee Press, 1975. Bibliography on pp. 215–227.

1274 Gordon, Asa H. *Sketches of Negro Life and History in South Carolina.* Columbia: University of South Carolina Press, 1971.

1275 Green, Jonathan. *Gullah Life Reflections: Traveling Exhibition of the Paintings of Jonathan Green.* Durham: North Carolina–Charleston University Art Museum, 1988. Bibliography on pp. 14–16.

1276 Green, Lorenzo J., and Carter G. Woodson. *The Negro Wage Earner.* Washington, DC: Association for the Study of Negro Life and History, 1930. Bibliography on pp. 369–380.

1277 Greer, Georgeanne. *American Stoneware: The Art and Craft of Utilitarian Pottery.* Exton, PA: Schiffer, 1981. Bibliography on pp. 277–280.

1278 Grider, Sylvia A. "Shotgun Shacks of the Texas Panhandle." In *A Time to Purpose: A Chronicle of Carson County and Area*, ed. Jo Randel. Hereford, TX: Pioneer Books, 1972, 434–436.

1279 Gullory, Queen Ida, and Naomi Wise. *Cookin' with Queen Ida: "Bon Temps"*

Creole Recipes (and Stories) from the Queen of Zydeco Music. Rocklin, CA: Prima, 1990.

1280 Hall, Carrie A., and Rose G. Kretsinger. *The Romance of the Patchwork Quilt in America.* New York: Bonanza Books, 1935.

1281 Harris, Middleton, et al., comps. *The Black Book.* New York: Random House, 1974.

1282 Hechtlinger, Adelaide H. *American Quilts, Quilters and Patchwork.* New York: Galahad, 1974.

1283 Hemphill, Herbert W., Jr., ed. *Folk Sculpture U.S.A.* New York: The Brooklyn Museum, 1976.

1284 Hill, W. B. *Rural Survey of Clarke County, Georgia, with Special Reference to the Negroes.* Athens: University of Georgia, 1915. Phelps-Stokes Fellowship Studies, no. 2.

1285 Hollis, Sara. "Afro-American Artists: A Handbook." Ph.D. dissertation, Atlanta University, 1985. Bibliography on lvs. 323–332.

1286 Holstein, Jonathon. *The Pieced Quilt: An American Design Tradition.* New York: Galahad Books, 1973. Bibliography on pp. 188–189.

1287 Hooks, Rosie L. "The African Diaspora Program: A Photo Essay." In *Black People and Their Culture*, ed. Linn Shapiro. Washington, DC: Smithsonian Institution, 1976, 11–26.

1288 Horowitz, Elinor L. *Contemporary American Folk Artists.* New York: J. B. Lippincott, 1975. Bibliography on p. 139.

1289 Hudson, Ralph. *Afro-American Art: A Bibliography.* Washington, DC: National Art Education Association, 1970.

1290 Jackson, Luther P. *Free Negro Labor and Property Holding in Virginia, 1830–1860.* New York: American Historical Association, 1942.

1291 Jennings, Paula T. *Mississippi Folk Arts and Folklife Collections: A Directory.* Jackson: Mississippi Arts Commission, 1983.

1292 Johnson, Guion G. *A Social History of the Sea Islands.* New York: Negro Universities Press, 1969.

1293 Katz, Elaine S. *Folklore for the Time of Your Life.* Birmingham: Oxmoor House, 1978. Bibliography on pp. 239–242.

1294 Klamkin, Marian, and Charles Klamkin. *Wood-carvings: North American Folk Sculptures.* New York: Hawthorn Books, 1974. Bibliography on pp. 205–206.

1295 Lamb, Venice. *West African Weaving.* London: Duckworth, 1975.

1296 Latrobe, Benjamin H. B. *Impressions Respecting New Orleans.* New York: Columbia University Press, 1951.

1297 Leuzinger, Elsy. *Africa: The Art of Negro Peoples.* New York: Crown, 1960.

1298 Lewis, Ronald L. *Coal, Iron, and Slaves: Industrial Slavery in Maryland and Virginia, 1715–1865.* Westport, CT: Greenwood Press, 1979. Bibliography on pp. 255–274.

1299   Lewis, Samella. *Art: African American*. New York: Harcourt, Brace, Jovanovich, 1978. Bibliography on pp. 233–239.

1300   Livingstone, Jane, and John Beardsley, with a contribution by Regina Perry. *Black Folk Art in America, 1930–1980*. Jackson, MS: Center for the Study of Southern Culture, 1982. Bibliography on pp. 179–185.

1301   Marcus, J. A. *Uncle Gabe Tucker: Reflections, Songs, Spirituals*. Philadelphia: J. B. Lippincott, 1883.

1302   Michels, Barbara, and Bettye White. *Apples on a Stick: The Folklore of Black Children*. New York: Coward-McCann, 1983.

1303   Mier, August, and Elliot Rudwick. *From Plantation to Ghetto*. New York: Hill and Wang, 1966. Bibliography on pp. 253–267.

1304   Mikell, I. Jenkins. *Rumbling of the Chariot Wheels*. Columbia, SC: The State Co., 1923.

1305   Montell, William L. *The Saga of Coe Ridge*. Knoxville: University of Tennessee Press, 1970. Bibliography on pp. 216–224.

1306   Myers, Robin. *Black Craftsmen Through History*. Brooklyn, NY: The Institute of Joint Apprenticeship Program, Workers Defense League, A. Philip Randolph Fund, 1969.

1307   Newton, James E., and Ronald L. Lewis. *The Other Slaves: Mechanics, Artisans, and Craftsmen*. Boston: G. K. Hall, 1978.

1308   Nichols, Gene. *The Geechee Cook Book*. Savannah, GA: Southern Printers, 1973.

1309   North Carolina Museum of Art. *Afro-American Artists, North Carolina, USA, North Carolina Museum of Art, November 9–December 31, 1980*. Raleigh, NC: The Museum, 1980.

1310   Old Slave Mart Museum, Charleston, South Carolina. *Catalog of the Old Slave Mart Museum and Library, Charleston, South Carolina*. 2 vols. Boston: G. K. Hall, 1978.

1311   *Old Time Tennessee Recipes*. New York: Greenberg, 1946.

1312   Olmstead, Frederick L. *A Journey in the Seaboard Slave States in the Years 1853–54*. New York: Dix and Edwards, 1856.

1313   Opala, Joseph A. *The Gullah: Rice, Slavery and the Sierra Leone-American Connection*. Freetown, Sierra Leone: USIS, 1979.

1314   Perry, Reginia A. *Selections of Nineteenth Century Afro-American Art*. New York: Metropolitan Museum of Art, 1976.

1315   Peto, Florence. *Historic Quilts*. New York: American Historical Society, 1930.

1316   Pinchbeck, Raymond B. *The Virginia Negro Artisan and Tradesman*. Richmond, VA: William Byrd Press, 1926. Phelps-Stokes Fellowship Papers, no. 7.

1317   Polley, Robert L., ed. *America's Folk Art: Treasures of American Folk Art and Crafts in Distinguished Museums and Collections*. New York: Putnam, 1968.

1318   Porter, James A. *Modern Negro Art*. 1943. Reprint, New York: Arno Press, 1960. Bibliography on pp. 183–192.

1319 *Profiles of Black Museums*. Washington, DC: African American Museum Association; Nashville, TN: American Association for State and Local History, 1988.

1320 Ramsay, John. *American Potters and Pottery*. New York: Tudor, 1947. Bibliography on pp. 244–251.

1321 Ransom, Roger L., and Richard Sutch. *One Kind of Freedom: The Economic Consequences of Emancipation*. Cambridge and New York: Cambridge University Press, 1977. Bibliography on pp. 374–393.

1322 Rawick, George P., ed. *The American Slave: A Composite Autobiography*. 19 vols. Westport, CT: Greenwood Press, 1973–1976.

1323 Richardson, Harry V. "The Negro in American Religious Life." In *The American Negro Reference Book*, ed. John P. Davis. Englewood Cliffs, NJ: Prentice-Hall, 1966, 400.

1324 Roach, Margaret S. "The Traditional Quiltmaking of North Louisiana Women: Form, Function, and Meaning." Ph.D. dissertation, University of Texas at Austin, 1986. Bibliography on lvs. 319–330.

1325 Roach, Susan. "The Kinship Quilt: An Ethnographic Semiotic Analysis of a Quilting Bee." In *Women's Folklore, Women's Culture*, ed. Rosen A. Jordan and Susan J. Kalcik. Philadelphia: University of Pennsylvania Press, 1985, 54–64.

1326 Rosengarten, Theodore. *All God's Dangers: The Life of Nate Shaw*. New York: Knopf, 1974.

1327 Rowell, Charles H. "Afro-American Literary Bibliographies: An Annotated List of Bibliographical Guides for the Study of Afro-American Literature, Folklore, and Related Areas." M.A. thesis, Ohio State University, 1972. Bibliography on lvs. 206–208.

1328 Scarborough, Donald D. *An Economic Study of Negro Farmers as Owners, Tenants, and Croppers*. Athens: University of Georgia, 1924. Phelps-Stokes Fellowship Papers, no. 7.

1329 Seward, Adrienne L. "Early Black Film and Folk Tradition: An Interpretive Analysis of the Use of Folklore in Selected All-Black Cast Feature Films." Ph.D. dissertation, University of Indiana, 1985. Bibliography on lvs. 268–296; filmography on lvs. 263–267.

1330 Shapiro, Linn, ed. *Black People and Their Culture: Selected Writings from the African Diaspora*. Washington, DC: Smithsonian Institution, 1976.

1331 Sieber, Roy. *African Textiles and Decorative Arts*. New York: Museum of Modern Art, 1972. Bibliography on pp. 229–238.

1332 Singleton, Theresa A., ed. *The Archaeology of Slavery and Plantation Life*. Orlando: Academic Press, 1985.

1333 Smart-Grosvenor, Verta Mae. *Vibration Cooking, or the Travel Notes of a Geechee Girl*. New York: Ballantine Books, 1970.

1334 Stahl, Annie L. W. "The Free Negro in Ante Bellum Louisiana." M.A. thesis, Louisiana State University, 1934. Bibliography on lvs. 134–139.

1335 Stavisky, Leonard P. "The Negro Artisan in the South Atlantic States, 1800–1860: A Study of Status and Economic Opportunity with Special Reference to

Charleston.'' Ph.D. dissertation, Columbia University, 1958. Bibliography on lvs. 259–285.

1336   Stearns, Charles. *Black Man of the South and the Rebels.* New York: American News Co., 1872.

1337   Sterkx, Herbert E. *The Free Negro in Antebellum Louisiana.* Rutherford, NJ: Fairleigh Dickinson University Press, 1972. Bibliography on pp. 316–337.

1338   Stoney, Samuel G. *This Is Charleston: A Survey of the Architectural Heritage of a Unique American City.* Charleston: Carolina Art Association, 1944.

1339   Taylor, Ellsworth. *Folk Art of Kentucky.* Lexington: University of Kentucky Fine Arts Gallery, 1975.

1340   Taylor, Orville W. *Negro Slavery in Arkansas.* Durham, NC: Duke University Press, 1958.

1341   Teilhet, Jehanne. *Dimensions in Black.* La Jolla, CA: La Jolla Museum of Art, 1970.

1342   Thomas, Valerie M. *Ancient African: Traditional and Contemporary Hairstyles for the Black Woman.* New York: Col-Bob Association, 1973.

1343   Thurm, Marcella. *Exploring Black America: A History and Guide.* New York: Atheneum, 1975.

1344   Tindall, George B. *South Carolina Negroes, 1877–1900.* Chapel Hill: University of North Carolina Press, 1964. Bibliography on pp. 311–326.

1345   Trechsel, Gail A., ed. *Black Belt to Hill Country: Alabama Quilts from the Helen and Robert Cargo Collection.* Birmingham, AL: Birmingham Museum of Art, 1982. Bibliography on p. 92.

1346   Twining, Mary A. ''An Examination of African Retentions in the Folk Culture of the South Carolina and Georgia Sea Islands.'' Ph.D. dissertation, Indiana University, 1977. Bibliography on lvs. 188–213.

1347   University of Montevallo Gallery. *Alabama Folk Art: The Gallery, University of Montevallo, Alabama, March 25–April 11, 1980.* Montevallo, AL: The University, 1980.

1348   Vick, Oscar. *Gullah Cooking: Creative Recipes from an Historic Past from the Low Country of South Carolina.* Charleston, SC: The Author, 1989.

1349   Vlach, John M. *The Afro-American Tradition in Decorative Arts.* Cleveland, OH: Cleveland Museum of Art, 1978. Bibliography on pp. 169–173.

1350   Vlach, John M. *By the Work of Their Hands: Studies in Afro-American Folklife.* Ann Arbor, MI: UMI Research Press, 1991.

1351   Vlach, John M. *Charleston Blacksmith: The Life and Work of Philip Simmons.* Athens: University of Georgia Press, 1981. Bibliography on pp. 151–154.

1352   Wadsworth, Anna, ed. *Missing Pieces: Georgia Folk Art: 1770–1976.* Atlanta: Georgia Council on the Arts and Humanities, 1976.

1353   Wahlman, Maude S., and James R. Ramsey, eds. *Spirit of Africa: Traditional Art from the Nokes Collection.* Memphis, TN: Memphis State University Gallery, 1982. Bibliography on pp. 65–68.

1354 Wahlman, Maude S., James R. Ramsey, and John Scully. *Black Quilters*. New Haven: Yale Art and Architecture Gallery, 1979.

1355 Walter, Eugene. *American Cooking, Southern Style*. New York: Time-Life Books, 1971.

1356 Waring, Dennis. *Making Wood Folk Instruments*. New York: Sterling, 1990.

1357 Waters, Donald J., ed. *Strange Ways and Sweet Dreams: Afro-American Folklore from the Hampton Institute*. Boston: G. K. Hall, 1983.

1358 Weatherford, W. D. *Negro Life in the South: Present Conditions and Needs*. 1915. Reprint, Miami, FL: Mnemosyne, 1969.

1359 Wharton, Vernon L. *The Negro in Mississippi, 1865–1890*. Chapel Hill: University of North Carolina Press, 1947.

1360 Wiggins, William, Jr. "January 1: The Afro-American's 'Day of Days.' " In *Prospects* 4, ed. Jack Salzman. New York: Burth Franklin, 1979, 351–354.

1361 Wikramanayake, Marina. *A World in Shadow: The Free Black in Antebellum South Carolina*. Columbia: University of South Carolina Press, 1973. Bibliography on pp. 195–212.

1362 Williams, Geoffrey. *African Designs from Traditional Sources*. New York: Dover, 1971.

1363 Wilson, Eugene M. *Alabama Folk Houses*. Montgomery: Alabama Historical Commission, 1975.

1364 Wise, Edith C., and Gerard C. Wertkin. *Southern Folk Art: A Bibliographical Guide to Sources in the Library of the Museum of Folk Art*. New York: Museum of Folk Art, 1985.

1365 Wood, Peter H. *Black Majority: Negroes in Colonial South Carolina from 1670 through the Stono Rebellion*. New York: Knopf, 1974. Bibliography on pp. 344–346.

1366 Woofter, Thomas J. *Black Yeomanry: Life on St. Helena Island*. New York: Henry Holt, 1930.

1367 Wrightman, Orrin S., and Margaret D. Cate. *Early Days of Coastal Georgia*. St. Simons Island, GA: Fort Frederika Association, 1955.

1368 Writer's Program of the Work Projects Administration in the State of Virginia. *The Negro in Virginia*. New York: Hastings House, 1940.

1369 Yetman, Norman, ed. *Life Under the Peculiar Institution: Selections from the Slave Narrative Collection*. New York: Holt, Rinehart, and Winston, 1970.

ARTICLES

1370 Adler, Elizabeth M. "It Takes a Smart Guy to . . . Take a Look at a Rock and Do Like That: George 'Baby' Scott (1865–1945), a Carver and His Repertoire." *Mid-SF* 3 (1975): 147–160.

1371 Alexander, Margaret W. "Black and White Threads in Mississippi Folk Culture." *Miss FR* 20, no. 2 (Fall 1986): 163–167.

1372 Anthony, Carl. "The Big House and the Slave Quarters." *Land* 20 (1976): 9–15.

1373   Ascher, Robert, and Charles H. Fairbands. "Excavation of a Slave Cabin." *Hist Arc* (1971): 3–17.

1374   Barfield, Rodney. "North Carolina Black Material Culture: A Research Opportunity." *NCF* 27 (1979): 61–66.

1375   "Basket Weavers of Charleston." *South Liv* (October 1970): 22, 26.

1376   Bell, H. S. "Plantation Life of the Negro in the Lower Mississippi Valley." *SW* 28 (1899): 313–314.

1377   Black, Patti C., and William Ferris. "The Shotgun, the Dogtrot, and the Row House . . ." *South V* 1 (1973): 28–32.

1378   Bolton, H. Carrington. "Decorations of Graves of Negroes in South Carolina." *JAFL* 24 (1891): 214.

1379   Bonner, James C. "Plantation Architecture of the Lower South on the Eve of the Civil War." *JSH* 11 (1945): 37–80.

1380   Bradford, S. Sidney. "The Negro Ironworker in Ante-Bellum Virginia." *JSH* 25 (1959): 194–206.

1381   Bradley, Arthur G. "A Peep at the Southern Negro." *Mac* 39 (1878): 61–68.

1382   Brewer, J. Francis. "Master Ironworkers Came to Practice Art in City." *Charleston Courier*, August 21, 1932.

1383   Bronner, Simon J. "Pictoral Jokes: A Traditional Combination of Verbal and Graphic Processes." *TFSB* 44 (1978): 189–196.

1384   Bronner, Simon J. "Saturday Night in Greenville: A Black Tale and Music Session in Context." *FF* 14 (1981): 85–120.

1385   Burrison, John A. "Afro-American Folk Pottery in the South." *SFQ* 42, nos. 2–3 (1978): 175–199.

1386   Burrison, John A. "Alkaline-Glazed Stoneware: A Deep South Pottery Tradition." *SFQ* 39 (1975): 377–403.

1387   Chase, Judith W. "American Heritage from Ante-Bellum Black Craftsmen." *SFQ* 42 (1978): 136–158.

1388   Clark, James. "Burley Tobacco Culture: A Northampton Slave's Account." *NCF* 16 (1968): 15–19.

1389   Cochran, Robert, Martha Cochran, and Christopher Pierle. "The Preparation and Use of Bear Grass Rope: An Interview with Robert Simmons, Mississippi Folk Craftsman." *NYFQ* 30, no. 3 (1974): 185–196.

1390   "Craze for Quilts." *Life 1972* 17 (May 5, 1972): 74–80.

1391   Davis, Henry C. "Negro Folklore in South Carolina." *JAFL* 27 (1914): 241–254.

1392   Dew, Charles B. "Black Ironworkers and the Slave Insurrection Panic of 1856." *JSH* 41 (August 1975): 321–328.

1393   Dew, Charles B. "David Ross and the Oxford Iron Works: A Study of Industrial Slavery in the Early Nineteenth-Century South." *William M Q*, 3rd ser. 31 (April 1974): 189–224.

1394   Dickens, Dorothy. "Food Preparation of Owner and Cropper Farm Families in the Shortleaf Pine Area of Mississippi." *SFQ* 22 (1943): 56–63.

1395   Dickens, Dorothy, and Robert Ford. "Geophagy (Dirt Eating) Among Mississippi Negro School Children." *American Sociological Review* 7 (1942): 59–65.

1396   Dowd, Jerome. "Art in Negro Homes." *SW* 30 (1901): 90–95.

1397   Dozier, Richard E. "Black Architects and Craftsmen." *BW* (May 1974): 5–7.

1398   Eudy, John. "A Mississippi Log Wagon." *J Miss H* 20 (1968): 143–150.

1399   Evans, E. Raymond. "The Strip House in Tennessee Folk Architecture." *TFSB* 42 (1976): 163–166.

1400   Ferris, William R. "Black Folk Arts and Crafts: A Mississippi Sample (Photo Essay)." *SFQ* 42, no. 2–3 (1978): 209–241.

1401   Ferris, William R. "Folk Architecture: A Key to the Past." *Miss A* 4 (1973): 5–20.

1402   Ferris, William R. "If You Ain't Got It in Your Head, You Can't Do It with Your Hands: James Thomas, Mississippi Delta Folk Sculptor." *SI* 3 (1970): 89–101.

1403   Ferris, William R. "Mississippi Folk Architecture: A Sampling." *Mid-SF* 1 (1973): 71–85.

1404   Ferris, William R. "Mississippi Folk Architecture: Two Examples." *Miss FR* 7 (1973): 101–114.

1405   "Folk-Lore and Ethnology." *SW* 28 (1899): 112–113, 314–315.

1406   Franklin, John H. "James Boon, Free Negro Artisan." *JNH* 30 (April 1945): 150–180.

1407   Greene, Caroll, Jr. "Afro-American Artists: Yesterday and Now." *HWAY* 7 (3rd quarter, 1968): 10–15.

1408   Gunter, Carolyn P. "Tom Day, Craftsman." *Antiq* 10 (September 1928): 60–62.

1409   Handler, Jerome S. "A Historical Sketch of Pottery Manufacture in Barbados." *The Journal of the Barbados Museum Historical Society* 30 (1963): 129–153.

1410   Henderson, George W. "Life in the Louisiana Sugar Belt." *SW* 35 (1906): 207–215.

1411   Herring, James V. "The American Negro as Craftsman and Artist." *Crisis* 49 (1942): 116–118.

1412   Hilliard, Sam. "Hog Meat and Cornpone: Food Habits in the Ante-Bellum South." *Proc Am Phil Soc* 113 (1969): 1–13.

1413   Hinson, Glenn. "An Interview with Leon Berry, Maker of Baskets." *NCF* 27 (1979): 56–60.

1414   Howard, W. H. A. "In the Black Belt of Florida." *SW* 37 (1908): 284–290.

1415   Ingersoll, Ernest. "Notes and Queries: Decoration of Negro Graves." *JAFL* 5 (1892): 68–69.

1416   Jernegan, Marcus W. "Slavery and the Beginnings of Industrialism in America." *Am Hist Rev* 25 (1920): 220–240.

1417   Johnson, Rhonda S. "Harmon Young: Georgia Wood Sculptor." *SFQ* 42 (1978): 243–256.

1418   Joyner, Charles W. "The Creolization of Slave Folklife: All Saints Parish, South Carolina as a Test Case." *Hist Reflec* [Canada] 6, no. 2 (1979): 435–453.

1419   Kiah, Virginia. "Ulysses Davis: Savannah Folk Sculptor." *SFQ* 42 (1978): 271–286.

1420   Kniffen, Fred B. "Physiognomy of Rural Louisiana." *LHQ* 4 (1963): 271–286.

1421   Not used.

1422   Lee, Florence W. "Harvest Time in Old Virginia." *SW* 37 (1908): 566–567.

1423   Lemon, John W. "Agricultural Vignettes: The Conversation of Doubting Thomas." *SW* 34 (1905): 605–608.

1424   Lemon, John W. "Agricultural Vignettes: His Better Half." *SW* 35 (1906): 221–224.

1425   Lemon, John W. "Agricultural Vignettes: When the Race Problem Will Die." *SW* 35 (1906): 278–281.

1426   Lewis, Donald L. "Slavery on Chesapeake Iron Plantations Before and After the American Revolution." *JNH* 59 (July 1974): 242–254.

1427   Lewis, Pierce. "Common Houses, Cultural Spoor." *Land* 19, no. 2 (1975): 1–22.

1428   Little, M. Ruth. "Afro-American Gravemakers in North Carolina." *Markers: The Journal of the Association for Gravestone Studies* 6 (1989): 102–134.

1429   Long, Worth, and Roland Freeman. "Mississippi Black Folklife." *South Exposure* 3 (1975): 84–89.

1430   Lornell, Christopher. "Black Material Folk Culture." *SFQ* 42 (1978): 287–294.

1431   Lornell, Christopher. "Coy Thompson, Afro-American Corn Shuck Mop Maker: 'We Make Them Now to Show the Younger People How the Older Ones Come Up.' " *TFSB* 42 (1977): 175–180.

1432   McCann, Gary G., and Hilliard Saunders. "Cuisine d'Amour à la Creole." *LAFM* 6, no. 2 (1986–1987): 69–71.

1433   McIntire, Carl. "Slave Made Markers." *Jackson Clarion Ledger*, May 4, 1969.

1434   Metcalf, Eugene W. "Black Art, Folk Art, and Social Control." *Winterthur Portfolio* 18, no. 4 (1983): 271–289.

1435   "Minnie Evans, Folk Artist." *South Liv* (August 1970).

1436   A Mississippi Planter. "Management of Negroes Upon Southern Estates." *De Bow* 10 (1851): 621–627.

1437   Moe, John F. "Concepts of Shelter: The Folk Poetics of Space, Change and Continuity." *JPC* 11 (1977): 219–253.

1438   Montgomery, Charles J. "Survivals from the Congo of the Slave Yacht *Wanderer*." *AA* 10 (1908): 611–621.

1439   Moore, J. Roderick. "Folk Crafts." *Arts in Virginia* 12 (1971): 22–30.

1440   Moore, Janie G. "Africanisms among Blacks in the Sea Islands." *J Black Stud*, J. Bradford. "The Negroes of Cinclare Central Factory and Calumet Plantation, Louisiana." Bulletin of the Department of Labor, no. 38 (1902): 95–102.

1441 Nelson, Randy F. "George Black: A New Folk Hero." *NCF* 20, no. 1 (1972): 30–35.

1442 Newton, James E. "Slave Artisans and Craftsmen: The Roots of Afro-American Art." *BlS* 9 (November 1977): 35–44.

1443 Peck, Phil. "Afro-American Material Culture and the Afro-American Craftsman." *SFQ* 42, no. 2–3 (1978): 109–134.

1444 Perdue, Charles L. "Slave Life Styles in Early Virginia." *Proc Am Phil Soc* 2 (1973): 54–58.

1445 Perdue, Robert E., Jr. "African Baskets in South Carolina." *Econ Bot* 22 (1968): 289–292.

1446 Phillips, Yvonne. "The Shotgun House." *LA Stud* 2 (1963): 178–179.

1447 Picket, Andrew J. "The Red Lands of Alabama." *So Cul* 5 (1847): 10.

1448 Porter, James A. "Four Problems in the History of Negro Art." *JNH* 27 (1942): 9–36.

1449 Porter, James A. "Versatile Interests of the Early Negro Artist: A Neglected Chapter of American Art History." *Art Am* 24 (1936): 16–27.

1450 Reagon, Bernice. "Creating the Georgia Sea Island Festival." *SI* 26 (1977): 23–26.

1451 Sherwood, Henry R., ed. "The Journal of Miss Susan Walker, March 3rd to June 6th, 1862." *Q Pub Hist Phil Soc OH* 7 (1912): 3–48.

1452 Showers, Susan. "A Weddin' and a Buryin' in the Black Belt." *N Eng Mag* 18 (1898): 478–483.

1453 A Small Farmer. "Management of Negroes." *De Bow* 11 (1851): 369–372.

1454 "Southern Folk Art." *Early Am L* 16, no. 3 (1985): 16–21.

1455 Spears, James E. "Favorite Southern Negro Folk Recipes." *KFR* 16 (1970): 1–5.

1456 Stavisky, Leonard. "Negro Craftsmanship in Early America." *Am Hist Rev* 54 (1949): 315–325.

1457 Stavisky, Leonard. "The Origins of Negro Craftsmanship in Colonial America." *JNH* 32 (1947): 417–429.

1458 Stokes, George. "Lumbering and Western Louisiana Cultural Landscapes." *AAG* 47 (1957): 250–266.

1459 "Tanner: Negro Painter." *Cur Lit* (October 1908).

1460 "Tanner—Story of Artist's Life." *World's Work* (June/July 1909).

1461 Taylor, Jerry. "They Call It the Black Diamond Railroad." *FF* 17, no. 2 (Summer 1983): 122–137.

1462 Not used.

1463 Not used.

1464 Torian, Sarah, ed. "Ante-Bellum and War Memories of Mrs. Telfair Hodgson." *GHQ* 27 (1943): 350–356.

1465 Towne, Laura M. "Pioneer Work on the Sea Islands." *So Work* 30 (1901): 396–401.

1466 Twining, Mary. "Harvesting and Heritage: A Comparison of Afro-American and African Basketry." *SFQ* 42 (1978): 159–174.

1467 Van Horn, Donald. "Carve Wood: The Vision of Jesse Aaron." *SFQ* 42 (1978): 257–270.

1468 Vermeer, Donald E. "Geophagy in a Mississippi County." *AAG* 65 (1975): 414–424.

1469 Vlach, John M. "The Fabrication of a Traditional Fire Tool." *JAFL* 86 (1973): 54–57.

1470 Vlach, John M. "Shotgun Houses." *Nat Hist* (February 1977): 51–57.

1471 Wahlman, Maude S. "Religious Symbols in Afro-American Folk Art." *NY Folkl* 12, no. 1–2 (1986): 1–24.

1472 West, Pamela. "The Rise and Fall of the American Porch." *Land* 20, no. 3 (1976): 42–47.

1473 Williams, W. T. B. "The Negro in Gloucester County, Virginia." *SW* 35 (1906): 103–106.

1474 Winkop, Aileen P. "The Crafting of Sea Island Baskets." *Nat An Rev* (September 1979): 28–31.

1475 Work, Monroe N. "The Negroes of Warsaw, Georgia." *SW* 37 (1908): 29–40.

5

Witchcraft, Superstitions, Voodoo, and Hoodoo

MONOGRAPHS

1476 Ashanti, Faheem C. *Rootwork and Voodoo in Mental Health*. Durham, NC: Tone Books, 1987. Bibliography on pp. 237–248.

1477 Avery, Myrta L. *Dixie After the War*. New York: Doubleday, Page, 1906.

1478 Bach, Marcus. *Inside Voodoo*. New York: New American Library, 1968.

1479 Bartlett, Napier. *Stories of the Crescent City*. New Orleans: n.p., 1869.

1480 Beard, James M. *K.K.K. Sketches, Humorous and Didactic*. Philadelphia: Claxton, Remsen, and Heffelfinger, 1877.

1481 Bell, Michael E. "Pattern, Structure, and Logic in Afro-American Hoodoo Performance." Ph.D. dissertation, Indiana University, 1980.

1482 Berry, Brewton. *You and Your Superstitions*. Columbia, MO: Lucas Bros., 1940.

1483 Bodin, Ron. *Voodoo: Past and Present*. Lafayette: Center for Louisiana Studies, University of Southwestern Louisiana, 1990. Bibliography on pp. 99–101.

1484 Brewer, J. Mason. *Dog Ghosts and Other Texas Negro Folktales*. Austin: University of Texas Press, 1958.

1485 Brown, Handy N. *Necromancer, or Voo-Doo Doctor*. New York: AMS Press, 1976.

1486 Buel, J. W. *Mysteries and Miseries of America's Great Cities*. San Francisco: A. L. Bancroft, 1883.

1487 Burton, Thomas G., and Ambrose N. Manning, eds. "A Collection of Folklore by Undergraduate Students of East Tennessee State University." Johnson City: East Tennessee State University Research Advisory Council, 1970.

1488 Cothran, Michael C. "Hoodoo: A Belief System Among Self-Identified Blacks in Tuscaloosa County.'' M.A. thesis, University of Alabama, 1980. Bibliography on lvs. 146–150.

1489 Courlander, Harold, and Rémy Bastien. *Religion and Politics in Haiti: Two Essays*. Washington, DC: Institute for Cross-Cultural Research, 1966. Bibliography on pp. 69–81.

1490 D'Argent, Jacques. *Voodoo*. Los Angeles: Sherbourne Press, 1970.

1491 Davis, Wade. *The Serpent and the Rainbow*. New York: Simon and Schuster, 1985. Bibliography on pp. 274–284.

1492 Denning, Melita, and Osbourne Phillips. *Voudon Fire: The Living Reality of Mystical Religion*. St. Paul, MN: Llewellyn, 1979.

1493 Deren, Maya. *Divine Horsemen: The Living Gods of Haiti*. 1953. Reprint, New Paltz, NY: McPherson, 1983. Bibliography on pp. 339–340.

1494 Dorson, Richard M. *Buying the Wind*. Chicago: University of Chicago Press, 1964.

1495 Gandolfo, Charles M. *Voodoo in South Louisiana*. New Orleans: New Orleans Historic Voodoo Museum, 1985.

1496 Gilford, Henry. *Voodoo, Its Origins and Practices*. New York: Watts, 1976. Bibliography on pp. 101–102.

1497 Gover, Robert. *Voodoo Contra*. York Beach, ME: S. Weiser, 1985.

1498 Hand, Wayland D. *Popular Beliefs and Superstitions from North Carolina*. Durham, NC: Duke University Press, 1964.

1499 Haskins, James. *Voodoo and Hoodoo: Their Tradition and Craft as Revealed by Actual Practitioners*. Bronx, NY: Original Pubs., 1988. Bibliography on pp. 219–220.

1500 Hurston, Zora Neale. *Tell My Horse*. Philadelphia: J. B. Lippincott, 1938.

1501 Hurston, Zora Neale. *Voodoo Gods: An Inquiry into Native Myths and Magic in Jamaica and Haiti*. London: J. M. Dent & Sons, 1939.

1502 Huxley, Francis. *The Invisibles: Voodoo Gods in Haiti*. New York: McGraw-Hill, 1966.

1503 Hyatt, Harry M. *Hoodoo, Conjuration, Witchcraft, Rootwork: Beliefs Accepted by Many Negroes and White Persons, These Being Orally Recorded Among Blacks and Whites. Hannibal*, MO: Western, 1970.

1504 Johnson, F. Roy. *Witches and Demons in History and Folklore*. Murfreesboro, NC: Johnson, 1969.

1505 Kennedy, Stetson. *Palmetto Country*. New York: Duell, Sloan, and Pearce, 1942.

1506 Kerboull, Jean. *Voodoo and Magic Practices*. London: Barris and Jenkins, 1978. Bibliography on pp. 191–192.

1507 Kristos, Kyle. *Voodoo*. Philadelphia: Lippincott, 1976. Bibliography on p. 108.

1508 Laguerre, Michel S. *Voodoo and Politics in Haiti*. New York: St. Martin's Press, 1989.

1509 Laguerre, Michel S. *Voodoo Heritage*. Beverly Hills, CA: Sage, 1980. Bibliography on pp. 219–223.

1510 Lavigne, Jeanne de. *Ghost Stories of Old New Orleans*. New York: Rinehart, 1946.

1511 Loederer, Richard A. *Voodoo Fire in Haiti*. Garden City, NY: Doubleday Doran, 1935.

1512 Mallisham, Ivy J. "Hoodoo: An Integration of Cultural Belief and Psychological Practice." Psy.D. dissertation, Hahnemann University, 1983. Bibliography on lvs. 70–73.

1513 Mars, Louis. *The Crisis of Possession in Voodoo*. n.p.: Reed & Cannon & Johnson, 1977. Bibliography on pp. 67–71.

1514 Martinez, Raymond J. *Mysterious Marie Laveau, Voodoo Queen: And Folk Tales Along the Mississippi*. Jefferson, LA: Hope, 1956. Bibliography on p. 96.

1515 Mayer, Charles F. *Hoodoo, Voodoo, and Bugaboo: Strange Superstitions, Curious Customs, and Freakish Folk-Lore*. Dallas: Century Feature Syndicate, 1939. Bibliography on pp. 87–96.

1516 Métraux, Alfred. *Voodoo*. London: Sphere Books, 1974. Bibliography on pp. 379–390.

1517 Mitchell, Henry. *Black Belief*. New York: Harper and Row, 1975.

1518 Montell, William L. *Ghosts Along the Cumberland: Deathlore in the Kentucky Foothills*. Knoxville: University of Tennessee Press, 1975.

1519 Ott, Bryan M. "Voodoo in New Orleans, 1990: Contemporary Beliefs and Ritual Practices." M.A. thesis, University of Wisconsin-Madison, 1991.

1520 Owen, Mary A. *Old Rabbit, the Voodoo, and Other Sorcerers*. London: T. F. Unwin, 1893.

1521 Pelton, Robert W. *The Complete Book of Voodoo*. New York: Putnam, 1972. Bibliography on pp. 247–254.

1522 Pelton, Robert W. *Voodoo Charms and Talismans*. New York: Drake, 1973. Bibliography on pp. 200–209.

1523 Pelton, Robert W. *Voodoo Secrets from A to Z*. South Brunswick, NJ: A. S. Barnes, 1973. Bibliography on pp. 127–138.

1524 Pelton, Robert W. *Voodoo Signs and Omens*. South Brunswick, NJ: A. S. Barnes, 1974. Bibliography on pp. 277–284.

1525 Rigaud, Milo. *Secrets of Voodoo*. New York: Arco, 1970.

1526 Saxon, Lyle. *Old Louisiana*. New Orleans: Robert L. Crager, 1950.

1527 Smith, Austine. *Haiti Is Waiting: The Story of One Woman's Encounter with Voodoo Practices and Her Oppression and Deliverance*. Tulsa, OK: Christian Pub. Ser., 1985.

1528 South Carolina Writers' Program. *South Carolina Folk Tales: Stories of Animals and Supernatural Beings*. Columbia: WPA, 1941.

1529 Tallant, Robert. *Voodoo in New Orleans*. New York: Macmillan, 1946. Bibliography on p. 248.

1530 Teagarden, J. B. Hollis. "Voodooism." M.A. thesis, University of Chicago, 1924. Bibliography on lvs. 50–51.

1531 Thomas, Daniel L., and Lucy B. Thomas. *Kentucky Superstitions*. Princeton, NJ: Princeton University Press, 1920.

1532 *Le Voodoo à la Nouvelle Orléans: Strolling Tour of Voodoo in the Vieux Carré*. New Orleans: Voodoo Museum, 1975.

1533 Williams, Joseph J. *Voodoos and Obeahs: Phases of West India Witchcraft*. New York: AMS Press, 1970. Bibliography on pp. 237–248.

ARTICLES

1534 Adams, George C. S. "Rattlesnake Eye." *SFQ* 2, no. 1 (1938): 37–39.

1535 Adams, Samuel C., Jr. "The Acculturation of the Delta Negro." *Social Forc* 26 (1947): 202–205.

1536 Adams, Samuel H. "Dr. Bug, Dr. Buzzard and the U.S.A." *True* (July 1949): 33, 69–71.

1537 Anderson, John Q. "The New Orleans Voodoo Ritual and Its Twentieth-century Survivals." *SFQ* 24 (June 1960): 135–143.

1538 Bacon, A. M., and Miss Herron. "Conjuring and Conjure-Doctors in the Southern United States." *JAFL* 9 (1896): 143–147, 224–226.

1539 Barkus, E. M. "Folktales from Georgia." *JAFL* 13 (1900): 19–32.

1540 Bass, Ruth. "The Little Man." *Scrib M* 97 (1935): 120–123.

1541 Bass, Ruth. "Mojo." *Scrib M* 87 (1930): 83–90.

1542 Bayard, Samuel P. "Witchcraft Magic and Spirits on the Border of Pennsylvania and West Virginia." *JAFL* 51 (1938): 47–59.

1543 "Beliefs of Southern Negroes Concerning Hags." *JAFL* 7 (January–March 1894): 66–67.

1544 Bergen, Fanny D. "Louisiana Ghost Story." *JAFL* 12 (1899): 146–147.

1545 Bergen, Fanny D. "On the Eastern Shore." *JAFL* 2 (1889): 295–300.

1546 Bolton, H. C. "Decoration of Graves of Negroes in South Carolina." *JAFL* 4 (1891): 2–4.

1547 Brandon, Elizabeth. "Superstitions in Vermillion Parish." *PTFS* 31 (1962): 108–118.

1548 Brown, Hugh S. "Voodooism in Northwest Louisiana." *LAFM* 2, no. 2 (1965): 74–86.

1549 Burman, Ben L. "Mississippi Roustabout." *Harper* 180 (1940): 635–643.

1550 Burt, W. C. "The Baptist Ox." *JAFL* 34 (1921): 397–398.

1551 Byers, James F. "Voodoo: Tropical Pharmacology or Psychosomatic Psychology?" *NYFQ* 26 (1970): 305–312.

1552 Cannon, W. B. "Voodoo Death." *AA* 44 (1942): 169–181.

1553 Chesnutt, Charles W. "Superstitions and Folklore of the South." *Mod C* 13 (1901): 231–235.

1554 Clayton, Edward. "The Truth About Voodoo." *Ebony* (April 1951): 54–61.

1555 Cobbs, Hamner. "Superstitions of the Black Belt." *Ar* 11 (1958): 55–65.

1556 Cocke, Ed. "Voodoo." *New Orleans Magazine* 4 (January 1970): 50–53.

1557 Cooley, Gilbert E. "Conversations About Hoodoo." *Ind Folk* 10, no. 2 (1977): 201–216.

1558 Cross, Tom P. "Folklore from the Southern States. *JAFL* 22 (1909): 251–255.

1559 Cross, Tom. P. "Folklore in North Carolina." *Stud Philol* 16 (1921): 217–287.

1560 Culin, S. "Concerning Negro Sorcery in the U.S." *JAFL* 3 (January–March 1890): 281–287.

1561 Not used.

1562 Dana, M. "Voodoo, Its Effect on the Negro Race." *MET M* 17 (1908): 529–538.

1563 Dance, Darryl. "In the Beginning: A New View of Black American Etiological Tales." *SFQ* 41 (1977): 53–64.

1564 "Divination with the Sifter and Crossing the Back." *JAFL* 5 (1892): 63–64.

1565 "*Don't* Superstitions and Birds of Ill Omen." *SW* 24, no. 28 (1899): 449–450.

1566 Dorson, Richard M. "Negro Witch Stories on Tape." *MF* 2 (1952): 229–241.

1567 Douglas, S. W. "Difficulties and Superstitions Encountered in Practice among Negroes." *South Med J* 19 (1926): 957–959.

1568 Duval, Margaret L. "Legends of Wilkinson County and the Surrounding Area." *LAFM* 3, no. 4 (1975 for 1973): 47–64.

1569 Ellis, A. B. "On Vodu Worship." *Pop Sci* 38 (March 1891): 651–663.

1570 Emmons, Martha. "Confidence from Old Nacogdoches." *PTFS* 7 (1928): 119–134.

1571 Emmons, Martha. "Dyin' Easy." *PTFS* 10 (1932): 55–61.

1572 Evans, David, Don S. Rice, and Joanne K. Partin. "Parallels in West African, West Indian and North Carolina Folklore." *NCF* 17, no. 2 (1969): 77–84.

1573 Evans, J. H. "Superstitions About Animals and Weather-lore." *SW* 25 (1896): 15–16.

1574 Firmin, Gloria. "Some Magical Practices Among New Orleans Blacks." *LAFM* 3, no. 4 (1975 for 1973): 42–46.

1575 Fitchett, E. Horace. "Superstitions in South Carolina." *Crisis* 43 (1936): 360–361, 370.

1576 Fortier, Alcée. "Customs and Superstitions in Louisiana." *JAFL* 1 (1888): 136–140.

1577 Gibbs, Samuel, Jr. "Voodoo Practices in Modern New Orleans." *LAFM* 3, no. 2 (1971): 12–14.

1578 Gittings, Victoria. "What William Saw." *JAFL* 58 (1945): 135–137.

1579 Gorn, Elliot J. "Black Spirits: The Ghostlore of Afro-American Slaves." *AM Q* 36, no. 4 (Fall 1984): 549–565.

1580 Granberry, Edwin. "Black Jupiter: A Voodoo King in Florida's Jungle." *Trav* 58, no. 6 (1932): 32–35, 54.

1581 Hall, Julian A. "Negro Conjuring and Tricking." *JAFL* 10 (1897): 241–243.

1582 Handy, Sarah M. "Negro Superstitions." *Lippinc* 48 (1891): 735–739.

1583 Haskell, Joseph H. "Sacrificial Offerings Among North Carolina Negroes." *JAFL* 4 (1891): 267–269.

1584 Hauptmann, O. H. "Spanish Folklore from Tampa, Florida: Superstitions." *SFQ* 2 (1938): 11–30.

1585 Hauptmann, O. H. "Spanish Folklore from Tampa, Florida: Witchcraft." *SFQ* 3 (1939): 197–200.

1586 Hawkins, John. "Magical Medical Practice in South Carolina." *Pop Sci* 70 (1907): 165–174.

1587 Hendricks, George D. "Voodoo Powder." *WF* 17 (1958): 132.

1588 Howell, W. W. "Reports of Voodoo Worship in Haiti and Louisiana." *JAFL* 2 (1889): 41–47.

1589 Hurston, Zora Neale. "Hoodoo in America." *JAFL* 44, no. 174 (October–December 1931): 318–417.

1590 "An Interview with a Hoodoo Curer." *LAFM* 3 no. 2 (1971): 44–47.

1591 Kane, Harnett P. "Reception by the Dead (Negro)." *JAFL* 5 (1892): 148.

1592 Kennedy, Louise. "Voodoo and Vodum." *JAFL* 3 (January–March 1890): 241.

1593 Lake, Mary D. "Superstitions About Cotton." *PTFS* 9 (1931): 145–152.

1594 Lee, F. W. "Christmas in Virginia Before the War." *SW* 37 (1908): 686–689.

1595 Lee, F. W. "Harvest Time in Old Virginia." *SW* 37 (1908): 566–567.

1596 "Louisiana Negro Superstitions." *JAFL* 18 (1905): 229–230.

1597 McCall, George J. "Symbiosis: The Case of Hoodoo and the Numbers Racket." *Soc Prob* 10 (1963): 361–371.

1598 McGlasson, Cleo. "Superstitions and Folk Beliefs of Overton County." *TFSB* 7 (1941): 13–27.

1599 Minor, M. W. "How to Keep Off Witches." *JAFL* 11 (1898): 176.

1600 Moore, R. "Superstitions from Georgia." *JAFL* 7 (April–June 1894): 305–306. (Supp).

1601 Moore, R. "Superstitions in Georgia." *JAFL* 5 (January–March 1892): 230–231.

1602 Not used.

1603 Moore, Ruby A. "Superstitions of Georgia." *JAFL* 9 (1896): 226–228.

1604 Mullon, Patrick. "The Function of Folk Belief Among Negro Fishermen of the Texas Coast." *SFQ* 33 (1969): 80–91.

1605 "Negro Superstitions Concerning the Violin." *JAFL* 5 (Jan.–March 1892): 329–330. (Supp.)

1606 "Negro Superstitions in South Carolina." *JAFL* 8 (1895): 251–252.

1607 "New Orleans Voodoo." *WF* 16 (1957): 60–61.

1608 Norris, Thaddeus. "Negro Superstitions." *Lippinc* 6 (July 1870): 90–95.

1609 Owens, William A. "Seer of Corsicana." *PTFS* 29 (1959): 14–31.

1610 Pendleton, Lewis. "Negro Folklore and Witchcraft in the South." *JAFL* 3 (1890): 201–207.

1611 Pitman, F. W. "Fetishism, Witchcraft, and Christianity Among the Slaves." *JNH* 11 (October 1926): 650–668.

1612 Post, Lauren C. "A Recollection of the Bleeding of Our Sick Mare by a 'Voodoo Doctor.' " *LAFM* 3, no. 5 (1975): 6–8.

1613 Price, Sadie F. "Kentucky Folklore." *JAFL* 14 (1901): 30–38.

1614 P. S. M. "Voodooism in Tennessee." *Atl* 64 (1889): 376–380; 75 (1895): 136–144, 714–720.

1615 Richardson, Clement. "Some Slave Superstitions." *SW* 41 (1912): 246–248.

1616 Roberts, Hilda. "Louisiana Superstitions." *JAFL* 40 (1927): 144–208.

1617 Royal, Aylett. "I's Sho' Nuff Lucky." *PTSF* 13 (1937): 137–145.

1618 Not used.

1619 Showers, Susan. "Snakes and Conjure Doctors." *SW* 27 (1898): 37.

1620 Snow, Loudell F. " 'I Was Born Just Exactly with the Gift': An Interview with a Voodoo Practitioner." *JAFL* 86 (1973): 272–281.

1621 "Sol Lockhart's Call (Negro Superstitions, Georgia)." *JAFL* 13 (1900): 67–70.

1622 Steagall, Archie. "The Voodoo Man of the Brazos (The Witchcraft Exploits of Negro Moe Green of Wharton)." *TFSB* 17 (1941): 113–114.

1623 Steiner, Roland. "Braziel Robinson Possessed of Two Spirits." *JAFL* 13 (1900): 226–228.

1624 Steiner, Roland. "Negro Conjuring." *Cur Lit* 32 (1902): 568–569.

1625 Steiner, Roland. "Observations on the Practice of Conjuring in Georgia." *JAFL* 14 (1901): 173–180.

1626 Steiner, Roland. "Superstitions and Beliefs from Central Georgia." *JAFL* 12 (1899): 261–271.

1627 "Superstitions of Negroes in New Orleans." *JAFL* 5 (1892): 330–332.

1628 Tartt, Ruby P. "Carrie Dyke's Midwife." *TFSB* 19 (1944): 21–28.

1629 Touchstone, Blake. "Voodoo in New Orleans." *LHQ* 13 (1972): 371–386.

1630 Waring, M. A. "Mortuary Customs and Beliefs of South Carolina Negroes." *JAFL* 7 (1894): 318–319.

1631 Waring, M. A. "Superstitions from South Carolina." *JAFL* 8 (1895): 251–252.

1632 Webb, Julie Y. "Louisiana Voodoo and Superstitions Related to Health." *Hea Se Me Hea Rep* 86, no. 4 (1971): 291–301.

1633 Williamson, George. "Superstitions from Louisiana." *JAFL* 18 (1905): 229–230.

1634 Wiltse, Henry M. "A Hoodoo Charm." *JAFL* 13 (1900): 212.

1635 Wolf, John Q. "Tales and Superstitions." *TFSB* 32 (1966): 56–57.

1636 Woodall, N. F. "Old Signs in Alabama." *JAFL* 43 (1930): 325–326.

6

Myths, Tales, and Customs

MONOGRAPHS

1637 Abrahams, Roger D. *Afro-American Folktales: Stories from Black Traditions in the New World*. New York: Pantheon Books, 1985.

1638 Abrahams, Roger D. *Jump-Rope Rhymes, a Dictionary*. Austin: University of Texas Press for the American Folklore Society, 1969.

1639 Abrahams, Roger D. *Talking Black*. Rowley, MA: Newbury House, 1976. Bibliography on pp. 93–98.

1640 Adams, Edward C. L. *Congaree Sketches. Scenes from Negro Life in the Swamps of the Congaree and Tales by Tad and Scip of Heaven and Hell with Other Miscellany*. Chapel Hill: University of North Carolina Press, 1927.

1641 Allen, Harriette B., ed. *Juba's Folk Games: A Collection of Afro-American Children's Games*. Nashville, TN: Juba, 1976.

1642 Aswell, James R. *God Bless the Devil! Liar's Bench Tales*. Knoxville: University of Tennessee Press, 1985.

1643 Bagley, Julian. *Candle-lighting Time in Bodidalee*. New York: American Heritage Press, 1971.

1644 Ballowe, Hewitt L. *Creole Folk Tales*. Baton Rouge: Louisiana State University Press, 1948.

1645 Ballowe, Hewitt L. *The Lawd Sayin' the Same: Negro Folk Tales of the Creole Country*. Baton Rouge: Louisiana State University Press, 1947.

1646 Bennett, John. *The Doctor to the Dead: Grotesque Legends and Folk-Tales of Old Charleston*. New York: Rinehart, 1946.

1647 Bennett, John. *Madam Margot: A Grotesque Legend of Old Charleston*. New York: Century, 1921.

1648   Berry, Pike. *Birthed into Glory*. Boston: Christopher, 1966.

1649   Bolick, Julian Stevenson. *Georgetown Ghosts*. Clinton, SC: Jacobs, 1956.

1650   Botkin, B. A., ed. *The American People in Their Stories, Legends, Tall Tales, Traditions, Ballads and Songs*. London: Pilot Press, 1946.

1651   Boyle, Virginia F. *Devil Tales*. New York and London: Harper, 1900.

1652   Brady, Margaret K. "Gonna Shimmy 'til the Sun Goes Down: Aspects of Verbal and Nonverbal Socialization in the Play of Black Girls." In *Folklore Annual of the University Folklore Association*, no. 6. Austin: University of Texas Press, 1974.

1653   Brewer, John M. *Aunt Dicey Tales; Snuff-dipping Tales of the Texas Negro*. Austin: University of Texas Press, 1956.

1654   Brewer, John M. *Dog Ghosts, and Other Texas Negro Folk Tales; The Word on the Brazos: Negro Preacher Tales from the Brazos Bottoms of Texas*. Austin: University of Texas Press, 1976.

1655   Brewer, John M. *Humorous Folk Tales of the South Carolina Negro*. Ann Arbor, MI: University Microfilms, 1976.

1656   Brookes, Stella Brewer. *Joel Chandler Harris—Folklorist*. Athens: University of Georgia Press, 1950.

1657   Brown, Carolyn S. *The Tall Tale in American Folklore and Literature*. Knoxville: University of Tennessee Press, 1987.

1658   Browne, Ray B. *Popular Beliefs and Practices from Alabama*. Los Angeles and Berkeley: University of California Publications, Folklore Studies, no. 9, 1958. Bibliography on pp. 262–271.

1659   *Bundle of Troubles, and Other Tarheel Tales by Workers of the Writer's Program of the Work Projects Administration in the State of North Carolina*. Durham: Duke University Press, 1943.

1660   Burton, Robert W. *De Remnant Truth: The Tales of Jake Mitchell and Robert Wilton Burton*. Tuscaloosa: University of Alabama Press, 1991.

1661   Campbell, Marie. *Folks Do Get Born*. New York: Rinehart, 1946.

1662   Carmer, Carl L. *The Hurricane's Children*. New York: D. McKay, 1967.

1663   Cobb, Lucy M., and Mary A. Hicks. *Animal Tales from the Old North State*. New York: E. P. Dutton, 1938.

1664   Cocke, Sarah. *Bypaths in Dixie: Folktales of the South*. New York: Gordon Press, 1976.

1665   Cocke, Sarah. *Old Mammy Tales from Dixie Land*. New York: E. P. Dutton, 1926.

1666   Cohn, David Lewis. *God Shakes Creation*. New York: Harper & Bros., 1935.

1667   Cothram, Jean, ed. *The Whang Doodle: Folk Tales from the Carolinas*. Orangeburg, SC: Sandlapper, 1987.

1668   Courlander, Harold. *Terrapin's Pot of Sense*. New York: Henry Holt, 1957.

1669   Dance, D. C. *Shuckin' and Jivin': Folklore from Contemporary Black Americans*. Bloomington: Indiana University Press, 1978.

1670   Dorson, Richard M., *American Negro Folktales*. Greenwich, CT: Fawcett, 1967.

1671 Dorson, Richard M. *Negro Tales*. Berkeley: University of California Press, 1954.

1672 Dorson, Richard M., ed. *Negro Folktales from Pine Bluff, Arkansas, and Calvin, Michigan*. Indiana University Folklore Series, no. 23. Bloomington, 1958.

1673 Duncan, Eula G. *Big Road Walker*. New York: Fred A. Stokes, 1940.

1674 Douglas, S. *The King of the Black Art & Other Folktales*. Aberdeen: Aberdeen University Press, 1987.

1675 Emmons, Martha. *Deep like the Rivers, Stories of My Negro Friends*. Austin, TX: Encino, 1969.

1676 Emrich, Duncan. *The Folklore of Love and Courtship*. New York: American Heritage Press, 1970.

1677 Fishburne, Ann Sinkler. *Belvidere: A Plantation Memory*. Columbia, SC: University of South Carolina Press, 1949.

1678 Gaudet, Marcia G. *Tales from the Levee: The Folklore of St. John the Baptist Parish*. Lafayette: Center for Louisiana Studies, University of Southwestern Louisiana, 1984.

1679 Goldstein, Kenneth S., and Dan Ben-Amos, eds. *Thrice Told Tales*. Lock Haven, PA: Hammerhill, 1970.

1680 Gonzales, Ambrose E. *The Black Border: Gullah Stories of the Carolina Coast*. Columbia, SC: State, 1922. Reprint, Spartanburg, SC: Reprint Co., 1991.

1681 Gonzales, Ambrose E. *The Captain: Stories of the Black Border*. Columbia, SC: State, 1924. Reprint, New York: Negro Universities Press, 1972.

1682 Gonzales, Ambrose E. *Laguerre: A Gascon of the Black Border*. Freeport, NY: Books for Libraries Press, 1924.

1683 Gonzales, Ambrose E. *Two Gullah Tales: "The Turkey Hunter" and "At the Crossroads."* New York: Purdy Press, 1926.

1684 Gonzales, Ambrose E. *With Aesop Along the Black Border*. Columbia, SC: State, 1924. Reprint, New York: Negro Universities Press, 1969.

1685 Green, Paul. *Home to My Valley*. Chapel Hill: University of North Carolina Press, 1970.

1686 Hamilton, James. *An Account of the Late Intended Insurrection Among the Portions of the Blacks of This City*. Charleston, SC: A. E. Miller, 1822.

1687 Harris, Joel Chandler. *Aaron in the Wildwoods*. Boston: Houghton Mifflin, 1897.

1688 Harris, Joel Chandler. *Balaam and His Master, and Other Sketches and Stories*. Boston: Houghton Mifflin, 1891.

1689 Harris, Joel Chandler. *The Bishop and the Boogerman*. New York: Doubleday, Page, 1909.

1690 Harris, Joel Chandler. *The Chronicles of Aunt Minervy Ann*. New York: Scribner's, 1899.

1691 Harris, Joel Chandler. *Daddy Jake the Runaway*. New York: Century, 1889.

1692 Harris, Joel Chandler. *Free Joe and Other Georgian Sketches*. New York: Collier, 1887.

1693   Harris, Joel Chandler. *Little Mr. Thimblefinger and His Queer Country: What the Children Saw and Heard There*. Boston: Houghton Mifflin, 1894.

1694   Harris, Joel Chandler. *The Making of a Statesman*. New York: McClure, Phillips, 1902.

1695   Harris, Joel Chandler. *Mingo, and Other Sketches in Black and White*. Boston and New York: Houghton Mifflin, 1884.

1696   Harris, Joel Chandler. *Mr. Rabbit At Home*. Boston and New York: Houghton Mifflin, 1895.

1697   Harris, Joel Chandler. *Nights with Uncle Remus*. Boston: Houghton Mifflin, 1883.

1698   Harris, Joel Chandler. *On the Plantation*. New York: Appleton, 1892.

1699   Harris, Joel Chandler. *Plantation Pageants*. Boston: Houghton Mifflin, 1899.

1700   Harris, Joel Chandler. *Seven Tales of Uncle Remus*. Ed. Thomas H. English. Atlanta, GA: Emory University Sources and Reprints, 1948.

1701   Harris, Joel Chandler. *Stories of Georgia*. New York: American Book, 1896.

1702   Harris, Joel Chandler. *Tales from Uncle Remus*. New York: Houghton Mifflin, 1881.

1703   Harris, Joel Chandler. *The Tar-Baby and Other Rhymes by Uncle Remus*. New York: Appleton, 1904.

1704   Harris, Joel Chandler. *Told by Uncle Remus. New Stories of the Old Plantation*. New York: McClure, Phillips, 1905.

1705   Harris, Joel Chandler. *Uncle Remus and Brer Rabbit*. New York: Frederick A. Stokes, 1907.

1706   Harris, Joel Chandler. *Uncle Remus and His Friends: Old Plantation Stories, Songs and Ballads, with Sketches of Negro Character*. Boston: Houghton Mifflin, 1892.

1707   Harris, Joel Chandler. *Uncle Remus and the Little Boy*. Boston: Small, Maynard, 1910.

1708   Harris, Joel Chandler. *Uncle Remus, His Songs and His Sayings*. New York: D. Appleton, 1880.

1709   Harris, Joel Chandler. *Uncle Remus Returns*. Boston: Houghton Mifflin, 1918.

1710   Harris, Joel Chandler. *The Witch Wolf; An Uncle Remus Story*. Cambridge, MA: Bacon & Brown, 1921.

1711   Hendricks, W. C. *Bundle of Troubles and Other Tarheel Tales*. Durham: Duke University Press, 1943.

1712   Hessy, Anne. *Giant Treasury of Brer Rabbit*. New York: Derrydale Books, 1991.

1713   Hewitt, Leonard Ballowe. *The Lawd Sayin' the Same*. Negro Folk Tales of the Creole Country. Baton Rouge: Louisiana State University Press, 1947.

1714   Heyward, J. *Brown Jackets*. Columbia, SC: State Co., 1925.

1715   Heyward, J. S. *Brown Jackets*. Columbia, SC: State Co., 1923.

1716   Higgins, W. H. "Juneteenth: Afro-American Customs of the Emancipation." In

The Old Tradition Way of Life: Essays in Honor of Warren E. Roberts, ed. Robert E Wells. Bloomington: Indiana University Folklore Institute, 1989, 146–158.

1717   Hobson, A. *In Old Alabama; Being the Chronic of Miss Mouse, the Little Black Merchant*. New York: Doubleday, Page, 1903.

1718   Hobson, Arthur Palmer. *Humor of the Old Deep South*. New York: Macmillan, 1936.

1719   Jones, Bessie, and Bess Lomax Hawes. *Step It Down: Games, Plays, Songs, and Stories from the Afro-American Heritage*. New York: Harper and Row, 1972.

1720   Jones, Charles Colcock. *Negro Myths from the Georgia Coast Told in the Vernacular*. Boston: Houghton Mifflin Co., 1888. Reprint, 1925.

1721   Kane, Harnett T. *The Southern Christmas Book*. New York: David McKay, 1958.

1722   Lavigne, Jeanne de. *Ghost Stories of Old New Orleans*. Illus. by Charles Richards. New York: Rinehart, 1946.

1723   Lee, F. H., ed. *Folk Tales of All Nations*. New York: Tudor, 1946.

1724   Leiding, Harriette K. *Street Cries of an Old Southern City*. Charleston, SC: Dagget Printing, 1910.

1725   Lester, Julius. *Black Folktales*. New York: Grove Weidenfeld, 1991.

1726   Lewis, George. *Impressions of America and the American Churches from Journal of the Rev. G. Lewis*. Edinburgh: W. P. Kennedy, 1845.

1727   Lyons, Mary E. *Raw Head, Blood Bones: African American Tales of the Supernatural*. New York: Scribner's, 1991.

1728   Martin, Margaret Rhett. *Charleston Ghosts*. Columbia SC: University of South Carolina Press, 1963.

1729   McBryde, John McLaren. *Brer Rabbit in the Folk-Tales of the Negro and Other Races*. Sewanee TN: University Press at the University of the South, 1911.

1730   McDowell, Katherine Sherwood Bonner. *Dialect Tales*. New York: Harper & Bros., 1883.

1731   McDowell, Katherine Sherwood Bonner. *Swannee River Tales*. Boston: Roberts Brothers, 1884.

1732   Meine, Franklin J. *Tall Tales of the Southwest*. New York: Knopf, 1930.

1733   Merrick, George Byron. *Old Times on the Upper Mississippi*. Cleveland: Arthur H. Clark, 1909.

1734   Montell, William Lynwood. "Supernatural Tales Collected from Negroes and Whites in Monroe and Cumberland Counties, Kentucky." M.A. thesis, Indiana University, 1963.

1735   Odum, Howard W. *Cold Blue Moon, Black Ulysses Afar Off*. Indianapolis: Bobbs-Merrill, 1931.

1736   Osofsky, Gilbert, ed. *Puttin' On Ole Massa: The Slave Narratives of Henry Bibb, William Wells Brown, and Solomon Northup*. New York: Harper & Row, 1969.

1737   Owen, Mary A. *Voodoo Tales: As Told Among the Negroes of the Southwest*. New York: G. P. Putnam's Sons, 1893.

1738 Parsons, E. D. *Folk Tales of the Sea Islands, South Carolina*. Philadelphia: American Folklore Society, 1923.

1739 Plumpp, Sterling. *Black Rituals*. Chicago: Third World Press, 1972.

1740 Raper, Arthur F. *Preface to Peasantry: A Tale of Two Black Belt Counties*. Chapel Hill: University of North Carolina Press, 1936.

1741 Raum, Green. *The Existing Conflict Between Republican Government and Southern Oligarchy*. Washington, DC, 1884. Reprint, New York: Negro Universities Press, 1969.

1742 Rees, Ennis. *Brer Rabbit and His Tricks*. Birmingham, AL: Hopscotch Books, 1988.

1743 Robb, Bernard. *Welcum Hinges*. New York: Dutton, 1942.

1744 Roberts, John. *From Trickster to Badman: The Black Folk Hero in Slavery and Freedom*. Philadelphia: University of Pennsylvania Press, 1989. Bibliography on pp. 223–229.

1745 Sanfield, Steve. *The Adventures of High John the Conqueror*. New York: Orchard Books, 1989. Bibliography on pp. 109–113.

1746 Saxon, Lyle, Edward Dreyer, and Robert Tallant. *Gumbo-Ya-Ya: A Collection of Folk Tales*. Boston: Houghton Mifflin, 1945.

1747 Scott, F. *That Passing Laughter: Stories of the Southland*. Birmingham: Southern University Press, 1968.

1748 Short, Sam. *Tis So: Negro Folk Tales*. Baton Rouge: Claiors, 1972.

1749 Simms, W. G. *Guy Rivers, the Outlaw: A Tale of Georgia*. London: J. Clements, 1841.

1750 Simms, W. G. *Guy Rivers: A Tale of Georgia*. New York: Redfield, 1855.

1751 Simms, W. G. *Mellichampe*. 2 vols. New York: Harper & Bros., 1836.

1752 Simms, W. G. *The Sword and the Distaff, or 'Fair, Fat, and Forty': A Story of the South, at the Close of the Revolution*. Philadelphia: Lippincott, Grambo, 1853.

1753 Smith, Reed. *Gullah*. Columbia: University of South Carolina Bulletin 190, 1926.

1754 *South Carolina Folk Tales*. Columbia: Bulletin of the University of South Carolina, 1940.

1755 Sterling, Philip. *Laughing on the Outside: The Intelligent White Reader's Guide to Negro Tales and Humor*. New York: Grosset and Dunlap, 1965.

1756 Stoddard, Albert H. *Buh Partridge Outhides Buh Rabbit*. Savannah: The Author, 1939.

1757 Stoddard, Albert H. *Gullah Tales and Anecdotes of the South Carolina Sea Islands*. Savannah: The Author, 1940.

1758 Stoddard, Albert H. *How Buh Wasp Got His Small Waist*. Savannah: The Author, 1941.

1759 Stoney, S. G. *Black Genesis: A Chronicle*. New York: Macmillan, 1930.

1760 Strecker, John Kern. *Folk-lore Relating to Texas Birds*. Austin, TX: n.p., 1928.

1761 Turner, F. W. *Badmen, Black and White: The Continuity of American Folk Traditions.* Ph.D. dissertation, University of Pennsylvania, 1965.

1762 Whiting, Helen A. *Negro Folk Tales.* Washington, DC: Associated, 1967.

1763 Whitney, Annie Weston, and Caroline Canfield Bullock. *Folklore from Maryland.* Memoirs of the American Folklore Society, vol. 18. New York: American Folklore Society, 1925.

1764 Wiggins, Robert Lemuel. *The Life of Joel Chandler Harris.* Nashville, TN: M. E. Church Publishing House, 1918.

1765 Windham, K. T. *Alabama: One Big Front Porch.* Tuscaloosa: University of Alabama Press, 1991.

1766 *A Woman Rice Planter.* New York: Macmillan, 1913.

1767 Writer's Program. *South Carolina Folk Tales: Stories of Animals and Supernatural Beings.* Philadelphia: R. West, 1977.

1768 Young, Martha. *Plantation Bird Legends and Uncle Remus Stories.* New York: D. Appleton, 1916.

ARTICLES

1769 Adams, George C. S. "Rattlesnake Eye." *SFQ* 2 (1938): 37–38.

1770 "Alabama Folklore." *SW* 32 (1904): 49–52.

1771 Andrews, W. D. "Negro Folk Games." *Play* 21 (June 1923): 132–134.

1772 Asbell, Bernard. "A Man Ain't Nothin' but a Man." *American Heritage* 14 (1963): 34–37, 98.

1773 Backus, Emma M. "Animal Tales from North Carolina." *JAFL* 11 (1898): 284–292.

1774 Backus, Emma M. "Folk-Tales from Georgia." *JAFL* 13 (1900): 19–32.

1775 Backus, Emma M. "Negro Ghost Stories." *JAFL* 9 (1896): 228–230.

1776 Backus, Emma M. "Negro Tales from Georgia." *JAFL* 25 (1912): 125–136.

1777 Backus, Emma M. "Tales of the Rabbit from Georgia Negroes." *JAFL* 12 (1899): 108–115.

1778 Bacon, Alice Mabel, and Elsie Clews Parsons. "Folk-Lore from Elizabeth City Country, Virginia." *JAFL* 35 (1922): 250–327.

1779 Ballard, Lou Ellen. "Folktales of Southeast Alabama: An Original Collection." *LAFM* 2 (January 1961): 50–68.

1780 Ballard, Lou Ellen. "Some Tales of Local Color from Southeast Alabama." *SFQ* 24 (1960): 147–156.

1781 Banks, Frank D. "Old Time Courtship." *SW* 24 (January 1895): 14.

1782 Barker, Danny. "A Memory of King Bolden." *ER*, no. 37 (September 1965): 66–74.

1783 Barnette, V. G., and C. H. Herbert. "Why the Dog Cannot Talk and Why the Rabbit Has a Short Tail." *SW* 27 (1898): 36–37.

1784   Bastin, Bruce. "The Devil's Goin to Get You." *NCF* 21 (1973): 189–194.

1785   "Beliefs and Customs Connected with Death and Burial." *SW* 26 (1897): 18–19.

1786   "Beliefs of Southern Negroes Concerning Hags." *JAFL* 7 (1894): 66–67.

1787   Bennett, John. "Charleston Folk-Tales." *Negro D* 1 (September 1943): 33–36.

1788   Bolden, T. G. "Brer Rabbit's Box." *SW* 28 (January 1899): 25.

1789   Bolton, H. Carrington. "Decoration of Graves of Negroes in South Carolina." *JAFL* 4 (1891): 214.

1790   "Brer Rabbit Outdone." *SW* 25 (March 1896): 62.

1791   Not used.

1792   Brown, W. Norman. "Hindu Stories in American Negro Folklore." *Asia* 21 (1921): 703–707.

1793   Brunner, Theodore B. "Thirteen Tales from Houston County." *PTFS*, no. 31 (1962): 8–22.

1794   Burt, Mrs. W. C. "The Baptist Ox." *JAFL* 34 (1921): 397–398.

1795   Caldwell, Joan. "Christmas in Old Natchez." *JNH* 21 (1959): 257–270.

1796   Cameron, Rebecca. "Christmas at Buchoi, a North Carolina Rice Plantation." *North Carolina Booklet* 13 (July 1913): 3, 8–10. (Originally published in the *Ladies Home Journal* in 1891.)

1797   "The Ceremony of the 'Foot Wash' in Virginia." *SW* 25 (1896): 82.

1798   Chamberlain, Alexander F. "Negro Creation Legend." *JAFL* 3 (1890): 302.

1799   Cimino, Miriam Pope. "Muscadines for Pink Dorsets." *Scrib M* 91 (1932): 361–365.

1800   Clark, Joseph D. "North Carolina Popular Beliefs and Superstitions." *NCF* 18, no. 1 (1970): 1–68.

1801   Claudel, Calvin. "Creole Folk Tales." *SLM* 4 (1942): 7–13.

1802   Claudel, Calvin. "Four Tales from the French Folklore of Louisiana." *SFQ* 9 (December 1945): 191–208.

1803   Claudel, Calvin. "Louisiana Tales of Jean Sot and Boqui and Lapin." *SFQ* 8 (1944): 287–299.

1804   Claudel, Calvin. "Three Tales from the French Folklore of Louisiana." *JAFL* 56 (January 1943): 38–44.

1805   Cohen, H. "A Negro Folk Game in Colonial South Carolina." *SFQ* 16 (1952): 183–185.

1806   Colmant, B. "Four Preacher Tales from West Central Georgia." *TFSB* 42 (1976): 125–128.

1807   Comeaux, E. "Let the Cat Die." *LAFM* 5 (1981): 1–18.

1808   "Courtship in Old Virginia." *SW* 25 (February 1896): 38.

1809   Cross, Paulette. "Jokes and Black Consciousness." *FForum* 2 (1969): 140–161.

1810   "Customs of Slave Days." *SW* 26 (August 1897): 163.

1811   Dale, William. "Lore from Harkers Island." *NCF* 20 (1972): 139–144.

1812   Dauner, Louise. "Myth and Humor in the Uncle Remus Tales." *Am Lit* 20 (1948): 129–143.

1813   "Death and Burial Customs." *SW* 26 (January 1897): 18.

1814   Dickens, Dorothy, and Robert N. Ford. "Geophagy (Dirt-Eating) Among Mississippi Negro School Children." *American Sociological Review* 7 (1942): 59–65.

1815   Dixwell, John. "Mourning Customs of Negroes." *JAFL* 21 (1908): 365.

1816   Doar, David. "Negro Proverbs." *Charleston Museum Quarterly* 2 (1932): 23–24.

1817   Dobie, Bertha McKee. "The Death Bell of the Brazos." *PTFS*, no. 3 (1924): 141–142.

1818   Dobie, Bertha McKee. "The Ghost of Lake Jackson." *PTFS*, no. 7 (1928): 135–136.

1819   Dobie, Bertha McKee. "How Dollars Turned into Bumble Bees and Other Legends." *TFSB* 3 (1924): 52–56.

1820   "Dog and Rabbit." *SW* 27 (February 1898): 36.

1821   Dorson, Richard M. "Negro Tales from Bolivar County, Mississippi." *SFQ* 19 (1955): 104–116.

1822   Dorson, Richard. "Negro Tales of Mary Richardson." *MF* 6 (1956): 1–26.

1823   Eddins, A. W. "Brazos Bottom Philosophy." *PTFS*, no. 2 (1923): 50–51.

1824   Eddins, A. W. "Brazos Bottom Philosophy." *PTFS*, no. 9 (1931): 153–164.

1825   Eddins, A. W. "From the Brazos Bottom." *PTFS*, no. 26 (1954): 50–55.

1826   Eddins, A. W. " 'How Sandy Got His Meat'—A Negro Tale from the Brazos Bottom." *PTFS* no. 1 (1916): 47–49.

1827   Emmons, Martha. "Walk Around My Bedside." *PTFS*, no. 13 (1937): 130–136.

1828   Fauset, Arthur Huff. "Negro Folk Tales from the South (Alabama, Mississippi, Louisiana)." *JAFL* 40 (1927): 213–303.

1829   Fawcett, Bill. "How Slaves Were Named." *KFR* 22 (1976): 100.

1830   Ferris, William R., Jr. "Black Folktales from Rose Hill." *Miss FR* 7 (1973): 70–85.

1831   Figh, M. G. "Some Alabama Folktales." *Ala R* 16 (1963): 270–278.

1832   "Fish Stories." *SW* 26 (November 1897): 229.

1833   Flagg, Charles. T. "The Fool Hunter . . ." *SW* 28 (June 1899): 230.

1834   "Folk-Lore and Ethnology." *SW* 25 (1896): 38–39.

1835   "Folk-Lore and Ethnology." *SW* 26 (1897): 122–123, 163

1836   "Folk-Lore and Ethnology." *SW* 28 (1899): 32–33, 314–315.

1837   "Folk-Lore from St. Helena, South Carolina." *JAFL* 38 (April–June 1925): 217–238.

1838   "Folktales from Students in the Georgia State College." *JAFL* 32 (1919): 402–405.

1839   "Folk-Tales from Students in Tuskegee Institute, Alabama." *JAFL* 32 (July–September 1919): 397–401.

1840   "The Fool Hunter." *SW* 28 (1899): 230–232.

1841   "Foot Washing in Virginia." *SW* 25 (April 1896): 82.

1842   Fortier, Alcée. "Four Louisiana Folktales." *JAFL* 19 (1906): 123–126.

1843   Fortier, Alcée. "Louisiana Nursery Tales." *JAFL* 1 (1888): 140–145.

1844   Fortier, Alcée. "Louisiana Nursery Tales, II." *JAFL* 2 (1889): 36–40.

1845   Fowke, Gerard. "Brer Rabbit and Brer Fox: How Brer Rabbit Was Allowed to Choose His Death." *JAFL* 1 (1888): 148–149.

1846   "A Ghost Story." *SW* 27 (June 1898): 125.

1847   " 'A Ghost Story' and 'Story of a Fox and a Pig.' " *SW* 27 (1898): 124–125.

1848   "Gombo, the Creole Dialect of Louisiana." *Proceedings of the American Antiquities Society* (1935): 101–142.

1849   Not used.

1850   "Goose and Drake." *SW* 27 (April 1898): 76.

1851   Green, Paul. "Words and Ways: Stories and Incidents from My Cape Fear Valley Folklore Collection." *NCF* 16, no. 4 (1968): 1–148.

1852   "Hags and Their Ways." *SW* (February 1894): 26.

1853   Halpert, Herbert. "The Cante Fable in Decay." *SFQ* 5 (1941): 191–200.

1854   Harris, Joel Chandler. "The Sea Island Hurricanes." *Scrib M* 15 (1894): 229–247, 267–284.

1855   Hedin, Raymond. "Uncle Remus: Puttin' on Ole Massa's Son." *SLJ* 15, no. 1 (Fall 1982): 83–90.

1856   Hendrix, W. S. "The Hell Hounds." *PTFS*, no. 1 (1916): 75–77.

1857   Herron, Leonora. "Conjuring and Conjure Doctors." *SW* 24 (July 1895): 117.

1858   Hubbard, Dolan. "The Black Preacher Tale as Cultural Biography." *CLA* 30 (March 1987): 328–342.

1859   Hudson, Arthur Palmer. "Some Folk Riddles from the South." *SAQ* 42 (1943): 78–93.

1860   Hunter, Rosa. "Ghosts as Guardians of Hidden Treasure." *JAFL* 12 (1899): 64–65.

1861   Hurston, Zora Neale. "High John De Conquer." *Am Merc* 57 (1943): 450–458.

1862   "Irishman Stories Told by Negroes." *JAFL* 12 (1899): 226–230.

1863   Jackson, Bruce. "Stagolee Stories: A Badman Goes Gentile." *SFQ* 29 (1965): 188–194.

1864   Jackson, Margaret Y. "Folklore in Slave Narratives Before the Civil War." *NYFQ* 11 (1955): 5–19.

1865   Jamison, Mrs. C. V. "A Louisiana Legend Concerning Will o' the Wisp." *JAFL* 18 (1905): 250–251.

1866   Johnson, F. Roy. "Two John Stories." *NCF* 20 (1972): 120–122.

1867 Johnson, Mrs. John L. "Brer Terrapin Learns to Fly." *NCF* 2, no. 1 (1954): 14–15.

1868 Johnston, Mrs. William Preston. "Two Negro Tales." *JAFL* 9 (1896): 194–198.

1869 Keller, John E. "The Source of 'The Wolf, the Fox, and the Well.'" *NCF* 7 (1959): 23–25.

1870 Kruger-Kahloula, A. "The Sad Tale of Mr. Fox in the Cow's Belly: Stability and Transformation in an Afro-American Folktale." *CLA* 14 (1984): 97–124.

1871 Lake, Mary Daggett. "Pioneer Christmas Customs of Tarrant County." *PTFS*, no. 5 (1926): 107–111.

1872 Langhorne, E. "Black Music and Tales from Jefferson's Monticello." *Folk F Va* 1 (1979): 60–67.

1873 Lankford, G. "A Night with the Hants and Other Alabama Folk Experiences." *JAFL* 91 (July–September 78): 855–856.

1874 Lee, Rosa Fairfax. "How the Clock Saved 'Ole Mis,' a Colonial Tale of Jamestown Island." *SW* 40 (1911): 46–51.

1875 Lueg, Maurita Russell. "Russell Tales." *PTFS*, no. 28 (1958): 160–166.

1876 MacMillan, Dougald. "John Kuners." *JAFL* 39 (1926): 53–57.

1877 Martin, Malcolm J. "Zombies and Ghost Dogs on the Harvey Canal." *LAFM* 2, no. 4 (1968): 103–104.

1878 McBride, J. M. "Br'er Rabbit in the Folktales of the Negro and Other Races." *Sew R* 19 (April 1911): 185–206.

1879 McBride, John McLaren, Jr. "Brer Rabbit in the Folk Tales of the Negro and Other Races." *Sew R* 19 (1911): 185–206.

1880 McGhee, Z. "A Study in the Play Life of Some South Carolina Children." *Ped Sem* 7 (1900): 415–478.

1881 McIlhenny, Edward A. "Trubble, Brudder Alligator, Trubble." *PTFS* 14 (1938): 135–144.

1882 McLennon, M. "Origin of the Cat: A Negro Tale." *JAFL* 9 (1896): 71.

1883 Miller, Heather R. "The Candlewalk: A Midwinter Fire-Festival." *NCF* 19 (1971): 153–156.

1884 Milling, Chapman J. "A Passel uh Snakes." *Folk-Say* 3 (1931): 103–112.

1885 "Mississippi Negro Tales." *JAFL* 40 (1927): 213–303.

1886 "Mortuary Customs and Beliefs of South Carolina Negroes." *JAFL* 7 (1894): 318–319.

1887 Mulcahez, Mary L. "John Henry." *KFR* 24 (1978): 6–9.

1888 "Negro Fables." *RiM* 2 (1868): 505–507; 3 (1869): 116–118.

1889 "A Negro Ghost Story." *SW* 28 (November 1899): 449–450.

1890 "Negro Tales from Bolivar County, Mississippi." *SFQ* 19 (June 1955): 104–116.

1891 O'Connor, K. S. "How Mr. Polecat Got His Scent." *TFSB* 7 (1928): 137–138.

1892 Oertel, Hanns. "Notes on Six Negro Myths from the Georgia Coast." *JAFL* 2 (1889): 309.

1893 "Old-Time Burials." *FF* 6, no. 1 (1972): 9–25.

1894 Olsen, Douglas. "Legends and Tales from Alabama." *TFSB* 28 (1962): 31–36.

1895 Oster, Harry. "The Afro-American Folktale in Memphis: Theme and Function." *NALF* 3, no. 3 (1969): 83–87.

1896 Owens, M. A. "Ole Rabbit an' De Dawg He Stole." *JAFL* 3 (1890): 135–138.

1897 Owens, Tary. "Poetry from Texas Prisons." *Riata* (Spring 1966): 22–33.

1898 Parks, Lillian V. "Black Jests from Virginia." *Journal of the Folklore Society of Greater Washington* 4 (Spring 1973): 18–20.

1899 Parler, Mary Celestia. "The Forty-Mile Jumper." *JAFL* 64 (1951): 422–423.

1900 Parsons, Elsie C. "Folktales Collected at Miami, Florida." *JAFL* 30 (1917): 222–227.

1901 Parsons, Elsie C. "Provenience of Certain Negro Folk-Tales, Playing Dead Twice in the Road." *Folklore* 28 (1917): 408–414.

1902 Parsons, E. C. "Provenience of Certain Negro Folk-Tales, II. The Password." *Folklore* 29 (1917): 206–218.

1903 Parsons, E. C. "The Provenience of Certain Folk-Tales, III. Tar Baby." *Folklore* 30 (1919): 227–234.

1904 Parsons, E. C. "The Provenience of Certain Negro Folk-Tales, IV. Missing Tongues." *Folklore* 32 (1921): 194–201.

1905 Parsons, E. C. "The Provenience of Certain Negro Folk-Tales, V. The House Keeper." *Folklore* 34 (1923): 363–370.

1906 Parsons, E. C. "Tales from Guilford County, North Carolina." *JAFL* 30 (1917): 168–200.

1907 Partin, R. "Alabama Newspaper Humor During Reconstruction." *Ar* 17 (1964): 243–260.

1908 Payne, Mildred Y. "Night Rider Love and Legend." *KFR* 12 (1966): 59–66.

1909 Perkins, A. E. "Riddles from Negro School-Children in New Orleans, Louisiana." *JAFL* 35 (1922): 105–115.

1910 Porter, Kenneth W. "A Legend of the Biloxi." *JAFL* 59 (1946): 168–173.

1911 "Prison Folklore." *JAFL* 78 (October–December 1965): 317–329.

1912 "Proverbs and Sayings." *SW* 27 (July 1898): 145.

1913 "Rabbit and Busard." *SW* 26 (December 1897): 249.

1914 "Rabbit and Frog." *SW* 27 (November 1898): 230.

1915 Rich, Carroll Y. "Born with the Veil: Black Folklore in Louisiana." *JAFL* 89 (1976): 328–331.

1916 "The Rich Ghost." *SW* 26 (March 1898): 57.

1917 Richard, Mrs. M. B. "Easter Day on the Plantation." *Plant Miss* 3, no. 2 (1892): 12–14.

1918 Rickels, Patricia K. "Some Accounts of Witch Riding." *LAFM* 2, no. 1 (1961): 1–17.

1919 Roberts, John W. "Stackolee and the Development of a Black Heroic Idea." *WF* 42 (1983): 170–190.

1920 Rodman, L. T. "The Black Baby and the Bear." *NCF* 7 (1959): 28–30.

1921 Scarborough, W. S. "Creole Folk Tale." *SW* 25 (September 1896): 186.

1922 Sisk, Glenn. "Funeral Customs in the Alabama Black Belt, 1870–1910." *SFQ* 23 (1959): 169–171.

1923 Smiley, Portia. "Courtship Customs." *SW* 25 (January 1896): 15.

1924 Smith, Richard. "Richard's Tales." *PTFS* 25 (1953): 242–247, 251–253.

1925 Snyder, Howard. "Traits of My Plantation Negroes." *Cent* 80 (1921): 367–376.

1926 "Some Conjure Doctors." *SW* 26 (February 1897): 37.

1927 Spenney, Susan Di. "Riddles and Ring-games from Raleigh, North Carolina." *JAFL* 32 (1921): 110–115.

1928 Stewart, Sadie E. "Seven Folk-Tales from the Sea Islands, South Carolina." *JAFL* 32 (1919): 394–396.

1929 "Tales from Guilford County, North Carolina." *JAFL* 40 (1917): 168–208.

1930 "Tales of the Rabbit from Georgia Negroes." *JAFL* 28 (1899): 108–115.

1931 "Two Ghost Stories." *SW* 26 (June 1897): 122.

1932 "Uncle Si'ah and the Ghosts." *SW* (October 1903): 506.

1933 Watkins, Floyd C. "De Dry Bones in de Valley." *SFQ* 20 (1956): 136–149.

1934 Weldon, Fred O., Jr. "Negro Folktale Heroes." *PTFS* 29 (1959): 170–189.

1935 Whiting, B. J. "William Johnson of Natchez." *SFQ* 16 (1952): 145–153.

1936 Winslow, David J. "A Negro Corn-Shucking." *JAFL* 86 (1973): 61–62.

1937 Young, Virginia H. "Family and Childhood in a Southern Negro Community." *AA* 72 (1970): 269–288.

7

Folk Literature and Religion

MONOGRAPHS

1938 Adams., R. *Cyclopedia of African Methodism in Mississippi*. Natchez: n.p., 1902.

1939 *Afro-American Baptists: A Guide to Materials in the American Baptist Historical Society*. Rochester, NY: American Baptist Historical Society, 1985.

1940 Alho, Olli. *The Religion of the Slaves: A Study of the Religious Traditions and Behaviour of Plantation Slaves in the United States, 1830–1865*. Helsinki: Academia Scientiarum Fennica, 1976. Bibliography on pp. 313–334.

1941 Allen, Helen B. "The Minister of the Gospel in Negro American Fiction." M.A. thesis, Fisk University, 1937.

1942 Baker, Houston A. *Black Literature in America*. New York: McGraw-Hill, 1971.

1943 Banks, Mary Ross. *Bright Days in the Old Plantation Time*. Boston: Lea and Shephard; New York: Charles T. Dillingham, 1882.

1944 Barnes-Harden, Alene. "African-American Verbal Arts: Their Nature and Communicative Interpretation (A Thematic Analysis)." Ph.D. dissertation, State University of New York at Buffalo, 1980.

1945 Beck, Horace P., ed. *Folklore in Action: Essays for Discussion in Honor of MacEdward Leach*. Philadelphia: American Folklore Society, 1962.

1946 Bell, Bernard W. *The Folk Roots of Contemporary Afro-American Poetry*. Broadside Critics series no. 3. Detroit: Broadside Press, 1974.

1947 Bell, Bernard W., ed. *Modern and Contemporary Afro-American Poetry*. Boston: Allyn & Bacon, 1972.

1948 Blake, Susan. "Modern Black Writers and the Folk Tradition." Ph.D. dissertation, University of Connecticut, 1976. Bibliography on lvs. 183–200.

1949 Bontemps, Arna. "Rock, Church, Rock." In *Anthology of American Negro Lit-*

erature, ed. Sylvester C. Watkins. New York: Modern Library, 1944. Bibliography on pp. 457–481.

1950 Boulware, Marcus H. *Jive and Slang of Students in Negro Colleges.* Hampton, VA: Hampton Institute, 1947.

1951 Bradford, Roark. *Kingdom Coming.* New York and London: Harper & Bros., 1933.

1952 Bradford, Roark. *Let the Bank Play Dixie, and Other Stories.* New York: Harper & Bros., 1934.

1953 Bradford, Roark. *Ol' King David an' the Philistine Boys.* New York and London: Harper & Bros., 1930.

1954 Bradford, Roark. *Ol' Man Adam an' His Chillun.* New York: Harper & Bros., 1928.

1955 Bradford, Roark. *This Side of Jordan.* New York and London: Harper & Bros., 1929.

1956 Bradley, David H., Sr. *A History of the African Methodist Episcopal Zion Church.* Nashville, TN: Parthenon Press, 1956.

1957 Brasch, Ila W. *A Comprehensive Annotated Bibliography of American Black English.* Baton Rouge: Louisiana State University Press, 1974.

1958 Brawley, Edward M. *The Negro Baptist Pulpit: A Collection of Sermons and Papers by Colored Baptist Ministers.* Freeport, NY: Books for Libraries Press, 1971.

1959 Brewer, John Mason. *Aunt Dicey Tales: Snuff-Dipping Tales of the Texas Negro.* Austin, TX: University of Texas Press, 1956.

1960 Brewer, John Mason. *Dog Ghosts and Other Negro Folk Tales.* Austin, TX: University of Texas Press, 1958.

1961 Brewer, John Mason. *The Work on the Brazos: Negro Preacher Tales from the Brazos Bottoms of Texas.* Austin, TX: University of Texas Press, 1953.

1962 Bronsard, James F. *Louisiana Creole Dialect.* Baton Rouge: Louisiana State University Press, 1942.

1963 Brown, Sterling Allen. *The Negro in American Fiction.* Washington, DC: Associates in Negro Folk Education, 1937. Reprint, New York: Arno Press and the New York Times, 1969.

1964 Burdett, James. *Burdett's Negro Dialect Recitations and Readings.* New York: Excelsior, 1884.

1965 Byerman, Keith E. *Fingering the Jagged Grain: Tradition and Form in Recent Black Fiction.* Athens: University of Georgia Press, 1985.

1966 Cassidy, Frederic. "Sources of the African Element in Gullah." In *Studies in Caribbean Language*, ed. Lawrence D. Carrington, pp. 75–91. St. Augustine, Trinidad: Society for Caribbean Linguistics, 1983.

1967 Chapman, Abraham. *The Negro in American Literature and a Bibliography by and About Negro Americans.* Madison: Wisconsin State University, 1966.

1968   Clarke, Elmer T. *The Small Sects in America*. New York: Abingdon-Cokesbury Press, 1949.

1969   Clarke, Erskine. *Wrestlin' Jacob: A Portrait of Religion in the Old South*. Atlanta, GA: John Knox Press, 1979.

1970   Colcock, Erroll Hay, and Patti Lee Hay Colcock. *Dusky Land: Gullah Poems and Sketches of Coastal South Carolina*. Clinton, SC: Jacobs, 1942.

1971   Coleman, Richard. *Don't You Weep, Don't You Moan*. New York: Macmillan, 1935.

1972   Coles, Samuel B. *Preacher with a Plow*. Boston: Houghton Mifflin, 1957.

1973   Conference of Negro Writers. *The American Negro Writer and His Roots: Selected Papers*. New York: American Society of African Culture, 1959.

1974   *Confessions of a Negro Preacher*. Chicago: Canterbury Press, 1928.

1975   Conroy, Pat. *The Water Is Wide*. Boston: Houghton Mifflin, 1972.

1976   Cotten, Sallie S. *Negro Folk Lore Stories*. Charlotte, NC: Charlotte Federation of Women's Clubs, 1923.

1977   Creel, M. *Peculiar People: Slave Religion and Community-Culture Among the Gullahs*. New York: New York University Press, 1988.

1978   Creel, M. W. "Gullah Attitudes Toward Life and Death," In *Africanisms in American Culture*, ed. Joseph E. Holloway, pp. 69–97. Bloomington: Indiana University Press, 1990.

1979   Crum, Mason. *Gullah: Negro Life in the Carolina Sea Islands*. Durham: Duke University Press, 1940. Bibliography on pp. 347–351.

1980   Culp, Daniel W., ed. *Twentieth-Century Negro Literature*. Naperville, IL: n.p., 1902.

1981   Cunningham, I. A. E. *A Syntactic Analysis of Sea Island Creole*. Tuscaloosa: University of Alabama Press, 1992. Bibliography on pp. 176–180.

1982   Dangerfield, Henrietta G. *Our Mammy and Other Stories*. Lexington, KY: Hampton Institute Press, 1906.

1983   Davis, Allison. *Negro Churches and Associations in the Lower South*. Manuscript in the Schomburg Collection of the New York Public Library.

1984   Davis, Gerald L. *I Got the Word in Me and I Can Sing It, You Know: A Study of the Performed African-American Sermon*. Philadelphia: University of Pennsylvania Press, 1985. Bibliography on pp. 163–180.

1985   Deedes, Henry. *Sketches of the South and West*. Edinburgh: William Blackwood, 1869.

1986   Devereux, Margaret. *Plantation Sketches*. Cambridge, MA: Riverside Press, 1906.

1987   Dillard, J. L. "The Creolist and the Study of Negro Non-Standard Dialects in the Continental United States." In *Pidginization and Creolization of Languages*, ed. Dell Hymes. Cambridge, UK: Cambridge University Press, 1971.

1988   Dillard, J. L. "Non-standard Negro Dialects: Convergence or Divergence?" In *Afro-American Anthropology, Contemporary Perspectives*, ed. Norman E. Whitten, Jr., and John F. Szwed. New York: Free Press, 1970.

1989   DuBois, W. E. B. *The Negro Church: Report of a Social Study Made Under the Direction of Atlanta University; Together with the Proceedings of the Eighth Conference for the Study of the Negro Problems, Held at Atlanta University, May 26th, 1903.* Atlanta: Atlanta University Press, 1903.

1990   Dundes, Alan. *Mother Wit from the Laughing Barrel: Readings in the Interpretation of Afro-American Folklore.* Englewood Cliffs, NJ: Prentice-Hall, 1973.

1991   Earnest, Joseph B. "The Religious Development of the Negro in Virginia." Ph.D. dissertation, University of Virginia, 1914. Bibliography on lvs. 177–203.

1992   Faulk, John Henry. "Quickened by de Spurit: Ten Negro Sermons." M.A. thesis, University of Texas, 1940.

1993   Felton, Ralph A. *Go Down Moses: A Study of 21 Successful Negro Rural Pastors.* New Jersey: Department of the Rural Church, Drew Theological Seminary, 1952.

1994   Felton, Ralph A. *These My Brethren: A Study of 570 Negro Churches and 1542 Negro Homes in the Rural South.* Madison, NJ: Department of the Rural Church, Drew Theological Seminary, 1950.

1995   Fortier, Alcée. *Louisiana Folk Tales, in French Dialect and English Translation.* Memoirs of the American Folklore Society, vol. 2. Boston: Houghton Mifflin, 1895.

1996   Fortier, Alcée. *Louisiana Studies: Literature, Customs, Dialects, History and Education.* New Orleans: F. F. Hansell, 1894.

1997   Frazier, Edward F. *The Negro Church in America.* New York: Shocken Books, 1964.

1998   Freeman, Gordon. "Climbing the Racial Mountain: The Folk Element in the Works of Three Black Writers." Ph.D. dissertation, University of New Mexico, 1977. Bibliography on lvs. 417–433.

1999   Fuller, Thomas O. *History of the Negro Baptists of Tennessee.* Memphis, TN: Roger Williams College, 1936.

2000   Gielow, Martha S. *Old Plantation Days.* New York: Russell, 1902.

2001   Glenn, Norval D. "Negro Religion and Negro Status in the United States." In *Religion, Culture and Society*, ed. Louis Schneider. New York: Wiley, 1964.

2002   *God Struck Me Dead. Religious Conversion Experiences and Autobiographies of Ex-Slaves.* Philadelphia: Pilgrim Press, 1969.

2003   Green, Bennet Wood. *Word-Book of Virginia Folk-Speech.* Richmond: W. E. Jones, 1899.

2004   Green, Elizabeth L. *The Negro in Contemporary American Literature: An Outline for Individual and Group Study.* Chapel Hill: University of North Carolina Press, 1928.

2005   Grimes, Johanna L. "The Function of the Oral Tradition in Selected Afro-American Fiction." Ph.D. dissertation, Northwestern University, 1980. Bibliography on lvs. 222–227.

2006   Grindal, Bruce T. "The Religious Interpretation of Experience in a Rural Black Community." In *Holding on to the Land and the Lord: Kinship, Ritual, Land*

Tenure, and Social Policy in the Rural South, ed. Robert L. Hall and Carol B. Stack, pp. 89–101. Athens: University of Georgia Press, 1982.

2007 Not used.

2008 Harris, Joel Chandler. *The Story of Aaron, So Named the Son of Ben Ali*. Boston: Houghton Mifflin, 1896.

2009 Harris, Trudier. *Fiction and Folklore: The Novels of Toni Morrison*. Knoxville: University of Tennessee Press, 1991.

2010 Harrison, W. W. *The Gospel Among the Slaves: A Short Account of Missionary Operations Among the African Slaves of the Southern States*. Nashville: Publishing House of the Methodist Episcopal Church of the South, 1893.

2011 Hatcher, William E. *John Jasper, The Unmatched Negro Philosopher and Preacher*. New York: F. H. Revell, 1908.

2012 Hearn, Lafcadio. *An American Miscellany*. New York: Dodd, Mead, 1924.

2013 Hearn, Lafcadio. "The Creole Patois." In *An American Miscellany*. Vol. 2, ed. Albert Mordell. New York: Dodd, Mead, 1924.

2014 Hearn, Lafcadio. *Gombo Zhebes: Little Dictionary of Creole Proverbs, Selected from Six Creole Dialects*. New York: W. H. Coleman, 1885.

2015 Hemenway, Robert E. *Zora Neale Hurston: A Literary Biography*. Urbana: University of Illinois Press, 1977.

2016 Heyward, Du Bose. *Mamba's Daughters. A Novel of Charleston*. New York: Cowell, 1928.

2017 Heyward, Du Bose. *Porgy*. New York: Grosset and Dunlap, George H. Doran, 1925.

2018 Heyward, Mrs. (Jane Screven). *Brown Jackets*. Columbia, SC: State Co., 1923.

2019 Holliday, Carl. *A History of Southern Literature*. New York: Neale, 1906.

2020 Hood, James W. *The Negro in the Christian Pulpit or, The Two Characters and Two Destinies, as Delineated in Twenty-one Practical Sermons . . .* Raleigh, NC: Edwards Broughton, 1884.

2021 Horton, George Moses. *Poems by a Slave*. Raleigh, NC: Gale and Son, 1829.

2022 Hucks, J. Jenkins. *Plantation Negro Sayings on the Coast of South Carolina in Their Own Vernacular*. Georgetown, SC: Charles W. Rouse, 1899.

2023 Hughes, Langston, ed. *The Best Short Stories by Negro Writers: An Anthology from 1899 to the Present*. Boston: Little, Brown, 1967.

2024 Hurston, Zora Neale. *Jonah's Gourd Vine*. Philadelphia: J. B. Lippincott, 1934.

2025 Hurston, Zora Neale. "The Sermon." In *Negro Anthology*, ed. Nancy Cunard. London: Wishart, 1934.

2026 Hurston, Zora Neale. "Shouting." In *Negro Anthology*, ed. Nancy Cunard. London: Wishart, 1934.

2027 Jenkins, J. "To Make A Woman Black: A Critical Analysis of the Women Characters in the Fiction and Folklore of Zora Neale Hurston." Ph.D. dissertation, Bowling Green State University, 1978. Bibliography on lvs. 209–216.

2028 Johnson, Guy. "Hurston's Folk: The Critical Significance of Afro-American Folk

Tradition in Three Novels and the Autobiography.'' Ph.D. dissertation, University of California, Irvine, 1977. Bibliography on lvs. 154–157.

2029 Johnson, James Weldon. *God's Trombones: Seven Negro Sermons in Verse.* New York: Viking Press, 1927.

2030 Johnson, Ruby F. *The Religion of Negro Protestants: Changing Religious Attitudes and Practices.* New York: Philosophical Library, 1956. Bibliography on pp. 214–217.

2031 Jones, B. W. ''A Descriptive and Analytical Study of the American Negro Folktale.'' Ph.D. dissertation, George Peabody College for Teachers, 1967.

2032 Jones, Major J. *Black Awareness: A Theology of Hope.* Nashville, TN: Abingdon Press, 1971.

2033 Jones, Raymond J. *A Comparative Study of Religious Cult Behavior Among Negroes with Special Reference to Emotional Group Conditioning Factors.* Washington, DC: Howard University Studies in the Social Sciences, vol. 2, no. 2, 1939.

2034 Jones-Jackson, P. A. *The Status of Gullah: An Investigation of Convergent Processes.* Ann Arbor: University of Michigan Press, 1978.

2035 Jordan, Lewis G. *Negro Baptist History, U.S.A.* Nashville, TN: Sunday School Publishing, 1930.

2036 Kein, Sybil. *Gombo People: New Orleans Creole Poetry.* New Orleans: Gosserand, 1981.

2037 Kennedy, Robert Emmet. *Black Cameos: Decorations by Edward Larocque Tinker.* New York: A. & C. Boni, 1924.

2038 Kerry, Paul. ''The Negro Church.'' Ph.D. dissertation, California State University, 1973. Bibliography on lvs. 88–90.

2039 Koger, A. Briscoe. *History of the Negro Baptists of Maryland.* Baltimore: n.p., 1936.

2040 Lawton, Samuel Miller. *The Religious Life of South Carolina Coastal and Sea Island Negroes.* Abstract of Contribution to Education no. 242, George Peabody College for Teachers, Nashville, TN, 1939.

2041 Leffall, Delores. *The Black Church: An Annotated Bibliography.* Washington, DC: Minority Research Center, 1973.

2042 Levine, Lawrence. *Black Culture and Black Consciousness: Afro-American Folk Thought from Slavery to Freedom.* New York: Oxford University Press, 1977.

2043 Lockwood, John P. *Darkey Sermons from Charleston County: Composed and Delivered by John Palmer Lockwood (alias Rebrin Isrel Manigo).* Columbia, SC: State Co., 1925.

2044 Loggins, Vern. *The Negro Author: His Development in America to 1900.* New York: Kennikat Press, 1964. Bibliography on pp. 408–457.

2045 Lomax, Alan. *The Rainbow Sign: A Southern Documentary.* New York: Duell, Sloan and Pearce, 1959.

2046 Lomax, Alan, and Raoul Abdul, eds. *3,000 Years of Black Poetry.* New York: Dodd, Mead, 1970.

2047 Long, Charles S. *History of the A.M.E. Church in Florida*. Philadelphia: A.M.E. Book Concern Printers, 1939.

2048 Long, Deborah J. "The Negro Genius and the Folk Tradition: Jean Tomer and Zora Neale Hurston." Ph.D. dissertation, Brown University, 1972.

2049 Love, E. K. *History of the First African Baptist Church from Its Organization, January 20, 1798 to July 1, 1888, Including the Centennial Celebration, Addresses, Sermons, etc.* Savannah Morning Newsprint, 1888.

2050 Lubiano, Wahneema H. "Messing with the Machine: Four Afro-American Novels and the Nexus of Vernacular, Historical Constraint, and Narrative Strategy." Ph.D. dissertation, Stanford University, 1987. Bibliography on lvs. 229–239.

2051 Margolies, Edward. *Afro-American Fiction, 1853–1976: A Guide to Information Sources*. Detroit: Gale Research, 1979.

2052 Matthews, Geraldine, comp. *Black American Writers, 1773–1949: A Bibliography and Union List*. Complied by Geraldine O. Matthews and the African-American Materials Project Staff. North Carolina Central University at Durham, School of Library Science. Boston: G. K. Hall, 1975.

2053 Mayo, Sandra M. "The Cultural Roots of the Drama of Ed Bullins." Ph.D. dissertation, Stanford University, 1987.

2054 Mays, Benjamin E., and Joseph W. Nicholson. *The Negro's Church*. New York: Russell and Russell, 1933, 1957, 1969.

2055 Mays, Benjamin E., and Joseph W. Nicholson. *The Negro's God as Reflected in His Literature*. Boston: Chapman and Grimes, 1938.

2056 Mikell, I. Jenkins. *Rumbling of the Chariot Wheels*. Columbia, SC: State Co., 1923.

2057 Mitchell, Henry Heywood. *Black Preaching*. Philadelphia: J. B. Lippincott, 1970.

2058 Mixon, Winfield H. *History of the A.M.E. Church in Alabama*. Nashville, TN: A.M.E. Church Sunday School Union, 1902.

2059 Morales, Donald M. "African American Folk Survivals in Contemporary Black American Theater." Ph.D. dissertation, University of New York at Stony Brook, 1981. Bibliography on lvs. 255–266.

2060 Moore, Carman. *Somebody's Angel Child: The Story of Bessie Smith*. New York: Crowell, 1969.

2061 Moore, John J. *History of the A.M.E. Zion Church in America*. York, PA: Teachers' Journal Office, 1884.

2062 Neal, Larry. "Eatonville's Zora Neale Hurston: A Profile." In *Black Review No. 2*, ed. Mel Watkins. New York: William Morrow, 1972.

2063 Nelson, Hart M. *The Black Church in America*. Lexington: University Press of Kentucky, 1975.

2064 Neuffer, Claude Henry, ed. *Names in South Carolina*. Vol. 12. Columbia: Department of English, University of South Carolina, 1967.

2065 Nichols, Patricia C. "Creoles of the USA." In *Language in the USA*, ed. Charles A. Freeman et al., pp. 69–91. Cambridge, MA: Cambridge University Press, 1991.

2066 Nichols, Patricia C. "Variations Among Gullah Speakers in Rural South Carolina: Implications for Education." In *Language and the Uses of Language*, ed. Roger W. Shuy and Ann Shnukal, pp. 205–218. Washington, DC: Georgetown University Press, 1990.

2067 Nixon, N. M. "Gullah and Backwoods Dialect in Selected Works by William Gilmore Simms." Ph.D. dissertation, University of South Carolina, 1971.

2068 Olmsted, Frederick Law. *A Journey Through Texas*. New York: Dix and Edwards, 1857.

2069 Patterson, Pernet. *The Road to Canaan*. New York: Minton, Balch, 1931.

2070 Peterkin, Julia. *Black April*. Indianapolis: Bobbs-Merrill, 1927.

2071 Peterkin, Julia. *Bright Skin*. Indianapolis: Bobbs-Merrill, 1932.

2072 Peterkin, Julia. *The Collected Short Stories of Julia Peterkin*, ed. Frank Durham. Columbia: University of South Carolina Press, 1970.

2073 Peterkin, Julia. *Green Thursday*. New York: Knopf, 1924.

2074 Peterkin, Julia. "Gullah." In *Ebony and Topaz*, ed. Charles S. Johnson. New York: National Urban League, 1927.

2075 Peterkin, Julia. *A Plantation Christmas*. Boston: Houghton Mifflin, 1934.

2076 Peterkin, Julia. *Scarlet Sister Mary*. Indianapolis: Bobbs-Merrill, 1928.

2077 Pipes, William H. *Say Amen, Brother: Old-Time Negro Preaching: A Study in Frustration*. New York: William-Frederick Press, 1951. Bibliography on pp. 201–205.

2078 Pryse, Marjorie. *Conjuring: Black Women, Fiction, and Literacy Tradition*. Bloomington: Indiana University Press, 1985.

2079 Reid, Ira. *The Negro Baptist Ministry: An Analysis of Its Profession, Preparation, and Practices*. Philadelphia: H. and L. Advertising Co., 1952.

2080 Richardson, Harry Van Buren. *Dark Glory: A Picture of the Church Among Negroes in the Rural South*. New York: Phelps-Stokes Fund by Friendship Press, 1947.

2081 Rosenberg, Bruce A. *The Art of the American Folk Preacher*. New York: Oxford University Press, 1970.

2082 Rosten, Leo. *Religions in American: A Completely Revised and Up-to-Date Guide to Churches and Religious Groups in the United States*. New York: Simon and Schuster, 1963.

2083 Rowell, C. H. "Afro-American Literary Bibliographies: An Annotated List of Bibliographic Guides for the Study of Afro-American Literature, Folklore, and Related Areas." Ph.D. dissertation, Ohio State University, 1972.

2084 Sernett, Milton. *Afro-American Religious History: A Documentary Witness*. Durham, NC: Duke University Press, 1985.

2085 Sernett, Milton. *Black Religion and American Evangelicalism: White Protestants, Plantation Missions, and the Flowering of Negro Christianity*. Metuchen, NJ: Scarecrow Press, 1975. Bibliography on pp. 239–288.

2086 Shelby, Gertrude Mathews, and Samuel Gaillard Stoney. *Po' Buckra*. New York: Macmillan, 1930.

2087 Sherman, Joan R. "Afro-American Poets of the Nineteenth Century and Their Poetry." Ph.D. dissertation, Rutgers University, 1971.

2088 Sherman, Joan R. *Invisible Poets: Afro-Americans of the Nineteenth Century*. Urbana: University of Illinois Press, 1974. Bibliography on pp. 225–236.

2089 Simpson, George E. *Black Religions in the New World*. New York: Columbia University Press, 1978. Bibliography on pp. 383–399.

2090 *Sketches of Old Virginia Family Servants*. Philadelphia: Isaac Ashmead, 1847.

2091 Snyder, Howard. *Earth Born: A Novel of the Plantation*. New York: Century, 1929.

2092 Sperry, Margaret. *Portrait of Eden*. New York: Liveright, 1934.

2093 Stoeltje, Beverly. "'Bow-legged Bastard: A Manner of Speaking (Speech Behavior of a Black Woman)." In *Folklore Annual of the University Folklore Association*, nos. 4 and 5, ed. Tom Ireland, Joanne Krauss, and Beverly Stoeltje. (1972 and 1973).

2094 Street, James H. *Look Away! A Dixie Notebook*. New York: Viking, 1936.

2095 Sweet, William Warren. *The Story of Religions in America*. New York: Harper & Bros., 1930.

2096 Swisher, Robert A., and Jill A. Archer. *Black American Literature and Black American Folklore*. Bloomington: Indiana University Libraries, 1969.

2097 Talley, Thomas W. *Negro Folk Rhymes*. New York: Macmillan, 1922.

2098 Thomas, H. Nigel. *From Folklore to Fiction: A Study of Folk Heroes and Rituals in the Black American Novel*. Westport, CT: Greenwood Press, 1988. Bibliography on pp. 181–194.

2099 Thompson, Robert Farris. "Kongo Influences on African-American Artistic Culture." In *Africanisms in American Culture*, ed. Joseph Holloway, pp. 148–184. Bloomington: Indiana University Press, 1990.

2100 Thompson, Stith. *Motif-Index of Folk-Literature: A Classification of Narrative Elements in Folktales, Ballads, Myths, Fables, Medieval Romances, Exempla, Fabliaux, Jest-Books and Local Legends*. 6 vols. Bloomington: Indiana University Press, 1955.

2101 Tiller, Lessie. "The Gullah in American Literature." M.A. thesis, University of South Carolina, 1923. Bibliography on l. 47.

2102 Tinker, Edward L. *Gombo, The Creole Dialect of Louisiana*. Worcester, MA, 1936. Bibliography on pp. 31–46.

2103 Tirotta, R. *No Crystal Stair: A Bibliography of Black Literature*. New York: Office Adult Services, New York Public Library, 1971.

2104 Tracy, Steven C. "The Influence of the Blues Tradition on Langston Hughes' Blues Poems." Ph.D. dissertation, University of Cincinnati, 1985. Bibliography on lvs. 402–441.

2105   Tristano, Richard. *Black Religion in the Evangelical South*. Atlanta, GA: Glenmary Research Center, 1986.

2106   Turner, Darwin T., ed. *Black American Literature: Poetry*. Columbus, OH: Charles E. Merrill, 1969.

2107   Turner, Lorenzo Dow. *Africanisms in the Gullah Dialect*. Chicago: University of Chicago Press, 1949.

2108   Von Kolnitz, A. H. *Crying in de Wilderness*. Charleston, SC: Walker, Evans and Cogswell, 1935.

2109   Wagner, Jean. *Black Poets of the United States: From Paul Laurence Dunbar to Langston Hughes*, trans. Kenneth Douglas. Urbana: University of Illinois Press, 1973.

2110   Washington, Joseph R. *Black Religion: The Negro and Christianity in the United States*. Boston: Beacon Press, 1964. Bibliography on pp. 298–303.

2111   Washington, Joseph R. *Black Sects and Cults*. New York: Anchor Books, 1972.

2112   Weatherford, Willie D. *American Churches and the Negro: An Historical Study from Early Slave Days to the Present*. Boston: Christopher, 1957.

2113   Whaley, Marcellus S. *The Old Types Pass: Gullah Sketches of the Carolina Sea Islands*. Boston: Christopher, 1925.

2114   Wharton, Vernon Lane. *The Negro in Mississippi, 1865–1890*. Chapel Hill: University of North Carolina Press, 1947.

2115   Wheelbarger, Johnny J. *Black Religion: A Bibliography of Fisk*. University Library Materials Relating to Various Aspects of Black Religious Life. Nashville: Internship in Ethnic Studies Librarianship, Fisk University Library, 1974.

2116   Wiggins, William H., Jr. "The Black Folk Church." In *Handbook of American Folklore*, ed. Richard M. Dorson et al., pp. 145–154. Bloomington: Indiana University Press, 1983.

2117   Wilentz, Gay. "From Africa to America: Cultural Ties That Bind in the Works of Contemporary African-American Women Writers." Ph.D. dissertation, University of Texas at Austin, 1986. Bibliography on lvs. 276–287.

2118   Wiley, Bell Irvin. *Southern Negroes, 1861–1865*. New Haven, CT: Yale University Press, 1965.

2119   Williams, Charles. "The Conversation Ritual in a Rural Black Baptist Church." In *Holding on to the Land and the Lord: Kinship, Ritual, Land Tenure, and Social Policy in the Rural South*, ed. Robert L. Hall and Carol Stack, pp. 60–70. Athens: University of Georgia Press, 1982.

2120   Williams, Ethel L., and L. Brown Clifton, comps. *Afro-American Religious Studies: A Comprehensive Bibliography with Locations in American Libraries*. Metuchen, NJ: Scarecrow Press, 1972.

2121   Williams, John G. *"De Ole Plantation": Elder Coteney's Sermons*. Charleston, SC: Evans and Cogswell, 1895.

2122   Wilmore, Gayraud S. *Black Religion and Black Radicalism*. New York: Doubleday, 1972. Bibliography on pp. 307–329.

2123 Wolfe, Charles K. *Thomas W. Talley's Negro Folk Rhymes*. Knoxville: University of Tennessee Press, 1991.

2124 Wood, Clement. *Nigger*. New York: Dutton, 1922.

2125 Woodson, Carter Godwin. *The History of the Negro Church*. Washington, DC: Associated, 1921.

2126 Woofter, T. J., Jr. *Black Yeomanry: Life on St. Helena Island*. New York: H. Holt, 1930.

2127 Yonker, Thomas W. "The Afro-American Church in North Carolina, 1700–1900." M.A. thesis, Duke University, 1955.

ARTICLES

2128 Abrahams, R. "The Changing Concept of the Negro Hero." *PTFS* 31 (1962): 119–132.

2129 Baird, K. E. "Guy B. Johnson Revisited: Another Look at Gullah." *J Black Stud* 19 (1980): 425–435.

2130 Baldwin, L. V. "A Home in Dat Rock: Afro-American Folk Sources and Slave Visions of Heaven and Hell." *Journal of Religious Thoughts* 41 (1984): 38–57.

2131 Bascom, W. "Acculturation Among Gullah Negroes." *AA* 43 (1941): 43–50.

2132 Bell, Suzanne Comer. " 'Epaminondas': The African-American Silly Song." *SFQ* 46 (1989): 221–239.

2133 Benesch, K. "Oral Narrative and Literary Text: Afro-American Folklore in Their Eyes Were Watching God." *Callaloo* 11 (Summer 1988): 627–635.

2134 Bennet, J. "Gullah: A Negro Patois." *SAQ* 7 (1908): 332–347; (1909): 39–52.

2135 Bennet, J. "Note on Gullah." *SC His Mag* 50 (1949): 56–57.

2136 Bibb, L. D. "They Preach Black to Be the Ideal." *Negro Hist Bull* 28 (March 1965): 132–133.

2137 "A Bibliography of Bibliographies for the Study of Black American Literature and Folklore." *Black Ex* 55 (June 1969): 95–111.

2138 Bickerton, Derek. "An Afro-Creole Origin for Eena Meena Mina Mo." *Am Sp* 57 (Fall 1982): 225–228.

2139 Billingslee-Brown, A. "The Folk Aesthetic in Contemporary African-American Women's Fiction and Visual Art." *DAI* 51 (September 1990): 849A.

2140 Blok, H. P. "Annotations to Mr. Turner's Africanisms in the Gullah Dialect." *Lingua* 8 (September 1959): 306–321.

2141 Not used.

2142 Bradford, S. Sidney. "The Negro Ironworker in Ante-Bellum Virginia." *JSH* 25 (1959): 194–206.

2143 Bradley, F. W. "The Bo' Dollar." *SFQ* 25 (1961): 198–199.

2144 Bradley, F. W. "Gullah Proverbs." *SFQ* 1 (1937): 99–101.

2145 Bradley, F. W. "Southern Carolina Proverbs." *SFQ* 1 (1937): 57–101.

2146 Bradley, F. W. "A Word List From South Carolina." *PADS* 9–16 (April 1948–November 1951): 10–73.

2147 Browne, Ray B. "Negro Folktales from Alabama." *SFQ* 18 (1954): 129–134.

2148 Byrd, James W. "Black Collectors of Black Folklore: An Update on Zora Neale Hurston and J. Mason River." *LAFM* 6 (1986): 1–7.

2149 "A Camp-Meeting in Tennessee." *Harper* 26, no. 151 (1862): 97–101.

2150 Chamberlain, Alexander F. "Negro Dialect." *SCI* 12 (1888): 23–24.

2151 Christensen, A. "Spirituals and Shouts for Southern Negroes." *JAFL* 7 (April–June 1894): 154–155.

2152 Clark, Joseph D. "Proverbs and Sayings in North Carolina." *NCF* 16 (1968): 38–43.

2153 Cobbs, Hamner. "Negro Colloquialisms in the Black Belt." *Ala R* 5 (1952): 203–212.

2154 Cohen, Hennig. "Slave Names in Colonial South Carolina." *AS* 27 (1952): 102–107.

2155 "Coonjining." *AS* 8 (1933): 77–78.

2156 Cox, E. "Rustic Imagery in Mississippi Proverbs." *SFQ* 9 (1947): 263–267.

2157 Crabtree, Claire. "The Confluence of Folklore, Feminism and Black Self-Determination in Zora Neale Hurston's *Their Eyes Were Watching God*." *SLJ* 17 (Spring 1985): 54–66.

2158 Davenport, Frederick Morgan. "The Religions of the American Negro." *Contemporary Review* 88 (September 1905): 369–375.

2159 Dillard, J. L. "Creole, Cajuns, and Cable with Some Heart and a Few Assorted Babies: Review of Lafcadio Hearn, *Gombo Zhe'bes*, and George Washington Cable, *Creoles and Cajuns; The Negro Question*." *Carib Stud* (1963): 84–89.

2160 Dillard, J. L. "Creole Studies and American Dialectology." *Carib Stud* 12 (1973): 76–91.

2161 Dowd, Jerome. "Rev. Moses Hester: Sketch of a Quaint Negro Preacher in North Carolina." *Tri A* 9 (February 1896): 238–296.

2162 Dowd, Jerome. "Sermon of an Ante-Bellum Negro Preacher." *SW* 30 (1901): 655–658.

2163 Ellison, J. Malcus. "A Negro Church in Rural Virginia." *SW* 60 (1931): 67–73, 176–179, 201–210, 307–314.

2164 Ellison, Mary. "Black Perceptions and Red Images: Indian and Black Literary Links." *Phyl* 44 (March 1983): 44–55.

2165 Estes, David C. "Across Ethnic Boundaries: St. Joseph's Day in a New Orleans Afro-American Spiritual Church." *Miss FR* 21 (Spring-Fall 1987): 9–22.

2166 Estes, Phoebe Beckner. "The Reverend Peter Vinegar." *SFQ* 23 (1959): 239–252.

2167 Ferris, William R., Jr. "The Negro Conversion Experience." *KFQ* 15 (1970): 35–51.

2168 Ferris, William R., Jr. "The Rose Hill Service." *Miss FR* 6 (1972): 37–56.

2169   Figh, Margaret Gillis. "Folklore in Bill Arp's Works." *SFQ* 12 (1948): 169–174.

2170   Figh, Margaret Gillis. "Nineteenth-Century Outlaws in Alabama Folklore." *SFQ* 25 (1961): 126–135.

2171   Fishwick, Marshall. "Uncle Remus Versus John Henry: Folk Tension." *WF* (1961): 77–85.

2172   Fishwick, Marshall. "What Ever Happened to John Henry?" *So HR* 5 (1971): 231–236.

2173   Flowers, Paul. "Picturesque Speech." *TFSB* 10 (1944): 9–10.

2174   Ford, John E. "Religious Life in Jacksonville." *Crisis* 49 (January 1942): 25.

2175   Fox, Robert Elliot. "Blacking the Zero: Toward a Semiotics of Neo-Hoodoo." *BALF* 18 (Fall 1984): 95–99.

2176   Galoob, Debra. " 'Back in '32 When the Times Was Hard': Negro Toasts from East Texas." *Riata* (1963): 24–33.

2177   Garner, Thurmon. "Playing the Dozens: Folklore as Strategies for Living." *Q J Speech* 69 (February 1983): 47–57.

2178   Gaudet, Marcia. "Folklore in the Writings of Ernest J. Gaines." *Griot* 3, no. 1 (Winter 1984): 9–15.

2179   Genovese, Eugene D. "Black Plantation Preachers in the Slave South." *LA Stud* 11 (1972): 188–214.

2180   Gerber, A. "Uncle Remus Traced to the Old World." *JAFL* 6 (October–December 1893): 245–247.

2181   Goodwin, W. T., and Peter Gold. "From 'Easter Sunrise Sermon.' " *Alcheringa* 4 (1972): 1–14.

2182   Griska, Joseph M., Jr. "Uncle Remus Correspondence: The Development and Reception of Joel Chandler Harris' Writing, 1880–1885." *Ala R* 14 (Spring 1981): 26–37.

2183   Groom, Bob. " 'Who Killed Lula?' Notes on a Memphis Blues Ballad." *JEMFQ* 17 (Fall 1981): 155–158.

2184   Hair, P. E. "Sierra Leone Idioms in the Gullah Dialect of American English." *SLLR* 4 (1965): 79–84.

2185   Hampton, Bill. "On Identification and Negro Tricksters." *SFQ* 31 (1967): 55–65.

2186   Harrison, J. A. "Negro English." *ANQ* 7 (1884): 232–279.

2187   Hemenway, Robert. "Folklore Field Notes from Zora Neale Hurston." *BlS* 7 (1976): 39–46.

2188   Henderson, Stephen E. "The Blues as Black Poetry." *Callaloo* 5 (October 1982): 22–30.

2189   Hill, Mildred A. "Common Folklore Features in African and African American Literature." *SFQ* 39 (1975): 111–133.

2190   Holm, John. "On the Relationship of Gullah and Bahamian." *Am Sp* 58 (Winter 1983): 303–318.

2191 Holmes, Urban T. "A Study of Negro Onomastics." AS 5 (1930): 463–467.

2192 Hudson, Arthur Palmer. "Some Curious Negro Names." SFQ 2 (1938): 179–193.

2193 Hudson, Gossie Harold. "Zora Neale Hurston and Alternative History." MAWA R 1 (Summer-Fall 1982): 60–64.

2194 Hurston, Zora Neale. "Dust Tracks on a Road." Negro D 1 (January 1923, 1943): 75–81.

2195 Jackson, Bruce. "Prison Nicknames." WF 26 (1967): 48–54.

2196 Jackson, Luther P. "Religious Instruction of Negroes, 1830–1860, with Specific References to South Carolina." JNH 15 (1930): 72–114.

2197 Jackson, Luther P. "Religious Development of the Negro in Virginia from 1760 to 1860." JNH 16 (1931): 168–239.

2198 Jaskoski, Helen. "Power Unequal to Man: The Significance of Conjure in Works by Afro-American Authors." SFQ 38 (1974): 91–108.

2199 Jones-Jackson, Patricia. "The Audience in Gullah and Igbo: A Comparison of Oral Traditions." CLA 27 (December 1983): 197–209.

2200 Jones-Jackson, Patricia. "On Decreolization and Language Death in Gullah." Lang Soc 13 (September 1984): 351–362.

2201 Jones-Jackson, Patricia. "The Prayer Tradition in Gullah." Journal of Religious Thought 39 (Spring-Summer 1978): 21–23.

2202 Kane, Elisha K. "The Negro Dialects Along the Savannah River." Dialect N 5 (1925): 354–367.

2203 Kaplan, Bruce. "Gullah: The Unique Culture of America's Sea Islands: The African-American Language That Gave Us Uncle Remus Struggles To Survive." Utne Reader, no. 37 (January–February 1990): 23.

2204 Kirk, R. "Plight of the Colored Clerisy; Incidents at Selma, Alabama." Natl Rev 17 (June 29, 1965): 551.

2205 Kloe, Donald R. "Buddy Quow: An Anonymous Poem in Gullah-Jamaican Dialect Written circa 1800." SFQ 38 (1974): 81–90.

2206 Krapp, C. P. "The English of the American Negro." Am Merc 2 (1924): 190–195.

2207 Krueger, E. T. "Negro Religious Expression." AJS 38 (1932): 22–31.

2208 Lane, Bruce. "Review Essay: Gumbo." JAFL 94 (371): 131–147.

2209 Law, Robert Adger. "A Note on Four Negro Words." PTFS 6 (1927): 119–120.

2210 Legman, G. "Poontang." AS 25 (1950): 234–235.

2211 Light, Kathleen. "Uncle Remus and the Folklorists." SLJ 7 (1975): 88–104.

2212 Not used.

2213 Lomax, Ruby Terrill. "Negro Baptizing." PTFS 19 (1944): 1–8.

2214 Lomax, Ruby Terrill. "Negro Nicknames." PTFS 18 (1943): 163–171.

2215 Lumpkin, Ben Gray. "The Hawk and the Buzzard: How Tellers Vary the Story." NCF 18 (1970): 114–147.

2216 Mallard, John P. "Liberty County, Georgia." *GHQ* 2 (1918): 1–21.

2217 Not used.

2218 Marcel (W. F. Allen). "The Negro Dialect." *Nat* 1 (1865): 744–745.

2219 Mason, Julian. "The Etymology of 'Buckaroo.' " *AS* 35 (1960): 51–55.

2220 Meikleham, R. "A Negro Ballad." *JAFL* 6 (October–December 1893): 300–301.

2221 Mollette, Carlton W., III. "Afro-American Ritual Drama." *Bl W* 22, no. 6 (1973): 4–12.

2222 Montenyohl, Eric L. "The Origins of Uncle Remus." *FF* 18, no. 2 (Spring 1986): 136–167.

2223 Mosher, Marlene. "James Baldwin's Blues." *CLA* 26 (September 1982): 112–124.

2224 Moyd, Olin P. "Redemption: A Theology from Black History." *DAI* 38 (1977): 2867–2868A.

2225 Mufwene, Salikoko S., and Charles Gilman. "Equivocal Structures in Some Gullah Complex Sentences." *Am Sp* 64 (Winter 1989): 304–326.

2226 Mufwene, Salikoko S., and Charles Gilman. "How African Is Gullah, and Why?" *Am Sp* 62 (Summer 1987): 120–139.

2227 Mufwene, Salikoko S., and Charles Gilman. "Number Delimitation in Gullah: A Response to Mufwene." *Am Sp* 61 (Spring 1986): 333–360.

2228 Neal, Larry. "Zora Neale Hurston: A Profile." *South Exposure* (1974): 160–168.

2229 Nelson, Mildred M. "Folk Etymology of Alabama Place Names." *SFQ* 14 (1950): 193–214.

2230 Niles, John J. "Shout, Coon, Shout!" *MQ* 16 (1930): 516–530.

2231 O'Meally, Robert G. "Game to the Heart: Sterling Brown and the Badman." *Callaloo* 5 (February–May 1982): 43–54.

2232 Overton, Betty J. "Black Woman Preacher, a Literary View." *SQ* 23, no. 3 (Spring 1985): 157–166.

2233 Owens, Guy. "Playing the Dozens." *NCF* 21 (1973): 53–54.

2234 Payne, L. W. "A Word List from East Alabama." *Dialect N* 3 (1903): 279–328, 343–391.

2235 Peavy, Charles D. "Faulkner's Use of Folklore in *The Sound and the Fury*." *JAFL* 79 (1966): 437–447.

2236 Penrod, James H. "Minority Groups in Old Southwestern Human." *SFQ* 22 (1958): 121–128.

2237 Perry, H. R. "Appoints Negro Bishop; Louisiana-Born H. R. Perry." *Christ Cen* 82 (October 20, 1965): 1277–1278.

2238 Peterkin, Julia. "Seeing Things." *Am Mag* 105 (January 1928): 26–27, 115–116.

2239 Peterkin, Julia. "Vinner's Sayings." *Poet* 25 (1925): 240–243.

2240 Petesch, Donald A. "The Role of Folklore in the Modern Black Novel." *KFQ* 7 (1975): 99–110.

2241 Plant, Deborah G. "The Folk Preacher and Sermon in Zora Neale Hurston's *Dust Tracks on a Road*." *FF* 21, no. 1 (1988): 3–19.

2242 Pollitzer, W. S. "The Negroes of Charleston: A Study of Hemoglobin, Types, Serology and Morphology." *Am J Phys Anthro* 16 (1931): 241–263.

2243 Popkin, Z. F. "Heaven Bound: An Authentic Negro Folk Drama Out of Old Savannah." *TGM* (August 8, 1931): 14–17.

2244 Prevos, Andre. "The Legend of Mary Magdalene in Afro-Cajun Spirituals." *PQM* 8 (1984): 25–30.

2245 Puckett, Newbell N. "Religious Folk Beliefs of Whites and Negroes." *JNH* 16 (January 1931): 9–35.

2246 Raymond, Charles A. "The Religious Life of the Negro Slave." *Harper's Mag* 27 (1863): 479–488, 676–682, 816–825.

2247 Reaver, J. Russell. "Folk History from North Florida." *SFQ* 32 (1968): 7–16.

2248 Rhame, J. M. "Flaming Youth: A Story in Gullah Dialect." *Am Sp* 8 (1833): 39–43.

2249 Rickels, Patricia K. "The Folklore of Sacraments and Sacramentals in South Louisiana." *LAFM* 2, no. 2 (1965): 27–44.

2250 Roberts, John W. "Stackolee and the Development of a Black Heroic Idea." *WF* 42, no. 3 (July 1983): 179–190.

2251 Sides, Sudie D. "Slave Weddings and Religion." *History Today* 24 (1974): 77–87.

2252 Sisk, Glenn. "Churches in the Alabama Black Belt, 1875–1917." *Church Hist* 23 (1954): 153–174.

2253 Sledge, M. "The Representation of the Gullah Dialect in Francis Griswold's *A Sea Island Lady*." *DAI* 46 (January 1986): 1917A.

2254 Smiley, Portia. "Folk-Lore from Virginia, South Carolina, Georgia, Alabama, and Florida." *JAFL* 32 (1919): 357–383.

2255 Smiley, Portia. "The Foot Wash in Alabama." *SW* 25 (1896): 101–102.

2256 Snyder, Howard. "Plantation Pictures: The Ordination of Charles." *Atl* 127 (1921): 338–342.

2257 Snyder, Howard. "A Plantation Revival Service." *Yale R* 10 (1920): 169–180.

2258 Southall, E. P. "The Attitudes of the Methodist Episcopal Church, South, Toward the Negro from 1844 to 1870." *JNH* 16 (1931): 359–370.

2259 Spears, James E. "Black Folk Element in Margaret Walker's *Jubilee*." *Miss FR* 14 (Spring 1980): 13–19.

2260 Stanley, Oma. "Negro Speech of East Texas." *AS* 16 (1941): 3–16.

2261 Steiner, R. "Seeking Jesus, a Religious Rite of Negroes in Georgia." *JAFL* 14 (1901): 172.

2262 Steiner, R. "Sol Lockheart's Call." *JAFL* 13 (1900): 67–70.

2263 Stoddard, Albert H. "Origins, Dialect, Beliefs and Characteristics of the Negroes of the South Carolina and Georgia Coast." *GHQ* 28 (1944): 186–196.

2264 Tartt, Ruby Pickens. "Richard the Tall-Hearted, Alabama Sketches." *SWR* 29 (1944): 234–244.

2265 Thomas, Will H. "The Decline and Decadence of Folk Metaphor." *PTFS* 2 (1923): 16–17.

2266 Tinker, Edward Larocque. "Louisiana Gumbo." *Yale R* 21 (1932): 566–579.

2267 Turner, Darwin T. "Daddy Joel Harris and His Old-Time Darkies." *SLJ* 1 (1968): 20–41.

2268 Turner, Lorenzo Dow. "Notes on the Sounds and Vocabulary of Gullah." *PADS* 3 (1945): 13–18.

2269 Turner, Lorenzo Dow. "Problems Confronting the Investigation of Gullah." *PADS* 9 (1948): 74–84.

2270 Utley, Francis Lee. "Review of *Gullah: A Breath of the Low Country*, by Dick Reeves." *SFQ* 34 (1970): 365–368.

2271 Wakefield, Edward. "Wisdom of Gombo." *Nine Ct* 30 (1891): 574–582.

2272 Waugh, Elizabeth. "All God's Children: A Sunday on the Sea Island." *Trav* 77 (May 1941): 26–29, 45–46.

2273 West, Harry C. "Negro Folklore in Pierce's Novels." *NCF* 19 (March 1971): 66–72.

2274 West, Steve. "The Devil Visits the Delta: A View of His Role in the Blues." *Miss FR* 19, no. 1 (Spring 1985): 11–23.

2275 Whitten, Norman E., Jr. "Contemporary Patterns of Malign Occultism Among Negroes in North Carolina." *JAFL* 75 (1962): 311–325.

2276 Wilmore, Gayraud S. "New Negro and the Church." *Christ Cen* 80 (February 6, 1963): 168–171.

2277 Wilson, G. R. "The Religion of the American Negro Slave: His Attitude Toward Life and Death. *JNH* (January 1923): 27+.

2278 Wolfe, Bernard. "Uncle Remus and the Malevolent Rabbit." *Comt* 8 (1949): 31–41. (Reprinted in Dundes, no. NA 854.)

2279 Work, Monroe N. "Geechee and Other Proverbs." *JAFL* 32 (1919): 441–442.

2280 Work, Monroe N. "Geechee Folk-Lore." *So Work* 34 (November–December 1905): 633, 695.

2281 Wright, John S. "The New Negro Poet and the Nachal Man: Sterling Brown's Folk Odyssey." *BALF* 23 (Spring 1989): 95–105.

2282 Yates, Irene. "A Collection of Proverbs and Proverbial Sayings from South Carolina Literature." *SFQ* (1947): 187–199.

2283 Yates, Irene. "Conjures and Cures in the Novels of Julia Peterkin." *SFQ* 10 (1946): 137–149.

RECORDING

2284 Klatzko, Bernard. "In the Spirit, No. 1 and No. 2." Record notes to Origin Jazz Library LP records 12 and 13.

Appendix 1

Festivals

Afram-Fest (May)
Norfolk, VA 23501
(804) 838–4203

Africa in April Cultural Awareness Fest (April)
Memphis, TN 38101
(901) 785–2542

African-American Spirituals Concert
Drayton Hall Visitors' Services
3380 Ashley River Road
Charleston, SC 29402

African Extravaganza
Selma Convention Center
Selma, AL 36701

Annual African-American Heritage Festival (August)
Jacksonville, FL 32203
(904) 469–1299

Annual African American Heritage Festival (September)
Staunton, VA 24402
(800) 332–5219

Annual Black Family Reunion Celebration (June)
Atlanta, GA 30301
(404) 524–6269

Annual Black Heritage Festival (September)
Savannah, GA 31402
(912) 651–6417

Annual Down Home Family Reunion (August)
Richmond, VA 23232
(804) 649–1861

Annual Hampton Jazz Festival (June)
Hampton, VA 23670
(804) 838–4203

Annual Henry Street Heritage Festival (September)
Roanoke, VA 24022
(703) 345–4818

Annual Jubilee Festival (September)
Columbia, SC 29201
(803) 252–1770

Annual Labor Day Jazz Festival (September)
Augusta, GA 30903
(404) 821–8322

Annual South Carolina Humanities Festival (January)
(803) 521–4144

Annual Student Art Exhibition (April)
Orangeburg, SC 29115
(803) 536–7174

Annual Towne Point Jazz Festival (August)
Norfolk, VA 23501
(804) 627–7809

Annual Umoja Festival (September)
Portsmouth, VA 23705
(804) 393–8481

Black Arts Festival
Visitor Center
706 Caroline Street
Fredericksburg, VA 22401

Black Cultural Arts Festival
Recreation Department
Southern Pines, NC 28387

Black Cultural Festival
Cultural Center
Capitol Complex
Charleston, WV 25305

Camp Baskerville
Gumbo Stew Festival
P.O. Box 990
Pawley's Island, SC 29505

Capital City Kwanzaa Festival (December)
Elegba Folklore Society
Richmond, VA 23232
(804) 644–3900

Charleston Blues and Heritage Festival (April)
Charleston, SC 29402
(803) 723–1075

Charlotte Hawkins Brown Memorial Weekend
African-American Heritage Festival (May)
Sedalia, NC 27342
(910) 449–4846

Come See Me Festival (April)
Rock Hill, SC 29730
(800) 866–5200

Euwabu: A Day of Celebration
1444 Brattonsville Road
McConnells, SC 29726
(803) 684–2327

Florida Folk Festival (May)
White Springs, FL 32096
(904) 397–2192

Ft. Lauderdale Festival of the Arts (March)
Ft. Lauderdale, FL 33310
(305) 761–5360

Georgia Sea Islands Festival
P.O. Box 250
Brunswick, GA 31520

Goombay! Festival (August)
Asheville, NC 28801
(704) 257–4539

Greer Family Festival (May)
Greer, SC 29650
(803) 877–4841

Gullah Festival (May)
Gullah Festival of South Carolina, Inc.
P.O. Box 83
Beaufort, SC 29901
(803) 525–0628

Jubilee Festival
Mann-Simons Cottage

1403 Richland Street
Columbia, SC 29201

Juneteenth Festival
102 Cliffwood Court
Fountain Inn, SC 29644

Kuumba Festival
Greenville Cultural Exchange Center
P.O. Box 5482, Station B
Greenville, SC 29606

Kuumba Festival (Memorial Day Weekend)
Jacksonville, FL 32203
(904) 768–7766

"Ma Rainey" Blues and Jazz Festival (June)
Columbus, GA 31908
(706) 322–1613

Moja Arts Festival (September)
City of Charleston
Office of Cultural Affairs
133 Church Street
Charleston, SC 29401
(803) 724–7305

New Orleans Jazz and Heritage Festival
Box 2530
1205 North Rampart Street
New Orleans, LA 70176

Peach Blossom Festival (April)
Johnston, SC
(803) 275–3635

Penn Center Heritage Festival (November)
Penn Center, Inc.
P.O. Box 126
St. Helena Island, SC 29920

People's Craft Market (April)
Rock Hill, SC 29730
(803) 329–5645

Springing the Blues (April)
Jacksonville, FL 32203
(904) 247–4242

Zora Neale Hurston Festival of Arts and Humanities (January)
Eatonville, FL 32751
(407) 647–2307

Appendix 2

Libraries and Archives

Archive of Folk Culture
American Folklife Center
Library of Congress
Washington, DC 20540
(202) 287–5510
With emphasis on folk music, the collection contains approximately 200 broadsides, 100,000 pieces of ephemera, 200 maps, 12,000 discs, 15,000 tape recordings, 250 wire recordings, 8,000 cylinder recordings, 35,000 ms. cards, 100,000 ms. sheets, 5,000 photo prints, 60,000 photo negatives, 45,000 slides, and 4,000 reference books and journals.

Archives of American Minority Cultures
University of Alabama
Box S
University, AL 35486
(205) 348–5512
Concentrating on the history and culture of southern blacks, the collection contains 1,680 78rpm and 200 LP discs, 1,000 tape recordings, 207 cylinder recordings, 110 ms. cards, 6 linear feet of ms. sheets, 1,000 slides, 100 photo prints, 53 negatives, 5 motion pictures, 100 videotapes, 10 exhibitions and slide-tape programs, 300 reference books and journals, and subject files.

Atlanta Historical Society
Library/Archives
3101 Andrews Drive N.E.
Atlanta, GA 30305
(404) 261–1938
The collection has approximately 15,000 ms. sheets, 90,000 photo prints, 46,000 negatives, and 5,000 slides.

Avery Research Center for African American History & Culture
College of Charleston
125 Bull Street
Charleston, SC 29424
(843) 953–7608
Concentrating on the history and culture of African Americans in South Carolina and the low country. The collection contains approximately 150 personal manuscripts, 4,000 books on the African American experience, more than 500 audiocassettes and videocassettes, and numerous prints and photographs that reflect life in the South Carolina low country.

Center for Southern Folklore Archives
Box 40105
Memphis, TN 38174
(901) 726–4205
Items include the Historic Beale Street collection, 1,000 hours of tape, 20,000 photo prints, 40,000 negatives, 5,000 slides, 50,000 feet of motion pictures, and numerous artifacts.

Department of Archives and Special Collections
J. D. Williams Library
University, MS 38677
(601) 232–7408
This collection houses the W. R. Ferris and Arthur Palmer Hudson Folklore Collection of Mississippi folklore, which covers material such as culture, blues, and tales. It has 35 linear feet of ms. sheets, more than 10,000 photoprints, slides and negatives, and 7,000 pioneer postcards.

East Carolina University Folklore Archive
Department of English
Austin Building
Greeneville, NC 27834
(919) 757–6046
Concentrating on eastern North Carolina, the collection contains 4,500 ms. collections and 100,000 records of traditional items.

Florida Folklife Program
Florida Department of State
500 S. Bronough St.
Tallahassee, FL 32399
(850) 487–2073
In addition to the Stetson Kennedy materials, this collection contains 3,000 photo prints, 2,500 negatives, 10,000 slides, and 150 reference books and journals.

Georgia Folklore Society Archives
University of Georgia Library
Athens, GA 30602

John Edwards Memorial Collection
University of North Carolina
c/o Curriculum in Folklore
Greenlaw Hall
Chapel Hill, NC 27514
(919) 962–4065
With an emphasis on Piedmont country blues music, the collection has 14,000 78rpm, 8,000 45rpm, and 1,000 LP discs, 600 reels of tape, 1,500 ms. cards, 1,000 photo prints, 500 photo negatives, and 500 reference books and journals.

Kevin Barry Perdue Archive of Traditional Music
University of Virginia Folklore Archive
Room 303, Brooks Hall
University of Virginia
Charlottesville, VA 22903
(804) 924–6823
With strengths in the Piedmont blues tradition, the collections have 78rpm, LP, and aluminum discs; substantial ms. sheets; and 3,000 reference books and journals.

Mississippi Folklore Society
State of Mississippi
Archives Committee
Department of Archives and History
Box 571
Jackson, MS 39205
(601) 359–1424
This collection has WPA county histories and slave narratives and various photographs and recordings.

New Orleans Jazz Club Collections of the Louisiana State Museum
751 Chartres Street
New Orleans, LA 70176
(504) 568–6968
The collections include 3,000 78rpm, 200 45rpm, and 4,000 LP discs, 1,000 tape recordings and 20 cylinder recordings, 10,000 photo prints, 500 negatives, 200 slides, 100 motion pictures, 300 posters, 2,500 pieces of sheet music, files on 1,000 musicians, 500 reference books, and 100 journal titles.

Regional Culture Center
Arkansas College
Batesville, AR 72501
(501) 793–9813, ext. 253
This collection has 3,000 tape recordings, 50 linear feet of ms. sheets, 2,000 photo prints, 5,000 photo negatives, 3,000 slides, and 1,000 reference books and journals.

University of Mississippi Blues Archive
Farley Hall
University, MS 38677
(601) 232–7753
This collection houses the Kenneth S. Goldstein Folklore Collection, the *Living Blues*

archival collection, the Malaco Record Company archival collection, and the B. B. King record collection. It contains 20 linear feet of ephemera, 500 posters, 9,500 78rpm, 11,000 45rpm, and 11,000 LP discs, 5 feet of ms. sheets, 2,000 photo prints, and 12,300 reference works.

University of Mississippi Museum
University, MS 38677
(601) 232–7073
The collection contains photographs of southern folk customs and structures.

William Ransom Hogan Jazz Archive
Tulane University
Howard-Tilton Memorial Library
New Orleans, LA 70118
(504) 865–5688
This collection contains, among others, the John Robichaux, Nick LaRocca, and A1 Rose collections, 2,000 books, 6,000 photos, 1,700 oral history tapes, 10,000 pieces of oral history summaries, 36,400 phonograph records, 14,000 pieces of sheet music, and over 25,000 notes, clippings, and posters.

Appendix 3

State Folk Cultural Programs

ALABAMA

Alabama State Council on the Arts
Folklife Program
323 Adams Avenue
Montgomery, AL 36130–5801
(205) 261–4076

ARKANSAS

Arkansas Arts Council
Folk Arts Coordinator
The Heritage Center
225 E. Markham Street, Suite 200
Little Rock, AR 72201
(303) 866–5431

FLORIDA

Bureau of Florida Folklife Programs
Box 265
White Springs, FL 32096
(904) 397–2192

KENTUCKY

Folk Art Coordinator
Kentucky Center for the Arts
530 W. Main Street, Suite 400

Louisville, KY 40202
(502) 562–0100

LOUISIANA

Louisiana Folklife Program
Division of the Arts
Office of Program Development
Box 44247
Baton Rouge, LA 70804
(504) 925–3930

MARYLAND

State Folklorist
Maryland Arts Council
15 West Mulberry Street
Baltimore, MD 21201
(301) 685–6741

MISSISSIPPI

Mississippi Arts Commission
Box 1341
Jackson, MS 39202
(601) 354–7336

NORTH CAROLINA

Office of Folklife Programs
North Carolina Department of Cultural Resources
109 E. Jones Street, Room 316
Raleigh, NC 27611
(919) 733–7897

SOUTH CAROLINA

Folk Arts Coordinator
McKissick Museum
University of South Carolina
Columbia, SC 29208
(803) 777–7251

TENNESSEE

Folk Arts Coordinator
Tennessee Arts Commission
320 6th Avenue N.
Nashville, TN 37219
(615) 741–1701

TEXAS

Director
Texas Folklife Resources
Box 49824
Austin, TX 78765
(512) 482–9217

Appendix 4

Interviewees

Lease Ashe—Yonges Island, SC

Alma Brooks—Birmingham, AL

Leah Chase—New Orleans, LA

Joyce V. Coakley—Mt. Pleasant, SC

Mamie Cochran—Birmingham, AL

Blanche Davis—Birmingham, AL

Lucille Dennis—Charleston, SC

Luther Dennison—Pawleys Island, SC

Mattie Dudley—Birmingham, AL

Ardella M. Gayles—Birmingham, AL

Sadie Grady—Birmingham, AL

Beverly Jackson—Jacksonville, FL

Maggie McGill—Wadmalaw Island, SC

Willie McKinstry—Birmingham, AL

Several Members of The Menhaden Chanteymen—Beaufort, NC

Angela Mitchell—Charleston, SC

Gloria Mitchell—Charleston, SC

Loretta Nimmons—Charleston, SC

Julia Rhodes—Birmingham, AL

Peter Russell—Wadmalaw Island, SC

Vernon Sands—Jacksonville, FL

William Seabrook—Yonges Island, SC

Joseph Simmons—Charleston, SC
Phillip Simmons—Charleston, SC
Alice Washington—Cainhoy, SC
Dru Welch—Camden, AR
Bonnye White—Meridian, MS

Index

Numbers in *italic* are page numbers. All other references are to entry numbers.

Aching feet, remedy for, *11*
African Methodist Episcopal [AME] Church, *21*
Alabama, *24*, *42–43*, *48*, *51*, *55*, 0023, 0038, 0253, 0292, 0356–0357, 0359, 0433, 0586, 1078, 1214, 1345, 1363, 1447
Anansi, *1. See also* Folktales; Stories and Storytelling
Animals, *1*, *4*, *8*, *9*, 24, *25*, *41*, *46*; fictitious, *1*, *5*, *6*, *53*
Architecture, 1259, 1399, 1401, 1403–1404
Arkansas, *30*, *55*, 0008, 03655, 1340
Armstrong, Louis, 2, *28*, *37*, *44*, 0688, 1120–1121
Arthritis, remedies for, *2*
Arts, Decorative, 1331, 1349
Aunt Dicey, stories about, *2*

Babies, *4*, *5*, *10. See also* Children
Backache, folklore about, *2*
Bad luck, reasons for, *3*, *36*, *49. See also* Luck
Bad mood, reason for, *2*

Bad spirits, death and, *14. See also* Death; Funerals
Baking Soda, as a remedy for corns, *11*
Bands, 0712, 0847, 1170. *See also* Music; Musicians; *names of indiviual musicians*
Banjo, *26*, *37*, *49*, 0485, 1112
Basketmakers, *3*
Baskets and Basketry, *3*, *36*, *38*, 1375, 1113, 1445, 1466, 1474
Bateau (a type of boat), *5*
Beale Street, *4*, *34*, 0646. *See also* Blues
Beale Street Blues, *23*
Birth, folklore about, *4*, *9*, *18*, *36*, *51*. *See also* Midwives; Pregnancy
Birthmarks, reasons for, *4*, *5*
Black Bottom (a type of dance), *13. See also* Rainey, "Ma"
Black magic. *See* Hoodoo; Voodoo
Black snakes, folklore about, *46*
Blacksmith, *45*, 1351. *See also* Ironwork
"Blindness," convicts and, *19*
Blind Blake (Arthur Phelps), *5*
Blue doors, evil spirits and, *18. See also* spirits
Blues, *4*, *5*, *14*, *24*, *27*, *32*, *42*, 0450,

0475, 0507–0508, 0521, 0527–0528,
0546, 0559, 0563–0564, 0567, 0572,
0580, 0638, 0641–0645, 0648, 0662,
0705, 0707–0708, 0722, 0727, 0774–
0775, 0791, 0812, 0819, 0822–0823,
0826, 0835, 0845–0846, 0851, 0855,
0875, 0879, 0883–0885, 0888, 0909–
0910, 0913, 0920, 0922, 0924, 0940,
0947–0948, 0950, 0959–0960, 0974,
1021–1023, 1024, 1053, 1056, 1085,
1092, 1096–1097, 1108–1109, 1114,
1120, 1123, 1125, 1130, 1143, 1149–
1150, 1153, 1163, 1182, 1185, 1204,
1206, 1208, 2223. *See also* Music;
Musicians
Bluestone, use of, to break a spell, *6*
Boat building, *5*
Bolden, [Charles Joseph] "Buddy," *6*
Bones (a type of instrument), *26*
Boogie-woogie, *32, 34, 45*, 0987
Bowens, Cyrus, *6*
Brass Ankles (people of mixed races), *42*
Brer Fox, *24*. *See also* Harris, Joel Chandler; Stories and Storytelling; Uncle Remus
Brer Rabbit, *6, 23*, 1705, 1712, 1729, 1742, 1878–1879. *See also* Harris, Joel Chandler; Stories and Storytelling; Uncle Remus
Brewer, Mason J., *47*, 54, 0031
Broonzy, "Big Bill" [William Lee Conley], *7*
Bullwhip, use of, *5*
Burnett, Chester Arthur (Howlin' Wolf), *25*

Cakewalk (a type of dance), *13*
Calabash (turtle), *8, 22*
Calinda (a type of dance), *13*
Candles, *15*; meaning of, *8*
Caskets, *11*. *See also* Death; Funerals
Castor oil, as a remedy for corns, *11*
Chatman, Peter [Memphis slim], *34*
Chewing tobacco, used to heal cuts, *13*, 0421
Children, *1, 10, 15, 16, 18, 39, 40, 43, 44*
Claflin College, *47*
Clay eating, *15, 55*

Coach Snakes, folklore about, *46*
Coffins, *19, 21*. *See also* Death; Funerals
Colds, remedies for, *10, 24, 38, 49, 51*
Colic, *10*
Conjures, *53*, 0135, 0398, 2283. *See also* Conjure-Doctors; Conjuring; Hoodoo; Voodoo
Conjure-Doctors, *11, 22, 50*, 0135, 0397, 1538, 1619, 1857, 1926. *See also* Conjures; Conjuring; Hoodoo; Voodoo
Conjuring, 1581, 1624, 1625
Conley, William Lee, *7*
Cooling Board, *11, 19*. *See also* Death; Funerals
Copper, used to prepare the dead, *46*. *See also* Death; Funerals
Copper penny, used to heal cuts, *13*
Cortier, Eldzier, *11*
Coughs, remedy for, *49*
Cowpeas, *25*. *See also* Food
Creole Dialect, 0028, 1981
Creole Jazz Band, *12*. *See also* Creole Music
Creole Music, 0275, 0420, 0568, 0570, 0720, 0741, 0839
Creole People, *12*
Crudup, Arthur ["Big Boy"], *13*

"Dead Man Blues," *8*. *See also* Death; Funerals; Morton, "Jelly Roll"
Death, *4, 7, 11, 12, 14, 17, 19, 25, 35, 39, 42–43, 45*. *See also* Funerals
Delta Blues, *14*, 0884–0885, 0888, 0922, 0992, 1182. *See also* Blues
Dett, R[obert] Nathaniel, *14*
Discipline, saying about, *4*. *See also* Sayings/Proverbs
Domingo, John, *28*
Domino, Antoine "Fats," *15*
Dorsey, Thomas A., *15, 21*
Douglas, Lizzie [Memphis Minnie], *34*
Dr. Buzzard, 1536
Dreams, *16, 32*
Dress or Dressing (Conjuring), *16, 51*. *See also* Conjures; Conjuring

Easter Sunday, *12, 16*. *See also* Holidays; Religious Ceremonies

Edmonson, William, *17*
Ellington, "Duke" [Edward Kennedy], *17*

Fanner (a type of basket), *3*
Fat meat, used to heal cuts, *13*, *36*
Fats Waller, *30*
Feeler, use of in baptism, *2*
Fever, remedies for, *28*, *38*
Field peas, *25*. *See also* Food
Florida, *26*, *30*, 0132, 0359, 0402, 0812, 1414, 1585, 1900, 2047, 2254
Flu, remedy for, *38*
Fly Toe, remedy for, *53*
Folklore, *23*, *31*, *32*, 0007, 0016–0017, 0018–0019, 0020–0021, 0025–0026, 0039, 0054, 0057, 0067, 0072–0073, 0078, 0085, 0088, 0104, 0120, 0127, 0134, 0160, 0191, 0206, 0214, 0221, 0227, 0245, 0253, 0257, 0258, 0264, 0268–0270, 0280, 0281, 0287, 0310, 0313–0315, 0317, 0320, 0321, 0324–0325, 0334–0335, 0337–0341, 0350, 0353, 0356–0357, 0359, 0372–0374, 0403, 0404, 0411, 0579, 0795, 0862, 1264, 1293, 1302, 1325, 1327, 1329, 1357
Folktales, 0001, 0012, 0216, 0220, 0246, 0283, 0290, 0306, 0345, 1225, 1484, 1514, 1528, 1539, 1637, 1645, 1646, 1654–1655, 1664, 1667, 1670, 1672, 1674, 1713, 1723, 1725, 1729, 1738, 1746, 1748, 1754, 1762, 1767, 1774, 1779, 1787, 1828, 1830–1831, 1838–1839, 1879, 1900–1905, 1928, 1960, 1995, 2147
Food, *8*, *10*, *12*, *13*, *22*, *24*, *25*, *26*, *39*, *42*, *52*
Fuller, [Albert Fulton] "Blind Boy," *19*
Funerals, *16*, *19*, *42*, *45*. *See also* Death

Games, *24*, *37*
Garden of Gethsemane, *51*
Georgia, *22*, 0094, 0142, 0188, 0234–0235, 0248, 0299, 0322, 0359, 0364, 0428, 0456, 0716, 0804, 0815, 0853, 0866, 0909, 0926–0927, 0990, 1159, 1212, 1262, 1346, 1367, 1417, 1450, 1475

Ghosts, *20*, *25*, *39*, *46*, *54*, 1860, 1932. *See also* Spirits
Gillespie, "Dizzy" [John Birks], *20*
Good Luck, *14*, *18*, *20—21*, *25*, *27*, *43*. *See also* Bad luck
Gospel Music, *14*, *15*, *18*, *21*, *23*, *27*, 0450, 0457, 0521, 0560, 0580, 0662, 0755, 0791, 0855, 0970, 1110, 1126, 1128
Graves and Graveyards, *20*, *21*, *25*, *39*, *53*, 1378, 1415, 1789. *See also* Ghosts; Spirits
Gris-Gris (charms), *15*, *21*, *29*. *See also* Hoodoo; Voodoo
Gullah (language), *20*, *22*, *40*, *47*, 0060, 0409, 0771, 1348, 1680, 1683, 1753, 1757, 1966, 1970, 1979, 2034, 2066–2067, 2074, 2101, 2107, 2113, 2129, 2131, 2134–2135, 2140, 2144, 2184, 2190, 2193, 2199–2201, 2203, 2225–2227, 2248, 2253, 2269–2270
Gullah Jack, *22*, *28*. *See also* Conjure-Doctors
Gumbo, *13*. *See also* Food

Hags, *12*, *22*, *32*. *See also* Spirits
Hair, folklore about, *10*, *43*
Hambone (a rhymed chant), *23*, *30*. *See also* Slave Songs; Work Songs
Hampton Institute Choir, *14*, 0239, 0501
Handkerchief, used as a love charm, *33*
Handy, W. C. [William Christopher], *23*
Hardy, John, *23*
Harris, Joel Chandler, *23–24*, 0058, 0308
Headaches, cause of, *10*
Heart ailments, remedy for, *24*
Henry, John, *23*, 0024, 0084, 0140, 0297,1887
High Blood pressure, remedy for, *35*
Holidays, *1*, *14*, *17*, *25*, *30–31*, *34*, 0049
Hoodoo, *24*, 0389, 1481, 1488, 1499, 1503, 1512, 1515, 1557, 1589–1590, 1597, 1634. *See also* Voodoo
Horses, *34*
House, son, *25*
Howlin' Wolf [Chester Arthur Burnett], *25*
Humor, 0039, 0057, 0120, 0221

Hurston, Zora Neale, *26*, 2015, 2062, 2148, 2157, 2187, 2228, 2241
Hurt, [John Smith] "Mississippi," *26*

Illnesses, causes of, *5*, *9*. *See also names of individual illnesses*
Improvisation, blues, *5*
Instruments, *22*, *26*, *37*
Ironwork, *27*, *45*, 1380, 2142

Jackson, Mahalia, *15*, *21*, *27*, 0962, 1192
Jazz, *12*, *27*, *47*, 0435, 0438, 0469, 0472, 0477, 0486, 0496, 0502, 0524, 0530, 0566, 0576, 0580, 0583, 0587, 0588, 0592, 0628, 0630, 0670, 0682, 0685, 0691, 0714, 0737, 0739, 0745–0746, 0748, 0766, 0777, 0781–0782, 0789, 0845, 0882, 0930–0931, 0999, 1049, 1062, 1073, 1076, 1132, 1140, 1151, 1174, 1176, 1197. *See also* Musicians
Jefferson, Clarence "Blind Lemon," *5*, *27–28*
Jenkins, Daniel J., *28*
Jitterbug, *13*
Johnson, Robert, *25*, *29*, 0859, 0914, 1154
Johnson, William Geary "Bunk," *29*
Johnson, William H., *29*
Joplin, Scott, *29–30*
Jordan , Louis, *15*, *30*
Juke Joints, *13*, *30*, *38*, *53*
Jukebox, *30*
Juneteenth *2*, *30–31*, 1716

Kerosene, as a cold remedy, *10*
Kinkombo, *22*

Labor pains, *9*. *See also* Birth
Language, *22*. *See also* Gullah
Laurel tree, *4*
Leadbelly [Huddie Ledbetter], *31*
LeMenthe, Ferdinand Joseph ["Jelly Roll" Morton], *35*
Life everlasting (Rabbit Tobacco), *41*
Light-skinned black person, *7*
Locke, Alain, 0030
Loften, "Cripple" Clarence, *32*
Lomax, Alan, *32*

Lomax, John, *32*
Louisiana, *12*, *16*, *31*, *32*, *56*, 0028, 0032–0033, 0041, 0152, 0205, 0211, 0228, 0282, 0288, 0292, 0468, 0641, 0647, 0690, 0693, 0700, 1020, 1064, 1178, 1235, 1337, 1420, 1458, 1495
Love Charms, *32–33*
Luck, *3*, *14*, *20*
Lying, indications of, *5*, *31*

McGhee, "Brownie" [Walter Brown], *33*
McTell, "Blind Willie" [Willie Samuel], *33–34*
Measles, remedies for, *36*
Memorial Day, *14*
Memphis Minnie [Lizzie Douglas], *34*
Memphis Slim [Peter Chatman], *34*
Midwives, *21*, *43*, *51*. *See* also Birth; Pregnancy
Mississippi, *16*, *35*, 0020, 0067, 0085, 0120, 0292, 0295, 0310, 0403, 0412, 0529, 0791, 0846, 0890, 0912, 0939, 1147, 1161, 1236, 1258–1259, 1269, 1291, 1359, 1371, 1338, 1394–1395, 1403
Money, folklore about, *12*, *26*, *27*, *36*, *39*
Monkey Jars, *40*
Morton, "Jelly Roll" [Ferdinand Joseph LeMenthe], *35*
Mulattos, *36*, *55*
Music, *13*, *19*, *28*, *30*, *39*, *43*, *47*; Brass band, *6*; Dixieland, *15*; Rhythm and blues, *42–43*; Scat, *44*; Zydeco, *56*. *See also* Blues; Creole Music; Gospel; Instruments; Jazz; Musicians; Ragtime; Slave Songs; Songs; Work Songs
Musicians, *5*, *13*, *14*, *25*, *38*, *50*, *54*, *55*; Blues, *7*, *19*, *26*, *27–28*, *30*, *31*, *32*, *33–34*, *38*, *41*, *46*, *52*, *53*; Boogie-woogie, *32*, *34*, *45*; Bop, *20*; Gospel, *15*, *27*; Jazz, *2*, *6*, *23*, *29*, *35*, *37–38*; Ragtime, *29–30*; Rock and roll, *15*; Swing, *17*
Mustard Seeds, used as charms, *22–23*, *55*

National Baptist Convention, *21*, *27*
New Orleans, *8*, *27*, *29*, *37*, *48*, 0009,

0041, 0116, 0159, 0204, 0210, 0217, 0278, 0430, 0439, 0459, 0462, 0623, 0634, 0720, 0722, 0737, 0744, 0756, 0789, 1173, 1197, 1221, 1296
91st Psalm, *42*
North Carolina, *28, 36, 53–54*, 0026, 0265, 0307, 0339, 0340, 0412, 0805, 0807, 0923, 1027, 1079, 1215, 1243, 1254, 1374, 1428, 1559, 1773, 1796, 1800, 1906, 1929, 2161, 2275

Octoroons, *36, 37*
Okra Soup, 34. *See also* Food
Oliver, Joe "King," *37*
126th Psalm, *42*
Oro-stick (a type of toy), *7*
Ory, Edward "Kid," *37–38*

Page, "Hot Lips" [Oran Thaddeus], *38*
Palmetto trees, for baskets, *3, 38*
Parsons, Elsie Crews, *38*
Patten, Charley [Chatmon], *38*
Phelps, Arthur (Blind Blake), *5*
Pine Top Smith, *32*
Plantation dances, *14*
Plantations, *40*, 0002, 0093, 0133, 0153, 0196, 0199, 0264, 0299, 0344, 0347, 0410, 0526, 0561, 0624, 0751, 1032–1044, 1222, 1303, 1426, 2091, 2121, 2256–2257
Plants, *4, 7, 9, 12, 14, 19, 35, 38, 46, 49, 51*
Pneumonia, remedy for, *4*
Pottery, *40*, 1320
Poultices, *5, 40*
Pregnancy, *9, 18, 44*
Psalms (7, 12, 54, 59, 112, 138, 139), *8, 42*

Quadroons, *36*
Quilts, *40–41*, 1280, 1282, 1315, 1345

Rainey, "Ma" [Gertrude Melissa Pridgett], *41*
Ragtime, *23, 27, 29, 41*, 0555, 0882, 1124
Railroad songs, *28. See also* Music
Rain, folklore about, *41–42, 49*

Recipes, 1237, 1279, 1311, 1348, 1455. *See also* Food
Red flannel, *2, 19, 50*
Red rice, *34*
Religious ceremonies, *3, 7, 16–17, 30, 54*
Remedies, *2, 3, 4, 5, 6, 7–8, 10, 11, 13, 16, 19, 24, 28, 33, 35, 36, 38, 40, 42, 43, 46, 48, 49, 52, 53, 54*, 0379, 0392, 0395, 0406, 0410, 0412
Rheumatism, remedies for, *7, 19, 42*
Root doctor, protection against, *40*
Ryngo, Dr., *16*

Salt, *8, 24, 44, 48*
Salt peter, use of, to break a spell, *6*
Sapelo Island, *49*
Satan, stories about, *24*
Savannah, GA, *27*, 0101
Sayings/proverbs, *1, 4, 9, 16, 18, 20, 26, 36, 37, 38, 48, 49, 51, 54*
Scarlet Fever, remedy for, *10*
Sea Islands, *11, 20, 21, 22, 33, 38, 39, 44, 49–50, 53*, 0044, 0060, 0138, 0189, 0234, 0277, 0304, 0364, 0368, 0841, 1159, 1244, 1346, 1440, 1465, 1757, 1928, 1979
Sermons, 1958, 2025, 2029, 2043, 2049
Seventh Child, folklore about, *4, 44*
Simmons, Philip, *27, 45*, 1351
Slave Songs, *10, 11, 23, 45*, 0275, 0429, 0532, 0839, 0958
Slavery, 0050, 0083, 0086, 0153, 0165, 0238, 0632. *See also* Slaves
Slaves, *23*, 0202, 0312. *See also* Slavery
Smith, Clarence "Pine Top," *45*
Smith, Elizabeth "Bessie," *46*
Smith, Mamie, *5*
Snakes, folklore about, 46
Songs, *11*, 0433–0434, 0454, 0488, 0493, 0550, 0561, 0613, 0617, 0633, 0669, 0676, 0696, 0702–0703, 0716, 0720, 0751, 0773, 0785, 0787–0788, 0801, 0805, 0810, 0834, 0912–0927, 0976–0986, 1115, 1301, 1650. *See also* Music
Soot, used to heal cuts, *13*
South Carolina, *22, 24, 35, 36–38, 40–41, 44, 47, 48*, 0144, 0173, 0189,

0213, 0220, 0234, 0287, 0296, 0298, 0359, 0407, 0477, 0758, 0771, 0784, 0841, 0994, 1088, 1238, 1247, 1274, 1319, 1344, 1346, 1348, 1387, 1391, 1418

Spirits, *4, 9, 18, 19, 20, 22, 27, 45, 47, 52, 54. See also* Ghosts

Spirituals, *31,* 0449, 0458, 0480, 0484, 0499–0500, 0503, 0505, 0514, 0517, 0533–0534, 0539, 0557, 0565, 0580, 0594, 0603, 0610, 0614–0617, 0637, 0672, 0687, 0689, 0721, 0770, 0802, 0811, 0831–0832, 0850, 0870, 0892, 0919, 0928, 1023, 1029, 1078, 1089, 1142, 1148, 1165, 1178

St. John's Day, *34*

St. Helena Island, *34,* 0138–0139, 0250, 0303, 0437, 0612, 0889, 1245, 1366, 1837, 2126

Stories and Storytelling, *1, 6, 23–24, 28,* 0021. *See also* Folktales

Storyville, *6, 12, 37, 48*

Street Cries, *24, 48,* 0617, 0836

Sugar, as a remedy, *10*

Sulfur, as a remedy, *10, 48*

Superstitions, *3, 4, 6, 10, 11, 14, 18, 21, 27, 31, 33, 46, 50,* 0065, 0407, 0418, 1498, 1515, 1531, 1547, 1553, 1555, 1565, 1567, 1573, 1582, 1593, 1596, 1600–1603, 1605–1608, 1615–1616, 1621, 1626–1627, 1631–1633, 1635

Sweeping, folklore about, *3, 49*

Swing and bop, *15, 49*

Tennessee, 0230, 0353, 0521, 1006

Terry, "Sonny" [Saunders Terrell], *50*

Texas, *30,* 0065, 0372–0374, 0376, 0600, 0715, 0810, 0811, 1167, 1278, 1484, 1653–1654, 1760, 1959, 2068

37th Psalm, *42*

Tools, *2*

Toys, *7*

Turner, "Big Joe" [Joseph Vernon], *51*

Twentieth Psalm, *6*

27th Psalm, *42*

Uncle Remus, *24,* 0259, 0264, 0297, 00308, 0327, 0351, 1697, 1700, 1702, 1703–1710, 1768, 1855, 2171–2172, 2180, 2182, 2211, 2222. *See also* Brer Fox; Brer Rabbit; Harris, Joel Chandler; Stories and Storytelling

Urban blues, *4. See also* Blues

Vesey, Denmark, *22*

Virginia, *52,* 0191, 0237, 0257–0258, 0328, 0334, 0359, 0718, 0964, 1270, 1273, 1290, 1298, 1368, 1444

Voodoo, *15, 16, 17, 18, 21, 24, 34, 52, 56,* 1478, 1485, 1490, 1495, 1496, 1497, 1499, 1501, 1502, 1506–1509, 1513–1516, 1519–1525, 1527, 1529, 1532, 1537, 1551, 1554, 1556, 1562, 1577, 1580, 1587, 1588, 1592, 1612, 1620, 1622, 1629, 1632. *See also* Hoodoo

Walker, "T-Bone" [Aaron Thibault], *52*

Washboards, as instruments, *26, 30*

Washboard Band, *50*

Waters, "Muddy" [McKinley Morganfield], *53*

Whooping Cough, remedy for, *24*

Williams, "Big Joe" [Joe Lee], *54*

Williams, "Sonny Boy," *55*

Woodcarving, *6*

Work, John W., *55*

Work Songs, *11, 18, 24, 43, 45,* 0600, 0617, 0943, 1081, 1179, 1193

About the Authors

SHERMAN E. PYATT is an archivist at the Avery Research Center for African American History and Culture, at the College of Charleston. His previous publications include *Martin Luther King, Jr.: An Annotated Bibliography* (Greenwood, 1986) and *Apartheid: A Selective Annotated Bibliography, 1979–1987* (1990).

ALAN JOHNS has worked as a catalog librarian at The Citadel, the University of South Carolina at Spartanburg, and the University of Tennessee, Knoxville.

ISBN 0-313-27999-3

EAN

9 780313 279997

90000>

HARDCOVER BAR CODE